Asian Yearbook of International Economic Law

Volume 2023

The Asian Yearbook of International Economic Law (AYIEL) is dedicated to the rapidly developing legal field of International Economic Law (IEL) with a focus on Asia and the Pacific region. This region has been and still is one of the engines of world economy, and hosts a large number of economies of varying developmental levels, economic policies and legal jurisdictions. The AYIEL aims to publish top quality research outcomes in all areas of IEL, such as trade/WTO law, investment law, financial law, tax law, competition law, intellectual property law, dispute settlement, economic regulation and cooperation, regional economic integration, as well as other legal development of the Asian countries. While putting its focus in Asia, the AYIEL is not limited to IEL issues and developments in Asian countries. It consists of several major parts, including topical articles on the cutting-edge and profound issues of IEL, regional and national law relating to economic governance and integration, analysis of leading cases, book reviews and documentation. The editors of AYIEL are supported by an international Advisory Board consisting of world renowned scholars of IEL.

Marc Bungenberg • Manjiao Chi • Sufian Jusoh •
Prabhash Ranjan • Islambek Rustambekov
Editors

Asian Yearbook of International Economic Law 2023

Springer

Editors
Marc Bungenberg
Europa Institute
Saarland University
Saarbrücken, Germany

Manjiao Chi
Law School
University of International Business and Economics
Beijing, China

Sufian Jusoh
Institute of Malaysian & International Studies
National University of Malaysia
Bangi, Selangor, Malaysia

Prabhash Ranjan
Faculty of Legal Studies
South Asian University
New Delhi, India

Islambek Rustambekov
Tashkent State University of Law
Tashkent, Uzbekistan

ISSN 2662-7515 ISSN 2662-7523 (electronic)
Asian Yearbook of International Economic Law
ISBN 978-3-031-31049-2 ISBN 978-3-031-31050-8 (eBook)
https://doi.org/10.1007/978-3-031-31050-8

This Springer imprint is published by the registered company Springer Nature Switzerland AG
The registered company address is: Gewerbestrasse 11, 6330 Cham, Switzerland

Paper in this product is recyclable.

Preface

In today's globalized world, conflicts and challenges in international economic relations have become increasingly prevalent. This 2023 volume of the Asian Yearbook of International Economic Law welcomes three new volume editors – Sufian Jusoh, Prabhash Ranjan, and Islambek Rustambekov – to its editorial team. It also brings together a collection of insightful articles that shed light on key issues affecting various regions and actors in the realm of international trade, investment, and economic law, with a special focus on the Asian continent, or reactions especially linked to developments in Asia. By examining conflicts over industrial and trade policy, the role of international institutions, the dynamics of China's Belt and Road Initiative, the interplay of multilateral agreements, investment relations between China and Germany, the intersection of environmental regulation and investment law, the investment climate in Uzbekistan, the legitimacy of investor state dispute settlement, the significance of arbitration centres, and the impact of intellectual property rights in biotechnology, this volume, like its predecessor, discusses a broad range of topics. By virtue of its breadth and depth, this book provides valuable insights for scholars, policymakers, practitioners, and anyone interested in navigating the complexities of the evolving global economy.

We hope you enjoy reading these contributions and we look forward to receiving from you interesting manuscripts on developments related to International Economic Law in the Asian context, which you can send at any time to any one of the editors.

Saarbrücken, Germany — Marc Bungenberg
Beijing, China — Manjiao Chi
Bangi, Malaysia — Sufian Jusoh
New Delhi, India — Prabhash Ranjan
Tashkent, Uzbekistan — Islambek Rustambekov

Contents

Part I
International Economic Order

Difficult Times in Investment Relations Between China and Germany: The Cases of Siltronic/GlobalWafers and COSCO/HHLA

Marc Bungenberg and Philipp Reinhold

Contents

Abstract Global economic relations become more and more tense. In addition to the shift in power, which is particularly due to the economic rise of China, and the multiple crises, most recently the COVID-19 crisis, an increasing fragmentation of economic relations is becoming apparent, which is associated with a lack of consensus on the future of the world order and its basic principles. In this context, the EU and its Member States are now emphasising their strategic autonomy, which has already led to a number of reforms. One important example of the readjustment of the EU's autonomous trade policy is the area of Investment Screening. In the new investment control policies of the EU and its Member States, a greater reluctance to foreign investment can now be observed overall. This is particularly noticeable in Germany, which has traditionally been more open to business. In Germany—as in some other Member States—investments particularly related to China have repeat-

M. Bungenberg and P. Reinhold (✉)
Saarland University, Saarbrücken, Germany
e-mail: bungenberg@europainstitut.de; reinhold@europainstitut.de

M. Bungenberg et al. (eds.), *Asian Yearbook of International Economic Law 2023*,
Asian Yearbook of International Economic Law (2023) 2023: 3–22,
https://doi.org/10.1007/16517_2023_18, Published online: 13 April 2023

edly caused heated discussions for various reasons. This article looks at the legal and political changes that have taken place in the area of investment control in Germany and the EU in recent years. Overall, they point to a difficult future for investment relations with China.

1 Introduction

The relationship between the People's Republic of China and the Federal Republic of Germany remains difficult. Since the establishment of diplomatic relations between both countries in 1972, especially after China's reform and opening up in 1979, the volume of trade has increased rapidly, making China Germany's most important trading partner today.[1] In recent years, however, a variety of tensions have arisen that have a fundamental character and are subsumed under the concept of a 'systematic rivalry'.[2] This term not only describes the economic contrasts between the two systems, but also encompasses fundamental political divergences, which have become increasingly prominent. Already in 2020, *Joseph Borrell*, High Representative of the Union for Foreign Affairs and Security Policy, noted that there had been a 'greater divergence' between the EU and China in recent years, as China had become 'gradually more assertive, expansionist and authoritarian'.[3] In a speech at the European Parliament debate on EU-China relations on 22 November 2022, *Borrell* stated: 'China is becoming increasingly assertive and developing an increasingly vigorous competition. This is another reality, and I am [sorry] to announce that it will remain the way it is in the coming years. That is why we must have a clear, steady and sustained strategy towards China'.[4]

This assessment corresponds to that of the German government, which emphasises the need to realign relations with China. To this end, a new China Strategy

[1] China was Germany's most important trading partner in 2021 for the 6th consecutive year: https://www.destatis.de/EN/Themes/Economy/Foreign-Trade/trading-partners.html (last accessed on 12 January 2023).

[2] This term was introduced by the European Union in 2019. See European Commission and the High Representative of the Union for Foreign Affairs and Security Policy, Joint Communication to the European Parliament, the European Council and the Council, EU-China—A strategic outlook, JOIN(2019) 5 final, p. 1.

[3] Borrell J, The Sinatra Doctrine: Building a United European Front, Institut Montaigne, Analyses, 9 September 2020, https://www.institutmontaigne.org/en/analysis/sinatra-doctrine-building-united-european-front (last accessed on 12 January 2023).

[4] EEAS Press Team, China: Speech by High-Representative/Vice-President Josep Borrell at the EP debate on EU-China relations, 22 November 2022, https://www.eeas.europa.eu/eeas/china-speech-high-representativevice-president-josep-borrell-ep-debate-eu-china-relations_en (last accessed on 12 January 2023).

(61 pages)[5] has been drafted, which is based on three basic aspirations:[6] First, ways are to be found for continued cooperation with China to implement international goals, especially in the area of climate protection. Second, Germany's competitiveness and innovative capacity should be strengthened by maintaining technological sovereignty and reducing dependence on China, among other things. Third, Germany's economic and political partnerships are to be broadened and thereby diversified.

Within this new strategy, special mention is made of investment relations between Germany and China. When deciding whether to ratify the EU-China Comprehensive Investment Agreement (CAI), Germany wants to consider what impact the agreement will have on the human rights situation, especially with regard to forced labour. Given the numerous human rights allegations made against China by EU Member States, a positive conclusion of the agreement is therefore very unlikely.[7] At the same time, Germany wants to monitor its technology and critical infrastructure more closely and reduce dependencies. These objectives relate to the application and further development of EU and German rules on investment screening, which will be the focus of this contribution.

The following article focuses on two recent investment control cases that illustrate how Germany's attitude towards foreign investment, especially from China, has changed: *Siltronic/GlobalWafers* and *COSCO/HHLA*. Both cases play out against the background of a newly created investment control law system in the EU and a subsequent tightening of German investment screening (Sect. 2). The *Siltronic/GlobalWafers* case shows the discrepancy between the assessment of competition and investment control policy and contemporaneously led to the first court decisions in the field of investment screening in Germany (Sect. 3). The *COSCO/HHLA* case illustrates the internal political conflicts that can arise within Germany and the resulting uncertainties for investors, especially from China (Sect. 4). Finally, both cases have an influence on the current reform discussions in Germany and the EU on a further adjustment of investment control rules (Sect. 5).

---

[5] The new China strategy of the German government has not yet been published; however, a draft document has inter alia been leaked by the German publisher *Spiegel* in November 2022.

[6] See for an English summary, e.g. von der Burchard H, Germany weighs harder line on China and its 'massive human rights violations', Politico, 23 November 2022, https://www.politico.eu/article/germany-mulls-harder-line-on-china-new-deal-with-taiwan/ (last accessed on 12 January 2023).

[7] Apart from this, it should be pointed out that even if Germany ratifies the CAI, success is very uncertain, as demonstrated not least by the difficulties with the Comprehensive Economic and Trade Agreement between Canada and the EU (CETA). In November 2022, the Irish Supreme Court ruled that Ireland's parliamentary efforts to ratify the EU-Canada trade deal are unconstitutional. See Pogatchnik S, Ireland's top court rejects Canada-EU trade deal as unconstitutional, Politico, 11 November 2022, https://www.politico.eu/article/irelands-top-court-rejects-canada-eu-trade-deal-as-unconstitutional/ (last accessed on 12 January 2023).

2 The Tightening of Investment Screening in Germany and the EU

The treatment of foreign direct investment (FDI) in Europe has changed significantly in recent years. Apart from overall policy changes, which now explicitly emphasise the need for a 'strategic autonomy' of the EU,[8] this is particularly due to the introduction of a uniform EU Framework Regulation (EU) 2019/425,[9] which laid the floor for an EU-wide investment screening policy (Sect. 2.1). It not only has political significance, but has led to an adaptation and tightening of national screening rules in the majority of Member States, including Germany in particular (Sect. 2.2).

2.1 Birth of the EU-Screening-Regulation

The development of a common European approach in dealing with foreign direct investment has taken a long time and is far from complete. For a long time, the creation of common European rules was not considered realistic.[10] After the Treaty of Lisbon introduced an EU competence for FDI (Art. 207 TFEU), EU Commissioners *Tajani* and *Barnier* suggested to create a comprehensive screening mechanism at EU level in 2011.[11] In a resolution of 23 May, the European Parliament called for the introduction of an 'ex-ante evaluation of foreign strategic investment'.[12] Nevertheless, it took a long time before the Member States came out in favour of a common European approach in the area of foreign investment control. After a series of Chinese investments in Europe led to heated public debates, Germany, France and Italy sent a joint letter to Trade Commissioner *Cecilia Malmström* in 2017, setting out key points for a proposal on investment

[8] For an overview on this development, see Damen M, EU strategic autonomy 2013–2023—From concept to capacity, EPRS Briefing, PE 733.589—July 2022.

[9] Regulation (EU) 2019/452 of the European Parliament and of the Council of 19 March 2019 establishing a framework for the screening of foreign direct investments into the Union, OJ L 79I, 21.3.2019, pp. 1–14.

[10] Kretzschmar (2022), pp. 50 f.

[11] European Commission, Cabinet Newsletter of Vice President of the European Commission Tajani, No. 33 of 11 February 2011, http://ec.europa.eu/archives/commission_2010-2014/tajani/about/newsletter/files/2011-02/cabnews-33-20110211_en.pdf (last accessed on 12 January 2023). See Bungenberg and Reinhold (2022), pp. 32 f.

[12] European Parliament, Resolution of 23 May 2012 on EU and China: Unbalanced Trade? (2010/2301(INI)), P7_TA(2012)0218.

screening at EU level.[13] This ultimately led to the birth of the EU Screening Regulation.[14]

However, as not all Member States were convinced of the introduction of an investment screening mechanism until the very end and, moreover, the question of competence remained controversial, the parties only agreed on a common EU framework for the control of investments by EU Member States.[15] The EU Screening Regulation has established common obligations, such as the creation of redress mechanisms (Art. 3(5) EU Screening Regulation) or a prohibition of discrimination (Art. 3(2) EU Screening Regulation), whilst the decision on the introduction of investment controls and their implementation remains with the Member States themselves (Art. 1(3) EU Screening Regulation). Thus, there is no obligation for Member States to screen foreign investments so far.

Many were disappointed in view of this compromise, expecting the emergence of a two-tier review mechanism, as in merger control.[16] It is also in stark contrast to the US system of investment control.[17] However, this criticism does not consider that screening of foreign investments, unlike merger control, has so far lacked a common understanding of its necessity and scope.[18] For this reason, it is crucial that a common starting point for the development of an investment control system in Europe was first established. In this regard, important elements of this first EU-wide regulation on the screening of foreign investments were, on the one hand, the creation of a comprehensive cooperation mechanism between Member States and the EU Commission (horizontal cooperation mechanism) as well as between Member States and the Commission (vertical cooperation mechanism) (Art. 6–8 EU Screening Regulation) and, on the other hand, the integration of a uniform concept of a foreseeable impairment of public order or security (Art. 4 EU Screening Regulation). Equally important is that the regulation established the European Commission as a potential key player in the field of investment control.

---

[13] The first Member States' initiative 'Proposals for ensuring an improved level playing field in trade and investment' was published in February 2017: https://www.bmwi.de/Redaktion/DE/Downloads/E/eckpunktepapier-proposals-for-ensuring-an-improved-level-playing-field-in-trade-and-investment.pdf?__blob=publicationFile&v=4 (last accessed on 12 January 2023). The second initiative 'European investment policy: A common approach to investment control' followed on 28 July 2017, https://g8fip1kplyr33r3krz5b97d1-wpengine.netdna-ssl.com/wp-content/uploads/2017/08/170728_Investment-screening_non-paper.pdf (last accessed on 12 January 2023).

[14] See on the evolution of the EU Screening Regulation, e.g. Warchol (2020), pp. 56 ff.; Kretzschmar (2022), S. 52 f.; Bungenberg and Reinhold (2022), pp. 32 f.

[15] See on this aspect, e.g. Hindelang and Moberg (2020), pp. 1435–1445; Bungenberg and Blandfort (2021), pp. 167–170; Korte (2020), pp. 441–463; Bungenberg and Reinhold (2022), pp. 34 ff.

[16] See e.g. Hindelang and Moberg (2020), pp. 1435–1445; Bungenberg and Blandfort (2021), pp. 167–170; Korte (2020), pp. 441–463; Bugge (2020), pp. 467–476.

[17] See on a comparison between U.S. and EU investment screening, e.g. Jacobs (2019), pp. 105–117.

[18] On the following see already Bungenberg and Reinhold (2022), pp. 38 ff.

Since then, the Commission has made extensive use of its new powers, e.g. through repeated requests to Member States to introduce investment control, and through communications in the context of the COVID-19 crisis and the Ukraine war.[19] Considering that by the end of 2022 almost all Member States have introduced some form of investment control, or are at least planning or considering to do so, shows the success of this policy.[20] Due to changed political circumstances, it can be assumed that consensus on EU-wide investment screening has grown and further reforms are therefore foreseeable.

2.2 Development of Investment Control Law in Germany

Foreign investment control was first introduced in Germany in 2004 through a reform of the Foreign Trade and Payments Act (*Außenwirtschaftsgesetz*; AWG) and the Foreign Trade and Payments Ordinance (*Außenwirtschaftsverordnung*; AWV). A number of foreign investments were directed to the defence sector and it was feared that Germany would no longer be able to maintain its security infrastructure.[21] The reform introduced an authorisation requirement for cases in which a non-resident acquirer holds at least 25% of the direct or indirect share of voting rights in a German defence company or a crypto systems manufacturer after a transaction. This sector-specific reporting and authorisation requirement was supplemented by a cross-sectoral screening mechanism in 2009.[22] This expansion took place against the background of national and international discussions on the necessity and possibility of a national review of foreign direct investments to ensure public security and public order, in view of some non-transparent activities of foreign state funds. At the same time, Germany wanted to catch up with other western countries, such as the United Kingdom, France and the US[23]

[19] European Commission, Communication from the Commission Guidance to the Member States concerning foreign direct investment and free movement of capital from third countries, and the protection of Europe's strategic assets, ahead of the application of Regulation (EU) 2019/452 (FDI Screening Regulation), OJ C 99I, 26.3.2020, pp. 1–5; Communication from the Commission Guidance to the Member States concerning foreign direct investment from Russia and Belarus in view of the military aggression against Ukraine and the restrictive measures laid down in recent Council Regulations on sanctions (Council Regulation (EU) No 833/2014 concerning restrictive measures in view of Russia's actions destabilising the situation in Ukraine (OJ L 229, 31.7.2014, p. 1) and its amendments and Council Regulation (EC) No 765/2006 of 18 May 2006 concerning restrictive measures concerning restrictive measures in view of the situation in Belarus (OJ L 134, 20.5.2006, p. 1) and its amendments.), OJ C 151I, 6.4.2022, pp. 1–12.

[20] European Commission, Report from the Commission to the European Parliament and the Council, Second Annual Report on the screening of foreign direct investments into the Union, COM(2022) 433 final, pp. 7 ff.

[21] Roth (2004), p. 431; Dehne (2022), pp. 206 f.

[22] Willems (2008), p. 369; Dehne (2022), pp. 221 ff.

[23] Kollman (2009), pp. 205 f.

Nevertheless, at that time, Germany emphasised openness to foreign investment and a requirement for approval was therefore often viewed critically. However, the perception of foreign investments has changed in recent years. A political turning point was the acquisition of the German robotics manufacturer *KUKA* by the Chinese company *Midea* in 2016, viewed by many as a symbolic sell-out of German technology.[24] German politicians had explicitly wished for an alternative investor, preferably German or at least European.[25] However, such a 'white knight' did not appear on the scene until the very end. The Federal Ministry of Economic Affairs and Energy (today: Federal Ministry for Economic Affairs and Climate Action; BMWK) had carried out a preliminary examination of the transaction, but ultimately did not initiate a formal investigation because it did not see sufficient indications of a threat to public safety or public order. While the transaction could ultimately be completed, the debate about Chinese investments in Germany and Europe had only just gained momentum. Some pointed out that European competition could not keep up with the high takeover bid. Politicians criticised the lack of veto power and held out the prospect of legal adjustments. There was also growing criticism in the industry, pointing to a lack of reciprocity and unfair conditions in competition with China.

Since then, German investment control law has been reformed several times. In 2020 and 2021, cross-sector investment control has been comprehensively adapted to the content of the EU Screening Regulation.[26] In this context, lower intervention thresholds were established and further subcategories defined, for example for semiconductors, 3D printing and other emerging technologies. In addition, the standard of review was changed from the necessity of an 'actual and sufficiently serious threat' to a 'likely impairment'.

Cross-sectoral investment control today[27] covers any direct or indirect acquisition of a domestic company by non-EU/non-EFTA investors, provided that the respective share of voting rights reaches one of the thresholds listed in Sec. 56 AWV. The respective notification threshold depends largely on the company's listing under Sec. 55a(1) AWV. For companies within the meaning of Sec. 55a(1) nos. 1–7 AWV (e.g. operators of critical infrastructures or companies of the media industry), a threshold of 10% of the voting rights applies, which must be reached or exceeded. A threshold of 20% of the voting rights applies to companies within the meaning of Section 55a(1) nos. 8–27 AWV (e.g. developer or manufacturer of certain medical devices, robots, IT products and artificial intelligence applications, but also companies that extract critical raw materials or certain agricultural companies) and a

[24] Chazan G, German angst over Chinese M&A. FT Online, 9 August 2016, https://www.ft.com/content/e0897e24-598e-11e6-8d05-4eaa66292c32 (last accessed on 12 January 2023).

[25] Siemens CEO says not interested in robot maker Kuka, https://www.businessinsider.com/r-siemens-ceo-says-not-interested-in-robot-maker-kuka-2016-6 (last accessed on 12 January 2023).

[26] See e.g. Niestedt and Kunigk (2020), p. 2504; Barth and Käser (2021), p. 813.

[27] See for an overview in English language, e.g. Röhling F and Salaschek U, The Foreign Investment Regulation Review: Germany, 21 October 2022, https://thelawreviews.co.uk/title/the-foreign-investment-regulation-review/germany (last accessed on 12 January 2023).

threshold of 25% applies to all other companies. Sector-specific investment control applies to any complete acquisition of companies or the acquisition of a direct or indirect voting share of 10% by a foreigner, if these companies operate in particularly security-sensitive areas (Sec. 60(1) and (1a), 60a AWV) (e.g. the defense industry). Deviating from the cross-sectoral investment control, EU foreigners are also subject to sector-specific investment control under Sec. 60 (1) AWV, in addition to non-EU acquirers (Sec. 2(5) AWG).

Under Sec. 55(1) AWV, the BMWK examines whether a transaction is likely to impair the public order or security of the Federal Republic of Germany, of another Member State of the European Union or in relation to projects or programs of Union interest. Within this assessment, particular importance is attached to cases involving a company that falls under one of the sectors mentioned in Sec. 55a(1) AWV. A different standard of review applies in the context of sector-specific investment control, where the BMWK examines whether the acquisition is likely to 'impair essential security interests of the Federal Republic of Germany' (Sec. 60(1) AWV).

Following from the strengthening of its investment control in recent years, Germany has seen a steady increase in case numbers. While around 40–50 cases were dealt with between the years 2009 and 2016, the number rose to 106 by 2019 and 306 by 2022.[28] In terms of the countries of origin of foreign investors subject to investment screening, the US accounts for the largest share of cases, followed by the United Kingdom and the People's Republic of China.[29] Although China does not take first place, the cases often involved controversy, which will be shown below.

3 Technological Sovereignty and Security of Supply: *Siltronic/GlobalWafers*

Parallel to the tightening of German investment control, investments by Chinese investors were repeatedly discussed in public. This particularly includes the case of the failed takeover of *Siltronic*, a Munich-based silicon wafer producer, by the Taiwanese company *GlobalWafers*. *Siltronic* is one of the world's largest manufacturers of hyperpure silicon wafers for the semiconductor industry, which form the basis for modern micro- and nanoelectronics. *GlobalWafers* planned to acquire the company in 2020 for approximately €4.4 billion. Ultimately, however, the takeover failed because both parties were unable to meet the agreed long stop date of 31 January 2022 due to the length of the regulatory process.[30]

---

[28] Federal Ministry for Economic Affairs and Climate Action, Investment Screening in Germany: Facts & Figures, 9 January 2023, p. 9.

[29] Federal Ministry for Economic Affairs and Climate Action, Investment Screening in Germany: Facts & Figures, 9 January 2023, p. 11.

[30] Burger L and Rinke A, GlobalWafers' Siltronic deal fails as Germany misses deadline, Reuters, 1 February 2022, https://www.reuters.com/business/globalwafers-siltronic-deal-fails-german-govt-approval-misses-deadline-2022-01-31/ (last accessed on 12 January 2023).

What is special about this case is that, for the first time, an official insight into the way the BMWK examines investment control cases was provided, which revealed a number of fundamental problems. The BMWK does not publish any case reports. Occasionally, only brief press releases are issued, meaning information about 'critical' takeover bids only becomes known via the press or online postings by law firms based on their own cases or on leaked documents.[31] In the past, this is how the public became aware of, for example, *SGCC*'s prevented entry into the electricity grid operator *50Hertz*, or the first official prohibition decision by the BMWK in the *IMST* case.[32] Another reason why the *Siltronic/GlobalWafers* case is of particular interest is the fact that the different approach of a competitive versus an investment control policy assessment became apparent. In *Siltronic/GlobalWafers*, the German Federal Cartel Office (FCO) first cleared the merger from a competition perspective (Sect. 3.1). During the investment control procedure, the BMWK refused to take a decision, so that the parties could not meet their deadline for obtaining regulatory approvals (Sect. 3.2). *Siltronic* and *GlobalWafers* took legal action against the BMWK's conduct, resulting in the first court decisions in the field of investment control in Germany (Sect. 3.3).

3.1 Merger Control: Approval by the Federal Cartel Office

The FCO cleared the planned acquisition within the 1-month preliminary examination period on 8 February 2021.[33] The worldwide investigations of the FCO had shown that the merger was not expected to significantly impede effective competition, although *GlobalWafers* had steadily expanded its global market position through acquisitions in recent years, and *Siltronic* occupied a comparable market position to *GlobalWafers* in terms of market shares. The FCO's enquiries with a number of significant customers of silicon wafers had not revealed any significant concerns on the transaction with regard to possible non-coordinated effects of the merger and to the creation or strengthening of a joint dominant position of the remaining leading suppliers:

The market shares of both companies were below the presumption thresholds for a single dominant position under Sec. 18(4) of the (German) Act against Restraints

---

[31] See e.g. BMWK, Elmos chip factory cannot be sold to Chinese investor—cabinet blocks sale, https://www.bmwk.de/Redaktion/EN/Pressemitteilungen/2022/11/20221109-elmos-chip-factory-cannot-be-sold-to-chinese-investor-cabinet-blocks-sale.html (last accessed on 12 January 2023).

[32] See e.g. Freshfields (2020), German foreign investment authority takes off the gloves, https://www.freshfields.us/49bba2/globalassets/imported/documents/6ebb78e3-812b-4ac0-8df4-4474d13ae7a5.pdf (last accessed on 12 January 2023); Schoening F et al. (2020), This time's for real—German government prohibits acquisition of a tech company by a Chinese acquirer, https://www.engage.hoganlovells.com/knowledgeservices/news/this-times-for-real (last accessed on 12 January 2023).

[33] See Federal Cartel Office, Case Report of 11 March 2021, B8-25/21 (in German).

of Competition (*Gesetz gegen Wettbewerbsbeschränkungen*; GWB).[34] In the area of common, relatively standardised wafers, the FCO assumed that the products of the merging parties are in principle substitutable with each other, but also with the wafers of their larger and smaller competitors. Any additional scope for behaviour as a result of the merger was therefore considered to be limited in this area by the existence of sufficient current and potential alternative products.[35] The FCO also did not consider both companies to be particularly close competitors with regard to their specialisations and focus of supply.[36] In the case of wafers with very specific characteristics, which, however, only account for a small share of the wafer market, the customers' current alternative sources of supply may well be more limited. In these constellations, however, there is a mutual dependence between wafer supplier and customer from the FCO's point of view. Moreover, the countervailing power of demand was found to counteract the emergence of merger-related unilateral behavioural leeway.[37] The FCO pointed out that the buyers, who are often many times more financially powerful and have higher sales, pursue differentiated procurement strategies. These are characterised by 'multi-sourcing', regular bilateral price negotiations and volume shifts.

Due to the comparatively strong and symmetrical market position in terms of market shares after the merger, the FCO examined the question of whether the merger could threaten to create or strengthen a joint dominant position of the leading suppliers.[38] However, from the results of the investigation, the FCO was able to rule out this risk. It did consider the presumption thresholds of Sec. 18(6) GWB to be fulfilled both before and after the merger. However, a large number of factors argued against the possibility or further stabilisation of coordinated market behaviour:[39] According to the FCO's analysis, the market is characterised by a relatively high degree of transparency in certain competition-relevant areas. However, this does not only extend to the large wafer manufacturers, but also includes the customer. Due to customised production and bilateral contract negotiations, not all competition-relevant factors are transparent. According to the FCO's analysis, the market is characterised by high volatility and dynamics. Moreover, as suppliers specialising in wafer production, *Siltronic* and *GlobalWafers* do not encounter each other on other markets and the suppliers are not intertwined with each other, e.g. through significant reciprocal supply relationships. In the FCO's view, these facts limit the possibilities of effectively sanctioning competitive advances by individual suppliers. Furthermore, there was a significant incentive for suppliers to ensure the highest possible utilisation of their production capacities (among other things because of the high fixed costs of production). Finally, the FCO considered the countervailing buyer

[34] Federal Cartel Office, Case Report of 11 March 2021, B8-25/21 (in German), p. 3.

[35] Federal Cartel Office, Case Report of 11 March 2021, B8-25/21 (in German).

[36] Federal Cartel Office, Case Report of 11 March 2021, B8-25/21 (in German).

[37] Federal Cartel Office, Case Report of 11 March 2021, B8-25/21 (in German).

[38] Federal Cartel Office, Case Report of 11 March 2021, B8-25/21 (in German), p. 4.

[39] Federal Cartel Office, Case Report of 11 March 2021, B8-25/21 (in German).

power and the fact that buyers regularly renegotiate purchase prices as part of multi-sourcing strategies and shift quantities between the suppliers they qualify.

As a result, the FCO was able to rule out any competition concerns regarding the acquisition. Interestingly, however, it felt compelled to point out that the clearance had been granted solely based on the expected effects on competition, while the FCO was not competent to make an assessment based on foreign trade law.[40]

3.2 *Investment Control: Decision by Non-Decision*

Unlike merger review, the investment screening by the BMWK was associated with a number of difficulties and ultimately led to the failure of the takeover.[41] The starting point of the proceedings was an application by the two parties for the issuance of a 'certificate of non-objection' (*Unbedenklichkeitsbescheinigung*) in December 2020. Under Sec. 58(1) AWV, the BMWK shall certify, upon written or electronic application, that it does not object to an acquisition within the meaning of Sec. 55 AWV if there is no objection to the acquisition in terms of public order or security of the Federal Republic of Germany, of another Member State of the European Union, or in relation to projects or programmes of Union interest within the meaning of Art. 8 EU Screening Regulation. The certificate of non-objection shall be deemed to have been issued if the BMWK does not launch an assessment procedure within 2 months according to Sec. 14a(1) no. 1 AWG (Sec. 58(2) AWV).

By decision of 3 February 2021, the BMWK then initiated a cross-sectoral investment control procedure as, in the Ministry's view, the submitted documents provided grounds for a more in-depth investigation. At the same time, the Ministry asked for answers to a total of 15 questions about the project and requested an English summary which was sent to the European Commission. In a further letter, the BMWK requested the parties to provide a series of additional information, including the question of whether certain products were covered by the EU Dual-Use Regulation, but also the supply situation for wafers in Germany and Europe, and the question in which areas *Siltronic* or its products were superior to those of *GlobalWafers*.

On 14 June 2021, the BMWK submitted an offer to the parties to enter into negotiations on contractual arrangements to ensure the public order and security of the Federal Republic of Germany. The authority pointed out that for the duration of the contractual negotiations, the time limit under Sec. 14a(6)(2) AWG was suspended. *Siltronic* and *GlobalWafers* agreed to enter into such contract negotiations. However, as these were repeatedly delayed and did not progress, they sent letters to the BMWK in October and December 2021 pointing out the approaching

[40] Federal Cartel Office, Case Report of 11 March 2021, B8-25/21 (in German).

[41] The following procedure is reproduced in: Berlin Administrative Court, Decision of 27 January 2022, 4 L 111/22, paras. 3–12 (in German).

long-stop date and attempting to refute the BMWK's concerns, particularly the fear that the People's Republic of China could gain access to the technology in question through shareholdings or otherwise.

Thereupon, on 7 December 2021, the BMWK extended the investigation period under Sec. 14a(4) AWG, referring to 'special difficulties of a factual or legal nature'. The BMWK justified these difficulties with the significance of *Siltronic*. According to the BMWK, *Siltronic*'s technology is a sensitive high technology with high innovation dynamics, the technical assessment of which entails particular difficulties. This also concerned the assessment of future fields of application and its relevance for the European chip industry. The BMWK described *Siltronic* as one of the last remaining European-controlled manufacturers of coated high-purity wafers in the EU. As a pre-product for microchips, they are irreplaceable for the industry, as they are used in almost all future technologies. According to the BMWK, *Siltronic* is therefore a very important supplier and also produces dual-use products that are used in sensor technology, for example, radar technology or airspace surveillance. Another problem for the BMWK was that the acquisition was subject to approval by the Chinese competition authority. It assumed that conditions would be imposed that would benefit the Chinese semiconductor industry. The BMWK wanted to wait for this decision to be able to assess how the conditions would affect the acquisition and thus the investment screening process. From the BMWK's point of view, a possible outflow of technology and sensitive process know-how to China was a relevant aspect to be considered in the context of a possible impairment of public order and security in Germany and other EU Member States. In this respect, the BMWK also referred to a critical statement by the EU Commission and two other Member States.

Siltronic and *GlobalWafers* criticised this decision to extend the review in several letters to the BMWK, not only against the background of the concerns expressed therein, but also because of the risk of exceeding the long stop date. After the BMWK did not respond to a letter of 13 January 2022 containing an additional offer to meet the BMWK's concerns, the companies filed an application for interim relief with the Berlin Administrative Court on 18 January 2022. At the same time, they brought an action against the extension decision before the same court. However, as the application for interim relief was not successful, the long stop date could not be met and the takeover failed.

3.3 Decisions by the Berlin Administrative Court and the Higher Administrative Court Berlin-Brandenburg

With regard to the decisions of the Administrative Court of Berlin and the Higher Administrative Court of Berlin-Brandenburg, it must be considered that these concerned a special constellation, as *Siltronic* and *GlobalWafers* had initially applied for interim legal protection. The courts therefore only had a short period of time to reach their decisions. However, it became clear in both decisions which line of argumentation the courts generally take with regard to investment control: The BMWK is given a great deal of leeway and the concerns raised—correct or not—are given higher priority overall than the economic interests of the companies.

Siltronic and *GlobalWafers* applied to the Berlin Administrative Court for a declaration that a 'fiction of release' of the transaction under Sec. 58a(2) AWV had occurred. According to Sec. 58a(2) AWV, a clearance of the transaction shall deemed to have been issued if an assessment procedure pursuant to Sec. 55 AWV is not launched within the deadline cited in Section 14a(1) no. 1 AWG, or if the powers pursuant to Sec. 59 (1) and (3) AWV are not exercised in an assessment procedure launched and the deadlines cited in Sec. 14a (1) no. 2 AWG have expired. The court considered this application to be admissible in principle.[42] On the merits, however, the court held that the claim was not well-founded.[43]

First, the court rejected the special urgency of a decision on the merits.[44] The precondition for this is that the settlement of a provisional situation appears to be necessary to avert serious and unreasonable disadvantages which cannot be reached in any other way and which the decision on the merits would no longer be able to remedy.[45] The court was not convinced that exceeding the long stop date would cause such an unreasonable disadvantage to both companies. It lacked information on the expenses incurred so far and on the question of whether these would be lost after the deadline. Particularly, the court pointed out that the parties would not be prevented from initiating a new takeover procedure in a timely manner. The court also did not consider the significant drop in the price of *Siltronic*'s shares as an indication of a possible loss.

Second, the court found that even if a special urgency were to be assumed, a provisional release would have to be refused due to overriding reasons.[46] In this context, it weighed up the consequences, whereby it considered the disadvantages that the companies would have to accept if their urgent application was unsuccessful to be of secondary importance to those that would occur on the side of the BMWK if the application was granted.[47] It did not consider the intended transaction to be prevented forever as a result of an unfavourable court decision. In this context, the

---

[42] Berlin Administrative Court, Decision of 27 January 2022, 4 L 111/22, paras. 3–12 (in German), paras. 31–35.

[43] Berlin Administrative Court, Decision of 27 January 2022, 4 L 111/22, paras. 3–12 (in German), paras. 37–43.

[44] Berlin Administrative Court, Decision of 27 January 2022, 4 L 111/22, paras. 3–12 (in German), paras. 40–41.

[45] Berlin Administrative Court, Decision of 27 January 2022, 4 L 111/22, paras. 3–12 (in German), para. 40.

[46] Berlin Administrative Court, Decision of 27 January 2022, 4 L 111/22, paras. 3–12 (in German), paras. 42–43.

[47] Berlin Administrative Court, Decision of 27 January 2022, 4 L 111/22, paras. 3–12 (in German), para. 43.

court referred to the importance of *Siltronic* as the only significant manufacturer of wafers produced in the EU in the near future as a result of global digitisation and the associated worldwide demand for its products. In contrast, the court found that if the transaction were to be completed after 31 January 2022 as a result of the court decision, the associated consequences for the respondent would ultimately be irreversible. The court also considered the concerns raised by the BMWK as plausible for the assumption of a probable impairment of public order or public safety. In doing so, the court emphasised that the BMWK had a wide margin of appreciation; the density of judicial control had been significantly limited by the current wording of Sec. 55a AWV. In view of this standard, it did not appear to the court that the concerns cited were irrelevant from the outset. Above all, the feared outflow of know-how would already be realised directly with the takeover. Even if the takeover could be reversed, the court assumed that a transfer of knowledge, which could not be ruled out, would be irreversible and could have adverse effects.

This assessment by the Administrative Court was later confirmed by the Higher Administrative Court of Berlin-Brandenburg.[48] Unlike the Administrative Court, the Higher Administrative Court assumed a time limit suspension until the submission of the decision of the Chinese competition authority on 26 January 2022.[49] In this context, it did not consider the repeated requests for information by the BMWK to be arbitrary or superfluous, but rather logical. In addition, the Higher Administrative Court also confirmed the decision with regard to the weighing of consequences.[50] The court questioned whether a determination of the effect of fiction can be made at all by way of an interim order. Contemporaneously, it shared the view of the administrative court that the danger of an irreversible outflow of technology had to be given special consideration. In doing so, it disagreed with the companies that the Administrative Court had adopted the concerns of the BMWK unchecked, but justified the plausibility check, among other things, with the limited time for the decision.

4 Critical Infrastructure as a Subject of Political Dispute: *COSCO/HHLA*

The *Siltronic/GlobalWafers* case offered insights into the way the BMWK reviews foreign investments. It has become clear that the BMWK takes an overall view based on various indications to reach a decision, including the decision of foreign

[48] Higher Administrative Court of Berlin-Brandenburg, Decision of 31 January 2022, OVG 1 S 10/22.

[49] Higher Administrative Court of Berlin-Brandenburg, Decision of 31 January 2022, OVG 1 S 10/22, paras. 4–7.

[50] Higher Administrative Court of Berlin-Brandenburg, Decision of 31 January 2022, OVG 1 S 10/22, paras. 8–14.

authorities. The *COSCO/HHLA* case, on the other hand, is an example of the importance of political trends for the concrete outcome of investment control procedures. It shows that internal political disputes increase the unpredictability of German investment control, especially in cases involving Chinese investors.

On 21 September 2022, *COSCO Shipping Ports Limited* (COSCO) and *Hamburger Hafen und Logistik AG* (HHLA) signed an agreement for the acquisition of a 35% stake in *HHLA Container Terminal Tollerort* in the Port of Hamburg.[51] At that time, *COSCO* already held shares in numerous other European ports, including two-thirds of the shares in the port of Piraeus.[52] Whilst the city of Hamburg, *HHLA* and the German Chancellor *Olaf Scholz* (former mayor of Hamburg) were positive about the acquisition from the beginning, it was strongly criticised by the German Minister of Economics *Robert Habeck* in particular, but also by the German Foreign Office, the German Federal Intelligence Service and other governmental bodies.[53] The European Commission also expressed its opposition to *COSCO*'s entry, as did various other EU Member States and third countries.[54] In addition to the now common reservations about the state capitalist structures within the People's Republic of China, security policy concerns were expressed—reinforced by the experiences with Russia in the wake of the Ukraine war—that China could deliberately exploit its participation for strategic purposes as part of its expansionist drive, including a possible attack on Taiwan. However, due to the persistence of the German Chancellor, a stalemate was reached at the political level, which raised fears of a fictitious authorisation under Sec. 58a(2) AWV due to the passage of time.

As a result of political negotiations, it was finally agreed to allow an acquisition of 24.9% by *COSCO*.[55] It was argued that this would prevent a strategic shareholding in the terminal and reduce the acquisition to purely financial participation. In addition to this partial prohibition, *COSCO* was prohibited from being contractually

51 Mardell J, COSCO takes stake in Hamburg Port terminal, Merics, 30 September 2021, https://merics.org/de/tracker/cosco-takes-stake-hamburg-port-terminal (last accessed on 12 January 2023).

52 Mardell J, COSCO takes stake in Hamburg Port terminal, Merics, 30 September 2021, https://merics.org/de/tracker/cosco-takes-stake-hamburg-port-terminal (last accessed on 12 January 2023); Tatlow DK, China's Stake in World Ports Sharpens Attention on Political Influence, Newsweek, 10 September 2022, https://www.newsweek.com/2022/10/14/chinas-stake-world-ports-sharpens-attention-political-influence-1749215.html (last accessed on 12 January 2023).

53 Tao A, Olaf Scholz's China Gamble, The Diplomat, 21 December 2022, https://thediplomat.com/2022/12/olaf-scholzs-china-gamble/ (last accessed on 12 January 2023); Rinke A and Marsh S, German coalition divided over Chinese bid for Hamburg port terminal, Reuters, 14 September 2022, https://www.reuters.com/business/autos-transportation/german-coalition-divided-over-chinese-bid-hamburg-port-terminal-2022-09-13/ (last accessed on 12 January 2023).

54 Thierry Breton issues China warning ahead of Scholz's Beijing visit, Euractiv, 1 November 2022, https://www.euractiv.com/section/global-europe/news/thierry-breton-issues-china-warning-ahead-of-scholzs-beijing-visit/ (last accessed on 12 January 2023).

55 See the statement of HHLA on 26 October 2022: Federal Government approves investment by CSPL in operating company HHLA Container Terminal Tollerort, https://hhla.de/en/media/news/detail-view/federal-government-approves-investment-by-cspl-in-operating-company-hhla-ctt (last accessed on 12 January 2023).

granted veto rights over strategic business or personnel decisions. The compromise was not only criticised in public, but was also accompanied by a critical protocol note in which, in addition to the BMWK, the Foreign Office and the Federal Ministry of Finance, among others, were involved.[56] Since then, there have been political discussions about a further tightening of German investment control, including an adjustment of the decision-making structures.

This dispute had also immediate consequences for an overlapping transaction concerning the sale of the wafer production of *Elmos Semiconductor* to the Swedish competitor *Silex Microsystems*, which in turn belongs to the Chinese *Sai Group*.[57] This acquisition was prohibited shortly after the settlement in the *COSCO* case, with *Elmos* pointing out that positive signals had been sent by the BMWK in advance. One point of contention in the aftermath of the decision was the extent to which the technology in question could not be subsumed under the concept of 'technology sovereignty' because it was simply obsolete, while at the same time emphasising the importance of a signalling effect in this case. Similarly, a shareholding in *ERS electronic*, a company active in the semiconductor industry, was also blocked.[58]

5 Current Reform Discussions in Germany and the EU

The *COSCO/HHLA* case has led to new discussions on a reform of investment control law in Germany. It is more likely, however, that reform will first be sought at the EU level which will subsequently lead to a tightening of national rules. A reform of the EU Screening Regulation is already anticipated within the regulation itself. Under Art. 15(1) EU Screening Regulation, the European Commission is to carry out an evaluation of its functioning and effectiveness by 12 October 2023 and every 5 years thereafter. The Commission shall submit a report to the European Parliament and the Council, which may be accompanied by an appropriate legislative proposal (para. 2).

To this end, the European Commission commissioned the OECD to prepare a comprehensive study on the effectiveness and efficiency of the existing regulatory regime at EU level, published in November 2022.[59] In this study, the EU Screening

56 Germany agrees on compromise over China port bid, DW, 26 December 2022, https://www.dw.com/en/germany-agrees-on-compromise-over-china-port-bid/a-63547949 (last accessed on 12 January 2023).

57 German ministry seeks to block Chinese chip factory takeover, DW, 11 August 2022, https://www.dw.com/en/german-ministry-seeks-to-block-chinese-chip-factory-takeover/a-63681593 (last accessed on 12 January 2023).

58 Rinke A and Murray M, Germany blocks Chinese stake in two chipmakers over security concerns, Reuters, 10 November 2022, https://www.reuters.com/markets/deals/germany-block-chinese-takeover-semiconductor-firm-ers-electronic-handelsblatt-2022-11-09/ (last accessed on 12 January 2023).

59 OECD, Framework for Screening Foreign Direct Investment into the EU, Assessing effectiveness and efficiency, 2022.

Regulation is recognised as being of outstanding importance for the creation of a common European awareness, an intensive exchange between the Member States as well as a harmonisation of the regulatory conditions in the EU.[60] At the same time, a number of inefficiencies are pointed out, especially in the context of the cooperation mechanism.[61] The absence of investment control regimes in some Member States, the limited scope of application of existing national regulations, inadequacies within the procedure provided for by the EU Screening Regulation and a lack of overall strategy are named as significant impairments of effectiveness and efficiency.[62]

One of the subjects of recent reform considerations is an expansion of investment controls to include also capital exports ('outbound investment' or 'outward investment'). The EU is taking inspiration from parallel legislation in the United States, where such controls have been under discussion for some time.[63] This would lead to a considerable expansion of EU investment control, especially with regard to export-oriented Member States such as Germany. Primarily, one could think of security-based regulations within European export control, such as the Dual-Use Regulation.[64] In line with the EU's value-based trade policy, however, environmental and social policy reasons for a restriction would also be conceivable.

Other planned adjustments concern investment guarantees.[65] The German government announced that, particularly with regard to investments in China, a strategic adjustment of the granting of guarantees would be considered to diversify investment flows.[66] Germany issued investment guarantees with a total volume of €2.6 billion in 2021, about three times as much as in the previous year (€0.9 billion).[67] In the first half of 2022, the newly issued guarantee volume amounted to €1.0 billion (capital and earnings) with a number of 14 guarantees issued.[68]

---

[60] OECD, Framework for Screening Foreign Direct Investment into the EU, Assessing effectiveness and efficiency, 2022, pp. 14 ff.

[61] OECD, Framework for Screening Foreign Direct Investment into the EU, Assessing effectiveness and efficiency, 2022, pp. 23 ff.

[62] OECD, Framework for Screening Foreign Direct Investment into the EU, Assessing effectiveness and efficiency, 2022, pp. 51 ff.

[63] Bauerle Danzman and Kilcrease (2022).

[64] Regulation (EU) 2021/821 of the European Parliament and of the Council of 20 May 2021 setting up a Union regime for the control of exports, brokering, technical assistance, transit and transfer of dual-use items (recast), OJ L 206, 11.6.2021, p. 1–461.

[65] For Germany, see https://www.investitionsgarantien.de/en (last accessed on 12 January 2023).

[66] Germany to cap investment guarantees for China, The Business Times, 23 November 2022, https://www.businesstimes.com.sg/international/germany-cap-investment-guarantees-china (last accessed on 12 January 2023).

[67] Federal Ministry for Economic Affairs and Climate Action, Investment Guarantees Annual Report 2021, May 2022.

[68] Federal Ministry for Economic Affairs and Climate Action, Investment Guarantees Interim Report 2022, July 2022.

6 Outlook

In times of a worldwide crises, especially after the Russian attack and aggression against the Ukraine, China is openly seen in Europe more and more critical. As a result, investment relations between China and Germany are currently beset with considerable difficulties stemming from various political divergences. Security and industrial policy seem now very closely, almost inseparably, interconnected. Germany is fearing not only investments in critical infrastructure, but also might be seeing industrial policy as a criterium when discussing public order and security. Furthermore, reciprocity—what kind of investments in which sectors are permitted in especially China—still plays a crucial role in current discussions. It also plays a role in the EU's approaches in international and European procurement law, as well as, e.g. in the context of the new Foreign Subsidies Regulation. Overall, the German approach in investment screening, which is shared by a number of other Member States as well as the European Commission, points to a certain form of decoupling following from a very strict public order and security approach. In the long term, this will also affect other Asian companies whose corporate structures include Chinese shareholders. From today's perspective, the original enthusiasm for a speedy conclusion of a joint investment agreement with China, therefore, seems astonishing. Human rights issues, the idea of greater independence from Chinese imports, and, not least, China's role in the war in Ukraine preclude a successful conclusion. A future FTA is currently not even discussed any further. What should not be forgotten, however, is that in the area of investment control and other areas, a large number of private companies are the ones who suffer. From a business point of view, it seems necessary that the political objectives are at least be made transparent and that decisions, e.g. of the BMWK, thus become more predictable. Otherwise, costly takeover attempts threaten to fail, which in turn can lead to a loss of confidence in Germany and Europe as an investment hub. A further burden on the investment relationship would be to extend investment control to capital exports. At this point, it should be considered that European companies, for their part, have to invest abroad to remain competitive.

Overall, there are difficult times ahead in which it will be important to balance political and economic interests carefully and, in any case, to offer companies legal certainty as far as possible. For the relationship between Germany, the EU and China, however, the signs are currently pointing to further alienation from each other.

References

Barth C, Käser AC (2021) Erneute Novellierung der deutschen Investitionskontrolle – Die 17. Verordnung zur Änderung der Außenwirtschaftsverordnung. Neue Zeitschrift für Gesellschaftsrecht 24(19):813–820

Bauerle Danzman S, Kilcrease E (2022) Sand in the silicon: designing an outbound investment controls mechanism. Atlantic Council Issue Brief, 14 September 2022

Bugge TD (2020) Comment on exploring possibilities and limits of the EU and Member States to set up an investment screening mechanism in the light of union law. In: Hindelang S, Moberg A (eds) YSEC yearbook of socio-economic constitutions 2020. Springer, Cham, pp 467–476

Bungenberg M, Blandfort F (2021) Investment screening – a new era of European protectionism? In: Hahn M, Van der Loo G (eds) Law and practice of the common commercial policy – the first 10 years after the Treaty of Lisbon. Brill, Leiden, pp 161–184

Bungenberg M, Reinhold P (2022) The evolution of the EU investment control legal regime: decentralization as a unifying factor. In: de Jong B, Looijestijn-Clearie A, Tans S, Veenbrink M (eds) The rise of public security interest in corporate mergers and acquisitions, Radboud economic law series, vol 5. Wolf Legal Publishers, Nijmegen, pp 31–45

Dehne B (2022) Investitionskontrolle in Deutschland – Die Kontrolle der Beteiligung ausländischer Staatsfonds an deutschen Unternehmen durch das Außenwirtschaftsrecht. Nomos, Baden-Baden

Hindelang S, Moberg A (2020) The art of casting political dissent in law: the EU's Framework for the screening of foreign direct investment. Common Mark Law Rev 57(5):1427–1460

Jacobs J (2019) Tiptoeing the line between national security and protectionism: a comparative approach to foreign direct investment screening in the United States and European Union. Int J Leg Inf 47(2):105–117

Kollman K (2009) Prüfung ausländischer Investitionen in Deutschland. Außenwirtschaftliche Praxis 15:205–209

Korte S (2020) Exploring possibilities and limits of the EU and Member States to set up an investment screening mechanism in the light of union law. In: Hindelang S, Moberg A (eds) YSEC yearbook of socio-economic constitutions 2020. Springer, Cham, pp 435–465

Kretzschmar M (2022) Die Überprüfung drittstaatlicher Unternehmensakquisitionen zum Schutz der öffentlichen Ordnung und Sicherheit in der Europäischen Union – Grundlagen für eine unionsweite Rechtsangleichung. Nomos, Baden-Baden

Niestedt M, Kunigk N (2020) Novelle des Außenwirtschaftsrechts – Verschärfung der Investitionskontrolle. Neue Juristische Wochenschrift 73(35):2504–2509

Roth T (2004) Der Erwerb von Rüstungs- und Kryptounternehmen durch Gebietsfremde. Außenwirtschaftliche Praxis 10:431–434

Warchol J (2020) The birth of EU screening regulation. In: Hindelang S, Moberg A (eds) YSEC yearbook of socio-economic constitutions 2020. Springer, Cham, pp 53–75

Willems H (2008) Braucht Deutschland ein Kontrollrecht gegenüber ausländischen Investoren? Außenwirtschaftliche Praxis 14:369–373

Marc Bungenberg is Director of the Europa-Institut and a professor of public law, European law, public international law and international economic law and Jean Monnet Chair for the EU Constitutional Framework of International Dispute Settlement and the Rule of Law at Saarland University in Germany (since 2015), as well as visiting professor at the University of Lausanne/ Switzerland (since 2011). He has taught at inter alia Sydney, Geneva, Lucerne, Lausanne, Tashkent, Copenhagen, Hamburg, and Munich. He is the recipient of multiple research grants. He received his doctorate in law from the University of Hannover and wrote his habilitation treatise at the Friedrich-Schiller-University Jena. He holds an LL.M. from Lausanne University. His main fields of research are European (Common Commercial Policy, public procurement and state aid law) and international economic law, particularly international investment and WTO law.

Philipp Reinhold is a Research Associate at the Chair of Public Law, Public International Law and European Law and the Europa-Institut, Saarland University, Germany. He received his doctorate in law from Saarland University. He studied law at the University of Bonn and the Université de Lausanne and was, as a staff member of the German Monopolies Commission, involved in the drafting of Chapter IV ("Chinese State Capitalism: A challenge for the European market economy") of the Biennial Report XXIII ("Wettbewerb 2020").

China's Dilemma in Renewing Its Belt and Road Initiative

Leon Trakman

Contents

Abstract China faces difficult choices in renewing its Belt and Road Initiative [BRI] in the post-Pandemic era. With its primary BRI now extending from Asia to Africa, Latin America and beyond, China is depicted as a saviour rescuing developing states from their colonial roots and sublimation to the economic outreach of Western liberal states. Alternatively, China is envisaged as a new colonial landlord acquiring property through investment and exploiting local economies for its own economic and political good, at their expense. For those mediating between these two extremes, China is both well intended in seeking to promote global investment and to assist developing states, while sometimes aggressively seeking economic benefits for its outbound investors. Whether it is doing so primarily for its own good or for the wellbeing of its developing state partners, conciliators infer, would depend on the specific case. This article explores these dynamics in China's treaties

---

The author thanks Lynne Wade for her editorial assistance. The study was supported by research grants from the Australian Research Council and the Herbert Smith Freehills China International Business and Economic Law Centre (CIBEL).

L. Trakman (✉)
University of New South Wales, Faculty of Law, Sydney, NSW, Australia
e-mail: L.trakman@unsw.edu.au

M. Bungenberg et al. (eds.), *Asian Yearbook of International Economic Law 2023*,
Asian Yearbook of International Economic Law (2023) 2023: 23–52,
https://doi.org/10.1007/16517_2023_20, Published online: 19 April 2023

providing for settling investment disputes along its BRI. It examines how China might reframe these dispute resolution options in the future.

1 Introduction

The West's recent portrayals of China as a dominant inbound and outbound investment state is decidedly negative. China is depicted as entrenching its economic dominance along its global trade and investment highway, known as its Belt and Road Initiative [BRI], through one-sided Bilateral Investment Treaties [BITs] that it has devised and implemented in its own interests. China is portrayed as expanding its Free Trade Agreements [FTAs] to extend its competitive advantage through regional partnerships, while catering to domestic protectionism that is distrustful of liberalised trade. The image is of China replicating its planned domestic economy internationally, under the guise of its willingness to engage in free trade and investment. Critics portray China as expanding its planned people-control from its domestic to the international community. The derision is of China using its state sovereignty to subordinate other developing states with which it is engaged in investment relationships, rather than recognise their sovereign rights.[1]

This depiction of China is exemplified through the image of it directing traffic along an infrastructure pathway of its creation and direction.[2] Directing state and investor travel along that Belt and Road, China is envisaged as engaged in the planned orchestrating of foreign direct investment, imposing burdensome infrastructure loans on dependent states and extracting selective licensing rights. At the same time, it is depicted as extending treaty and contract protections for the benefit of its outbound investors on empire building missions across Asia, Africa and Latin America.[3]

An illustration of China allegedly directing developing host states along its BRI is reflected in criticisms of its control over the formulation of its investment treaties or investor-state contracts. Under scrutiny is the challenge that China positioned itself in its first model BIT to impose its national interest and police powers to expropriate or otherwise regulate the investments of inbound foreign investors. As China grew into the second largest outbound investor, it reframed its model treaties to protect foreign investors, inferentially to empower its own outbound investors to invoke

[1] SOEs are sometimes depicted as engaging in unfair competition in being arms of the Chinese state in engaging with other sovereign states and non-state entities. See OECD (2016) State-Owned Enterprises as Global Competitors: A Challenge or an Opportunity?, p. 15.

[2] See Office of United State Trade Representative, Joint Statement by the United States, European Union and Japan at MC11, 12 December 2017, https://ustr.gov/about-us/policy-offices/press-office/press-releases/2017/december/joint-statement-united-states (joint statement 'to eliminate these and other unfair market distorting and protectionist practices by third countries').

[3] Chi and Li (2021), pp. 125–150.

those protections against developing host states.[4] The insinuation is not that China invariably so engaged in fact. It is rather that it positioned itself to able to do so under treaty and customary international law when it considered it economically justified or politically expedient. These arguments of its treaty empowerment and disempowerment of developing states is not presented as being wholly distinct to China.[5] It is instead highlighted as part of its empowerment and a reason for prospective BIT partner states to be precautious in dealing with it.[6]

The accusation of China building a BRI to sublimate the sovereign authority of vulnerable developing states is arguably overstated. China has sound reason to act, not as a dominant intruder targeted developing states along its BRI, but as engaging in fair state-to-state and investor-state practices. If it is to enjoy the confidence and trust of actual and prospective state partners and their investors, it is well motivated to offer them shared BRI benefits. One key motivate is for it to facilitate economic growth in developing states, to encourage their loyalty to it, together with a sense of common purpose. Another is to espouse its support in raising productivity, domestic standards of living, and improving social and health care benefits in developing states.[7]

China nevertheless faces formidable obstacles in formulating an outbound investment framework in a new world order. In part, Western proponents of free trade, while insinuating that China is not committed to it, have themselves gradually shifted away from investment liberalisation. Their new world order is beset with decentralisation as wary Western states have restricted reliance on foreign sources of supply and reverted to protectionism. The Pandemic has accentuated this shift from delocalisation to localisation. Trade sanctions imposed by the US and its allies, accentuated during COVID-19, have undermined inbound and outbound investment opportunities for Chinese investors.[8] China's retaliation and spiralling countermeasures has caused a downward slope in reliance on international investment; and has also led to shared economic hardship.[9]

The picture going forward is not entirely bleak. In leaning towards compliance with international health safety measures, China is gradually reacting proactively to climate change initiatives, remedying ecological damage to the environment and redressing their intergenerational implications. It is doing so by supporting foreign

[4] See Henckels (2018), p. 2825; Giest (2017), p. 337.

[5] Desierto D, Laird I, Sourgens F (2017) Oxford University Press Investment Claims Summer Academy, https://oxia.ouplaw.com/page/IC-summer-academy-2017/the-reign-of-law-in-international-investment-decisionmaking.

[6] See Berger (2019) on ISDS claims brought by Chinese investors against foreign host states.

[7] Buser (2020) on China's changing and diverging BIT policies.

[8] See Fang and Hassler (2021) on COVID-related risks to China's FDI.

[9] Lew JL et al. (2021) Independent Task Force Report No. 79, China's Belt and Road: Implications for the United States, https://www.cfr.org/report/chinas-belt-and-road-implications-for-the-united-states/download/pdf/2021-03/TFR_Belt%20and%20Road%20Initiative_03172021_SinglePages.pdf.

investments in renewable energy.[10] It is doing so self-interestedly as well, in recognising the disastrous domestic health implications of environmental ingestion, but also the costs of remediation. China is engaging in signs, more symbolic than concrete, of collaboration with Western liberal states pursuing climate reform, epitomised by the United States' announcement of a climate agreement between it and China at the COP26 summit in Glasgow in November 2021.[11] China also emphasised at the end of 2022 the mutual benefit of reigniting its trade in raw materials with Australia at the end of 2022.[12] However, these statements represent little more than encouraging comments, without substantive actioning to date.

How China will reconcile its planned domestic economy and its liberalisation of outbound investment remains an open question. How it will expand further across the developing world is disputable. How it will cement its BRI outposts through enticing trade and investment agreements remains uncertain. How the West will react, economically, to China's political and military expansionism, such as in South-East Asia and Oceano, is speculative. However, countries in proximate regions to China are expressing concern about its expansionism. Australia has reacted with hostility to China's 2022 alliance with the Solomon Islands. However, political posturing is a stance adopted by both East and West, muddying the trade and investment waters to storm levels.[13]

This chapter evaluates these issues, not abstractly, but from the perspective of resolving international investment disputes between China and its developing state partners. It concentrates specifically on the resolution of disputes between host states and Chinese outbound investors in principle, policy and practice. It does so through the history of China's international investment treaties and practices. It acts in response to shifts from its leadership in inbound and outbound investor growth to its most recent declines in global investment. It presents reasons for such developments, and how they have been fuelled by criticisms and defences of China's BRI policies and practices. Importantly, it critically assesses how China is likely to address these issues through its choice of dispute resolution mechanisms; and whether it will employ those measures selectively or pervasively. It also evaluates how China will respond to the use of Investor State Dispute Settlement [ISDS], a process devised by the West, to which China has subscribed, but not assuredly in the future.

Section 2 identifies China's entry into the international investment regime and the obstacles it posed for it as a planned domestic economy. Section 3 evaluates China's strategic and functional challenges in liberalising its investment treaties. Section 4 explores the divergent dispute resolution options available to China in resolving disputes between its outbound investors and developing host states, along its once

[10] Cohen and Schneiderman (2017) on environmental protection in China's BITs.

[11] U.S. and China Announce Surprise Climate Agreement at COP26 Summit. BBC News, 11 November 2021, https://www.bbc.com/news/uk-59240244.

[12] See Gao (2022), p. 341.

[13] Rosenberg (2022).

fast growing but now declining Belt and Road. Section 5 examines the prospect of China retreating from its Belt and Road and why and how it might do so. Section 6 considers challenges China faces in developing its Belt and Road in the future. The Conclusion highlights the complex choices ahead as China seeks to reconcile changing tensions in achieving its BRI ambitions.

2 China's FDI Dilemma

Central to China's FDI direction is its appreciation of a global economic order that is beset by both structural and functional schisms between creditor and debtor states. That obstacle is accompanied by unequal access to resources in a diffusely conceived free-market order, complicated by COVID fallout.[14] In key respects China still falls into each of these categories, as a creditor and debtor state and as having unequal access to resources. It is no longer a predominantly debtor state, but its demands for investment in its domestic social programs such as in health, unemployment and pensions, are growing.[15] China is also under increasingly pressure to build its foreign exchange reserves to maintain its market, while foregoing ambitious expansionism in response to costly domestic social programs and a declining workforce.[16]

From an ideological perspective, it would be an overstatement to maintain that China's FDI regime has expanded beyond its planned domestic economy. Its resourcing of both is inextricably interwoven. Increasing loans to foreign states and their investors is countered by China's need to resource its social programs particularly given its aging population, reduced workforce and economic shortfalls.[17] This shift does not infer that China has decided to retreat significantly from its BRI program, although it does suggest a slowdown. China has a long history of success in expanding its foreign investment regime, in becoming the second-largest outbound investor-state, after the US. That development occurred well before the Pandemic and its economic sequela. It is likely to continue, albeit with intermittent setbacks.

Four decades of international investment growth in which China concluded over 130 BITs is remarkable by any measure.[18] Its achievements were reflected in its

[14] Wei (2021) on China's evolving BIT responses to investment liberalisation.
[15] Baláž et al. (2020).
[16] Amineh (2022), pp. 36–69.
[17] Xi (2014–2017), Full Catalogue Reference MARCXML.
[18] See UNCTAD, Investment Policy Hub, International Investment Agreements Navigator, https://investmentpolicy.unctad.org/international-investment-agreements/countries/42/china.

adoption of Western style investment treaties and sometimes referred to as China's NAFTA-isation of its BITs.[19] It was also embodied in China's 1993 adoption of the Convention on the Settlement of Investment Disputes [ICSID] enacted in 1966,[20] affirming its extension of investor protections in line with the West.[21]

China's investment liberalisation has progressed in stages. China's first Model BIT, devised in the 1980s, reflected a mixed liberal and protectionist bent. Its second Model in the mid-1990s and its third Model in 1998 both demonstrated its increasing willingness to extend investment liberalisation,[22] including to protect outbound investors from expropriation by foreign host states.[23] To that end, it relaxed its national security defences in its treaties and provided foreign investors with greater due process protection.[24] The fact that China was envisaged as denying transparency in regulating inbound investment further motivated its willingness to agree to such protections, although there is scant evidence of wide scale investor claims against China.[25]

China's treaty liberalisation of investor protections in its Model BITs was also incremental. China's first-generation BITs significantly limited such protections, notably denying inbound investor claims based on 'expropriation'. But China's later BIT Models removed these limits on investor claims.[26] China has more recently adapted its BITs case-by-case rather than uniformly based on its current third Model BIT.[27] To date, there are few ISDS claims against China. In no ISDS has the foreign investor prevailed against it. However, Chinese outbound investors have won ISDS claims against foreign host states.[28]

China's liberalisation of investor protections was tactical. The protection of investors reassured developing states that their outbound investors would not be disadvantaged in China. Those protections also benefitted China. They served as

[19] Chapter 11 of NAFTA deals with investment, including the resolution of investor-state disputes. See further Berger (2019), p. 843 on China's early reliance on NAFTA in resolving disputes.

[20] Convention on the Settlement of Investment Disputes Between States and Nationals of Other States, opened for signature 27 December 1945, 2 UNTS 134 (entered into force 14 October 1966) ('ICSID Convention'). The Preamble states: 'Considering the need for international cooperation for economic development, and the role of private international investment therein'.

[21] See, e.g. Parra (2017), Kinnear (2015) and Trakman (2012b).

[22] Shen (2013) on the evolution of China BITs.

[23] See Shan and Chen (2016) and Shan and Gallagher (2013).

[24] See Wei (2021) for a textual, comparative, and empirical analysis of China's BITs.

[25] Trakman et al. (2020), pp. 231–261.

[26] Pathirana D, A Look into China's Slowly Increasing Appearance in ISDS Case, International Institute for Sustainable Development, 26 September 2017, https://www.iisd.org/itn/en/2017/09/26/a-look-into-chinas-slowly-increasing-appearance-in-isds-cases-dilini-pathirana/.

[27] See Li and Bian (2020).

[28] See Gallagher and Shan (2009) and Trakman (2017).

inducements for developing states to encourage outbound investment to China. They also served as regulatory shields to China's investors venturing into those developing states.[29]

China's strategic aim, from the outset, was not to carbon copy liberalisation initiatives of the West, but to use such treaty liberalisation to satisfy its own economic ends.[30] Its caution was not to subordinate the economic model it embodied in the Beijing Consensus in favour of the liberalised model contained in the Washington Consensus.[31] Essentially, China retained its planned domestic economy, while shifting to accommodate free trade initiatives. Illustratively, it diverted from its planned market model in which its State-Owned Enterprises [SOEs] directed much of its outbound investment to State Sponsored Enterprises [SSEs] in which it retained a significant economic stake but less direct control. Its shift, in some measure, was in response to criticism that its outbound SOEs ought not to receive the protection accorded to private inbound investors, in that they were agents for the Chinese government. In foregoing its ownership of such entities, however, China did not relinquish its significant financial interest in them.[32]

China increasingly faces difficult choices in determining how it will modify its BIT programs to meet local, regional and global economic and political shifts. One option is to strive predominantly to find inventive new ways in which to secure its already formidable achievements as a capital exporter. Another is to revert more to its early BIT program in which it was predominantly a capital importer to attract investors to its domestic market. Another is for it to seek options that include both, such as to court new and renewed partnerships in developing states and to attract investors from those states to China.[33]

A strategic dilemma is how China will balance its domestically planned market model with its FDI regime that differs ideologically from its domestic model.[34] The related quandary is how China will respond tactically to Western states that are increasingly deglobalising their investment outreach and reverting to localisation.[35]

---

[29] See Yamada H, Forgotten Promises: Bilateral Investment Treaties Between CEE and China, CHOICE, 6 November 2020, https://chinaobservers.eu/forgotten-promises-bilateral-investment-treaties-between-cee-and-china/.

[30] See Skovgaard Poulsen LN and Gertz G, Reforming the Investment Treaty Regime A 'backward looking' Approach, Brookings Institution, 17 March 2021, https://www.brookings.edu/research/reforming-the-investment-treaty-regime/.

[31] See Chen (2017) on China's adoption, adaptation, and reconstitution of the Washington Consensus. On the Washington Consensus, see Rooney (2007), p. 704 explaining that, even after China had acceded to the Washington Convention, it did not provide for ICSID in its BITs for a number of years.

[32] See Chen (2023); see also Laruelle (2018).

[33] Li et al. (2022), pp. 902–919.

[34] See Wang and Wang (2021).

[35] See Clover Alcolea L, The COVID-19 Crisis: Core Investment Law Issues Revisited. TDM, 25 May 2020, https://www.transnational-dispute-management.com/Journal-advance-publication-article.asp?key=1822 on limited commentary on investor-state claims during the epidemic.

A difficulty question also relates to the extent to which China will reformulate its investment outreach programs, how it will address resistance to them in the West and conceivably internally, and how it will achieve longer term horizons through collaborative partnership across the globe. Added to these problems is how China will respond to domestic political constraints that impact on these initiatives.[36]

China's choices are hampered by complexities relating to its cultural and economic identity. In truth, China is a regional and global power, although its domestic economy is still emerging.[37] Pursuing ambitious BRI horizons in an economically unstable global space also entail China cultivating politically sensitive responses to them, including to compromise between and among them. Among these compromises is its need to balance its political ambition to remain a first world provider of foreign direct investment and to return a significant proportion of those benefits to support its own economically pressured social programs. In so engaging, it cannot avoid the reality that, in engaging in such balancing, at least 'several sources of instability and macroeconomic problems' could arise.[38]

Nor can China escape related hard questions. How should it plan to progress from a debtor to a creditor state when it retains attributes of both? How can it remould its model of investment multilateralism to recognise the ambivalence of vulnerable debtor states to globalisation and their localisation of trade and investment as current default positions?[39] How should it offset the current criticism that it more authoritarian than collaborative in directing travel along its BRI global pathway?

3 A Directional Shift?

A big floating balloon ahead is to identify, assess and decipher prospective shifts that China will undertake in engineering its future BRI ambitions in volatile investment markets. In broad principle, China has growing reasons to reform its IIAs away from a single Model, to implement Western-style BITs to which it remains supportive, and to accommodate developing states it is courting. It is further impelled by its transformation into a developed-developing state to ensure that its BRI expansion grows prolifically and profitably and continues to outpace growth in other BRIC countries such as India.[40]

[36] He (2019), pp. 180–195.

[37] Tekdal (2018), p. 273 on China's challenge in reconciling its regional and emerging identities in building its global identity.

[38] Ibid.

[39] See Chaisse (2019) on China's investment bilateral strategies with the US and the EU regional strategies within the Free Trade Area of the Asia Pacific and global strategies in extending its BRI.

[40] See Buser (2020).

China remains well motivated in principle to continue liberalising its investment treaties.[41] It also retains functional incentives to modernise its BIT models through tactical bifurcation, to suit disparate state-to-state partnerships. China is also motivated to render its treaties more consistent across different generations of BITs and to extend them to encompass developing partners states.[42] A further motivation is for China to pursue both regional and international investment agreements. A key consideration is for it to establish agreements that provide greater and more immediate revenue benefits than many of its current FDI initiatives with developing states. China's delicate balance then is to continue to make short-term economic sacrifices to support developing state partners in turn for longer term returns, but only for so long and so extensively as it can reasonably afford to make short-term outlays. That balance is most acute in it having to offset infrastructure and construction loans to developing states and investors with more secure and sustained returns.[43]

Some directional shifts in China's BRI policies, more properly extensions, are already evident. They include China's extension of its BRI beyond its existing markets in Asia, Africa and Latin America into a global investment road. Further expansions-in-waiting encompass China's effort to conclude mutually profitable investment treaties with selected Western enclaves, such as the EU,[44] notably in negotiating the still tentative EU-China Comprehensive Agreement on Investment.[45]

China's directional challenge is whether to reject or materially modify its existing model investment treaties in reconciling intertwined domestic, regional and international belts and roads in a cost effective and sustained manner. At least three hard choices lie ahead in it so deciding. The first is to establish different treaty models, not limited to a treaty bifurcation between developing and developed states. The second is to limit reliance on its home spun treaty models in favour of a multilateral investment agreement operating across a global community of states. The third is neither to model nor publicise its guidelines in negotiating investment treaties. China's pervasive objective in considering these three options, jointly or separately, is to enable it to conclude IIAs on a partner specific basis. Each option has its perceived benefits. For example, concluding IIAs piecemeal provides China with the opportunity to frame treaties with partner states on a needs-be basis and without being unduly hampered by model treaty predetermination. However, there is a cost

[41] See Deng (2021), pp. 737–740 on China's liberalisation to build the credibility of its BRI. See also Hsueh (2011) on China's evolving strategy in global liberalisation.

[42] See Wei (2021).

[43] See Carmody and Wainwright (2022), pp. 2830–2851.

[44] See Zhang M, How China and the EU can boost investment. World Economic Forum, 17 October 2016 https://www.weforum.org/agenda/2016/10/how-china-and-the-eu-can-boost-investment; Zeng (1999) maintaining that Chinese foreign investment laws have adopted market economic principles since 1993.

[45] See Grieger G, EU–China Comprehensive Agreement on Investment: Levelling the Playing Field with China [International Agreements in Progress], https://epthinktank.eu/2020/09/14/eu-china-comprehensive-agreement-on-investment-levelling-the-playing-field-international-agreements-in-progresswith-china/.

to doing so. Negotiating treaties piecemeal ordinarily takes time. Negotiating and drafting such treaties is also subject to derailment, more than in adapting boilerplate Model agreements to specific partner states.[46]

Each approach also has perceived strategic strengths and weaknesses in China's pursuit of global political and economic leadership. Each raises cost-benefit uncertainties for China in attempting to predict divergent costs and benefits in pursuing its disparate and sometimes conflicting treaty objectives. For example, in providing infrastructure and financial assistance to developing states, China is incentivised to consider whether the cumulative benefit of doing so outweighs the economic shortfalls in not being able to finance alternative investment opportunities elsewhere, not limited to home spun projects.[47]

Given that cost-benefit measurements cannot be accurate and that macro-global economic and political developments shift, China faces the prospect of miscalculating the cost-benefit of both its piecemeal and shared investment treaty models.[48] The worst-case scenario is that it will err in balancing its domestic and international investor treaty models and suffer material economic losses that it can ill-afford.

China's choice among these alternatives hinges materially on how it weighs the interrelated costs of each in relation to others. Making such choices is tenuous at best, particularly if China determines that its global investment undertakings will extend its domestic financial shortfalls. It can willingly absorb the short-term costs of specific projects if it anticipates being able to offset those costs with benefits secured from other BRI projects. It can resile from projects it considers lacking sufficient strategic, political and economic importance compared to the alternatives. In engaging in such assessments, China will need to evaluate their relevance costs and benefits both *ex ante* and for verification purposes, *ex post*. It will need to do according to normative criteria that it values, such as the value of linked partnerships in Southern and West Africa.[49]

A balanced strategy in the sequel to COVID is for China to adopt a measured response to often unknown further eventualities, such as the economic collapse of a developing state partner in which it has invested. If China concludes that its investments in that state could seriously deplete its foreign exchange reserves, it might decide to cushion that risk through an exit strategy. If it is concerned that exit will cause other states to plan prematurely for its exit in relation to them, it may halt or limit its withdrawal. If it faces condemnation from ideologically apposed and opportunistic competitor states, it may include these factors in its cost-benefit

[46] See Du (2022).

[47] See Li (2021) maintaining that 'the development orientation of the BRI . . . does not set rules as a threshold during its initial stage, thus providing opportunities for developing countries to participate in international economic cooperation'.

[48] See Banga R, Impact of Government Policies and Investment Agreements on FDI Inflow, ICRIER Working Paper No. 116, https://icrier.org/publications/impact-of-government-policies-investment-agreements-on-fdi-inflows/.

[49] See Afzaal (2022).

calculus.[50] A related cost-benefit assessment arising from China's choices encompasses the manner in and extent to which Chinese investors will be granted or denied access to foreign markets, and reciprocally, how foreign investors will secure or be denied access to Chinese markets.[51]

Obstacles to China's balancing of strategic options are formidable, particularly in deciding the manner in and extent to which to extend its BRI to developed states. For example, building investment bridges with the US is a formidable task, given decades of adversity between these great powers. That task appears easier in relation to the EU.[52] However, with the EU's recent announcement of its construction of competitor road to China's BRI, that task remains formidable, such as in China and the EU agreeing on state-to-state and investor-state dispute resolution options.[53]

An important consideration for China going forward is also to provide for the resolution of disputes in its treaties with partner host states. Dispute resolution is particularly significant in addressing tensions between host states and inbound investors in an era of global financial insecurity in which caution guides states, including China, to protect their outbound investors from the regulatory action of host states. Competing methods of dispute resolution encompass often controversial state-to-state and investor-state alternatives. These alternatives are growing, not only in importance, but in controversies surrounding their use as global economic tensions, including in relation to China, grow. These alternatives are discussed below.

4 How to Resolve Investment Disputes

Complex issues arise over how China will remould its BIT and IIA provisions for resolving state-to-state and investor state disputes in the immediate future. China's capacity to redesign and modify its IIA roadmap is well illustrated already in its design of dispute resolution mechanisms in BITs to meet new demands along its road. The question is to evaluate the extent to which it is incentivised to change that modelling. The related question is whether it will do so limitedly, incrementally, or radically.

China has sound reason in principle to reconsider the methods of resolving disputes between host states and inbound foreign investors, to ensure that they are both consistent with its planned-market ideology and efficient in operation. It also has sound economic reasons to reduce its BIT investment shields against inbound investors to protect its standing as an inbound host state, while also protecting its outbound investors in partner host states.

[50] See Schulhof et al. (2022).

[51] See Zhou (2020) on China's evolving rulemaking along its BRI.

[52] See Kao (2021).

[53] Fach Gómez (2021) on the absence of provision for ISDS in China-EU draft Agreement and uncertainty over its formulation.

As a foremost importer and exporter state, a central issue is for China to consider whether to rebalance its traditional shield against inbound investors with countervailing protections for its outbound investors. In refining its investment treaties proactively to satisfy these ends, it is also incentivised to remodel its International Investment Agreements [IIAs] progressively and collaboratively, and not peremptorily or autocratically. That refinement entails deciding how to accommodate Western-style BITs and FTA, while increasingly crafting them according to its own planning, design and transfiguration.[54]

What is especially challenging for China is in determining which dispute resolution options would suit it in redesigning its BRI roadmap. One option is for it to adopt an amalgam of models to accommodate economic, social, and political divergences among partner states across its Belt and Road. Another option is to adapt two dispute resolution models that recognise the dichotomy between developed and developing states.[55] A related option is for China to devise dispute resolution provisions to suit the localised needs of BIT partner states, but in compliance with pre-set dispute resolution boundaries.[56]

An experimental option is for China to trial dispute resolution pathways across partner states in Asia, Africa and Latin America and also in Europe, such as by adopting different options across states or within the same treaty.[57] That trial could address the exhaustion of local remedies; waiting periods before foreign investors can lodge Investor State Dispute Settlement [ISDS] claims; and limits placed on the scope of ISDS. These options could be reformulated incrementally (or radically) in accordance with China's ongoing gains-based analysis.[58]

The prevalent investor-state dispute resolution option, adopted in most of China's BITs, is ISDS. ISDS was initially modelled by wealthy Western countries to protect their outbound investors from being subject to regulat action be developing host states. More recently, developing host states have used ISDS to defend themselves against claims from inbound investors from such wealth states.[59]

What is uncertain is whether China will continue to adopt ISDS as a preferred mode of dispute resolution in its regional and international investment treaties. Complicating that choice is political and economic resistance to the use of ISDS, notably by developing states that maintain that it favours the outbound investors

[54] See Wang and Wang (2021).

[55] On China's infrastructure partnerships along with its Belt and Road, see OECD (2018) China's Belt and Road Initiative in the Global Trade, Investment and Finance Landscape, OECD Business and Finance Outlook, https://www.oecd.org/finance/Chinas-Belt-and-Road-Initiative-in-the-global-trade-investment-and-finance-landscape.pdf. On China's Best and Road initiatives in Africa, see Dollar D, Understanding China's Belt and Road Infrastructure Projects in Africa, Brookings Institute, 2019, https://www.brookings.edu/wp-content/uploads/2019/09/FP_20190930_china_bri_dollar.pdf.

[56] See Vaccaro-Incisa (2021) on the history of China's BIT's.

[57] See Cotula et al. (2016).

[58] See Chaisse (2021).

[59] Trakman (2016), pp. 129–194.

from wealthy Western states. That is the stated view of multiple Latin American states and states in Africa such as South Africa that now decline to adopt ISDS, and states in Asia, such as India, that have expressed concerns about its use.[60]

China could inherit such criticisms in adopting ISDS, in being perceived as a powerful BRIC host state whose outbound investors are economic resourced and politically empowered to utilise ISDS against host states to their advantage. That criticism is a disincentive for China to continue to utilise ISDS. Politically, too, China is incentivised not to replicate a dispute resolution measure that was devised by the developed West which developing states consider as the source of adverse and crippling awards against them. A further reason for China to avoid ISDS is the prospect of it being subject to ISDS claims from multinational inbound investors from the wealthy West in the future.[61]

Conversely, China is incentivised not to jettison ISDS from its investment treaties because most of its BITs provide for ISDS, and because that is consistent with global practice. China is further motivated to retain ISDS because it has seldom been subject to ISDS claims and has won or settled all cases against it. That success is attributed to the perception that it is powerful and tenacious adversary that will steadfastly defend its regulatory decisions from foreign investor claims.[62] ISDS also benefits Chinese SOEs and SSEs in lodging claims against developing and also developed host states. This benefit is attributed to a combination of their resources in bringing such claims and often the support they receive from China.[63]

In addressing the reluctance of some developing states to resort to ISDS institutions as favouring developed Western states, China could resort to ISDS institutions that are not so identified, without jettisoning ISDS itself. For example, it could exclude the Rules of the International Centre for the Settlement of Investment Disputes [ICSID] from resolving investor-state disputes from its treaty, given that the ICSID is criticised as being created by the West and a creature of the World Bank. It could opt instead for the Rules of the United National Commission on International Trade Law [UNCITRAL] that is not so identified.

As a further option, China could supplement rather than abandon ISDS. It could do so by engaging in discussion on alternative dispute resolution choices, such as establishing a multilateral investment court with an appeal division. China has already done so in deliberations before the United Nations Commission on International Trade Law Working Group III (UNCITRAL WG III).[64]

Should China favour an alternative, in whole or part, to ISDS, a further choice is for it to provide in its treaties for domestic courts to resolve investor claims against a

60 See Sornarajah (2015).

61 Zhao (2023), pp. 165–197.

62 Trakman et al. (2020), pp. 231–261.

63 See Trakman (2014) on limited ISDS claims brought China.

64 See UNCITRAL, Working Group III: Investor-State Dispute Settlement Reform, September 2021, https://uncitral.un.org/sites/uncitral.un.org/files/media-documents/uncitral/en/210921_status_of_work_wg_iii.pdf.

host state in that court's jurisdiction.[65] That adoption would reflect the wide practice of domestic courts hearing disputes brought by foreign corporations against the host state. The resistance to domestic courts so deciding is their perceived lack of independence from their governments, a criticism that is directed at authoritarian and also some other developing states.[66] The presupposition is that such domestic courts will decide in the host state's favour because they are dependent upon its directions.[67] China may share the concern of Western states in protecting its own outbound investors from domestic courts that it considers lack independence from the executive branch of government. That approach will also avoid the countervailing view among China's prospective partner states that reliance upon Chinese courts poses those same risks. [68]

China is therefore incentivised to avoid, or constrain, the use of both ISDS and domestic courts on grounds of alleged systemic bias: namely, that ISDS is biased against developing states, and that domestic courts lack independence from their host states. For China to avoid over-reliance upon the seeming gordian knot in electing between two irreconcilable choices, an alternative is for it to resort to international investment arbitration [IIA], such as under the auspices the China International Economic Trade Arbitration Association (CIETAC) which China has proposed for that purpose.[69] The rationale is that arbitration, modelled on international commercial arbitration, is a private dispute resolution process that is widely used, and that functions independently of governments, including the Chinese government.[70] The CEITAC option might satisfy some developing states, for these reasons and to avoid institutions that allegedly favour wealthy investors. However, advanced Western states are unlikely to agree to incorporating CEITAC into their investment treaties because it is a Chinese institution, however independent it is alleged to be from the Chinese State. These objections will be comparable to the institutional biases that developing states have lodged against the ICSID administering ISDS.[71]

A more pervasive option is for China to opt for a multilateral institution to resolve investment disputes. The problem in China proposing such a model *de novo* is in China being identified at its champion. Developed states that have brokered ISDS to date are likely to oppose it on both ideological and functional grounds, particularly if China is its primary broker. Just as developing states have been critical of ISDS as empowering investors from Western states, they and their investors are likely to be suspicious of a multilateral option brokered by a dominant planned economy.

---

[65] Hepburn (2023), pp. 18–34.

[66] Alvarez (2021), pp. 253–277.

[67] Trakman (2012a).

[68] Du (2022).

[69] Ibid. On CEITAC's adoption of ISDS, with the approval of the Chinese Government, see Chen (2018) and Chi (2020).

[70] Gu (2018), p. 1305.

[71] See Puig and Strezhnev (2017), pp. 731–761; Trakman (2012b), p. 603.

Should China ameliorate its proposed multilateral model to accommodate Western powers, it risks having its multilateral option being overhauled to suit a wider global community of states, contrary to its own preferences.[72]

Another option is for China to accept a multilateral investment court [MIC], along lines of the EU's International Investment Court.[73] At its best, this dispute resolution proposal could be modified to suit China. It could include the institutionalisation of an appellate tribunal with rules and procedures to govern its operation.[74] It could enable China to opt for it, while still retaining existing investor-state institutions, such as ISDS, intact. However, in endorsing this judicial option, China would be subject to the criticism for endorsing an institution that shares the limitations attributed to courts generally, such as relate to the appointment of judges, the conduct of court proceedings and the appellate process.[75] China would also likely be signing onto a treaty option that it does not lead, that has few signatories, and has terms with which third party states disagree. The comparative picture is not particularly encouraging. The EU's International Investment Court is incorporated into the EU's bilateral agreements with Canada, Singapore and Vietnam respectively, but these treaties have not been ratified A Multilateral Investment Court is touted theoretically, but has not been adopted in practice.[76]

No matter how the multilateral dispute option is conceived and constructed, it is fraught for China. That underscores China's own ambivalence towards the formulation and adoption of a multilateral dispute resolution option. Notably, no dispute resolution option is incorporated into the draft EU-China Agreement, a decision that is conspicuously left to subsequent agreement between China and the EU.[77] That might well have been an indication of the difficulty of China and the EU to reach such an agreement. It might also signal the fate of further attempts to reach one at this time. The absence of such an agreement in the EU-China draft treaty is likely to be replicated in China's multilateral treaty negotiations with other Western states, unless China agrees to modify those provisions significantly to suit otherwise reluctant co-signatories.[78]

Given obstacles to the primacy of the dispute resolution options discussed above, China could adopt a mixture of models on a case-by-case basis. That option would depend less on the model of dispute resolution that is formally adopted in advance,

---

[72] Akperlinova and Jastrzebski (2022), pp. 1–9.

[73] See Bungenberg and Reinisch (2020), p. 222.

[74] See Fach Gómez (2021).

[75] Ning and Qi (2018) on obstacles between the EU and China in institutionalising an international investment court; Bungenberg and Reinisch (2020) maintaining that an international investment court can protect rule of law, reduce costs in protecting foreign investments, provide greater legal transparency and consistency in law and the effective enforcement of MIC decisions.

[76] Ji and Chaisse (2022) and Zeng (2010).

[77] See Fan (2020).

[78] Fan (2020), pp. 635–638.

than upon a broadly based option that is not tailored wholly to investor-state disputes, but also to state-to-state dispute avoidance measures. One such dispute avoidance measure is for China to endorse diplomatic measures to resolve differences between partner states. That measure could be supplemented by state-to-state mediation, such as was initiated in China and the EU's efforts to negotiate a China-EU Bilateral Investment Treaty.[79]

The model of state-to-state diplomacy could be further formalised, such as through Treaties of Friendship, Navigation, and Commerce historically adopted by Western states in colonial and post-colonial eras.[80] The benefit of this option is the ability to resolve investment differences before they become disputes. A strategic obstacle to China adopting this option is to avoid being seen to replicate treaties of overlordship attributed to Western Treaties of Friendship in the past, and contrary to its socialist ideology.[81] Even if such practices are recast as hard bargaining, for China to extract concessions from its developing state partners, while being unwilling to reciprocate, could cause them to retreat for such practices. While different in nature, China's politicised 2022 alliance with the Solomon Islands illustrates how apprehensively that alliance was perceived by developing states in the Region who became fearful of its consequences for them. It was also a reason why Australia ratcheted up its investments elsewhere in the Region.[82]

A further perception in the West is that China's outbound investors, particularly SOEs and SSEs will replicate China's alleged economic domination of developing BRI states along its BRI. In place of collaboration with host states, its outbound investors will be depicted as exercising unfair bargaining power, lacking transparency and disregarding local laws. Such disparate bargaining power will be identified with the extent to which Chinese investors are granted access to BRI partner markets, without foreign investors from those partner states securing equal access to Chinese markets.[83]

A collateral concern is that host states, including but not limited to China, should be disempowered by treaty from using their sovereignty to regulate foreign investors in a manner that is deemed to be unfair or inequitable. China's response is to market its BRI as collaborative in a manner in which developing states consider as fair and equitable to them, their local markets and their outbound investors. A related tension for such states is to ensure that dispute resolution measures in umbrella treaties and investor-state contracts with China do not favour it and its outbound investors at their expense and that of their outbound investors.[84]

---

[79] See Zhao (2018).

[80] See Vandevelde (2017) on the United States' early post-war BITs.

[81] See Ameyaw-Brobbey (2021), surveying the US and China's divergent diplomatic efforts to establish their supremacy in over international investment regimes from 2017 to the commencement of the Pandemic.

[82] See Lei and Sui (2022).

[83] Rudolf (2021).

[84] Maçães (2021).

5 A Retreat?

A lingering question is whether China will reduce its outbound international investment regime and if so, how and to what extent it will do so. While a total retreat is unlikely and a temporary one is more probable now, its longer-term approach is more questionable. What is clear now is that China's very swift pathway along its Belt and Road into the second largest outbound investor is being tested.[85] What is less clear is how China will redress the current diminution of its outbound investment reach. On the positive side, China has recently announced its readiness to ameliorate trade and investment restrictions. Developing states that withdrew from its BRI over the last decade primarily due to concerns about China's capacity and willingness to continue to pursue such infrastructure ventures, have returned to the fold, but not *en masse*.[86] The reaction of developed states to China's somewhat tempered outreach to them remains muted at the time of writing.

What is important to acknowledge at this juncture is the financial and political obstacles to China expanding its BRI, even as those dynamics change. It is evident that China's financial dilemma is not exclusive to it. Financial markets are beset by inflationary pressures. Supply and labour shortages remain present in securing access to the supply of foreign goods and workers. States operating across the global community face competing demands for their financial reserves, forcing them to select between foreign and domestic infrastructure and construction projects.[87] Public policy and national security imposts, too, override otherwise lucrative outbound and inbound investment.

China also faces difficult strategic choices in determining whether to withdraw investing in offshore projects generally, proportionately, or selectively. If it is to do so selectively, as at present, its arduous task is in both deciding upon the selection of those projects and the criteria to govern that selection.[88] These tasks are further complicated by economic constrains upon it and its outbound investor imposed primarily by developed Western states. China concurrently faces the blacklisting of Chinese entities abroad, their selective exclusion by those states and the application of taxes and duties to those Chinese investors who are not so excluded. China is also subject to the crippling impact of global economic dislocation upon its economy.[89]

China's responses to these obstacles remains a work in progress. The central tension is how it will respond to them and whether it will do so disparately according to the nature and source of the restrictions. Much depends, too, on whether it responds proactively by changing international investment relationships, such as in

[85] Sági and Engelberth (2018).

[86] Zou et al. (2022).

[87] See Heinberg (2011).

[88] See Liao et al. (2021) for an empirical study on the correlation between China's outward FDI and growth of its domestic economy, particularly employment.

[89] See Fang and Hassler (2021) on COVID-related risks to China's FDI.

purporting to re-engage Australia proactively in trade and investment in late 2022 following Australia's shift from a conservative to a labour government.

China's ongoing conundrum is to determine strategically whether to act proactively or reactively in restricting foreign importation and investments, such as in raw materials, in the absence of cost-effective alternative sources of supply. Influencing such choices is China's dilemma in prohibiting or discouraging outbound investments, not only to developed Western states, but also to developing states that are drawn into conflicts such as in being courted by the US.[90] China is also motivated by the sequelae of imposing constraints on both inbound and outbound investment, such as reluctance of foreign entities to invest in China or withdrawing from such investments there. Sensitive, too, is how China will use a national security rationale to justify its actions, knowing that competitor states invoke public policy justifications for their actions.[91]

The immediate obstacles to China's consolidation of the BRI are significant but not surmountable. What China cannot afford, economically and politically, is the ongoing intensification of a 'cold war' as interstate hostilities continue to undermine its Belt and Road access to global trade and investment markets. New macro-structural obstacles have also intervened, such as the EU's announcement of its new Global Gateway in competition with China's BRI.[92] Such actions underscore China's need to tactically allay foreign investor withdrawal from its Belt and Road, and for it to allocate less readily available capital to sustain it.[93] Coupled with these concerns is China's need to address spiralling regulatory action of foreign states imposing entry restrictions on inbound Chinese investors, and to support those investor claims through diplomatic or other intervention.[94]

China does have significant institutional means of protecting its outbound investors from host state restrictions. Chinese contractors have supplied project equipment, materials, and managerial expertise to multiple developing states.[95] Its regional and affiliated banks, such as the Asian Infrastructure Development Bank [AIIB], have provided financial support to such projects.[96] Importantly, China has reportedly acquired international assets of approximately $1 trillion since the advent of the Pandemic to the first quarter of 2021, as evidence of both its BRI commitment and its continued viability as a global investor state.[97]

[90] See Sangaré (2021) on protective measures use in trade wars during the Pandemic.

[91] See McLaughlin (2020).

[92] See, e.g. Roushan A, EU to Announce Own Infrastructure Plan to Rival China's Belt and Road Initiative, 16 November 2021, http://www.republicworld.com/world-news/europe/eu-to-announce-own-infrastructure-plan-to-rival-chinas-belt-and-road-initiative.html.

[93] Liu and Dunford (2016) arguing for an open, inclusive and co-operative BRI model that aligns with China's achievements on its historical Silk Roads.

[94] On proportionality in ISDS, see Henckels (2015).

[95] Rizzi et al. (2018) on Chinese and international banks providing loans for OBOR [BRI] Initiative.

[96] See Zhao (2020) on the AIIB's importance, both regionally and globally, in financing China's BRI expansion.

[97] Ghauri et al. (2021) on China's changing global influence since the Pandemic.

6 Challenges Ahead

China's predicament in expanding or restricting investor protections is politically delicate and economically fraught. Should China strenuously expropriate and otherwise regulate inbound investments, foreign investors are likely to claim that it is engaging in unfair investment practices. They will assert that it is invoking its domestic security unreasonably to confiscate their assets; and that it is denying their rightful protections under customary international law.[98] China's defence will likely be that, as a host state, it has the sovereign authority to adopt such regulatory measures, consented to by treaty, and in compliance with international investment law.[99] Its collateral rationale will be that it has the authority to regulate inbound FDI according to its conception of the national interest and its police powers.[100]

China's defences are still unlikely to halt a potential progression in inbound investors' claims against it. Inbound investors from Australia have contemplated ISDS claims under the China-Australia Free Trade Agreement for China's alleged discrimination against them, causing them economic harm.[101] More pervasive action against China is being considered by the US, albeit expressed in general terms. A Task Force on the impact of China's BRI upon the United States has proposed 'a response that rests on four pillars: mitigating the economic risks of BRI, improving US competitiveness, strengthening the multilateral response to BRI, and protecting US security interests in BRI countries'.[102] That response is already taking place in the United States' retreat from negotiating a US-China trade and investment agreement, accentuated by accelerating economic sanctions and blame directed at China for global health and economic crises.[103]

Large-scale foreign investors, such as multilateral corporations, are also positioned to lodge ISDS claims against China. Well-healed companies have already proceeded against developed states such as Germany and Canada and secured ISDS awards.[104] Outbound US investors are also likely to receive US Government support

[98] Collins (2023); World Bank, Foreign Direct Investment – The China Story, 16 July 2010, https://www.worldbank.org/en/news/feature/2010/07/16/foreign-direct-investment-china-story.

[99] Desierto D, Laird I, Sourgens F (2017) Oxford University Press Investment Claims Summer Academy, https://oxia.ouplaw.com/page/IC-summer-academy-2017/the-reign-of-law-in-international-investment-decisionmaking.

[100] Henckels (2018) and Giest (2017).

[101] Mizen R, Exporters Mull ISDS Legal Action Against Beijing, 17 December 2020, https://www.afr.com/politics/federal/exporters-mull-isds-legal-action-against-beijing-20201216-p56o1l.

[102] Lew JL et al. (2021) Independent Task Force Report No. 79, China's Belt and Road: Implications for the United States, https://www.cfr.org/report/chinas-belt-and-road-implications-for-the-united-states/download/pdf/2021-03/TFR_Belt%20and%20Road%20Initiative_03172021_SinglePages.pdf.

[103] See deLisle (2021).

[104] See, e.g. Steinbock (2018).

in lodging ISDS proceedings against China, given concerns about China's growing BRI and the US Task Force's warning about China's expanding BRI.[105]

Realistic, too, are prospective investor claims against China for expropriating their investments on national security grounds including domestic economic instability caused by COVID-19. They will also likely raise procedural arguments against China and its BIT partner states for denying them fair and equitable treatment. The allegation will be that China is undermining due process protections along its self-created 'bumpy' BRI.[106]

In grounding its regulatory action, not limited to expropriation, on the debilitating effect of COVID-19 upon its domestic economy, China, along with its outbound SOE investors, will be denounced for subjecting vulnerable states and their local industries to economic subordination along its Belt and Road. China's BIT partner states are also likely to assert that Chinese SOEs are not legally entitled to investor protections in host states because they are state-owned and should not receive the protections accorded to foreign investors that are not state-owned.[107] China's likely response will be that, as destination states invoke ISDS to protect themselves from inbound Chinese investor claimants, it is justified in so defending against inbound investor claims against it.[108]

Whether these host state defences to China's outbound investors are overstated, incompletely substantiated, or replicate colonial state practice, they are unlikely to discourage developed Western states from imposing escalating trade sanctions on Chinese imports and investments.[109] Allied liberal states will likely continue to raise entry barriers to inbound investors from China in an accelerating saga of macroeconomic politics at work. Some of their rationalisations for imposing these entry barriers will be incendiary, such as the allegation that China deliberately created the COVID virus, or intentionally planned the Pandemic's global spread. The issue is not whether these propositions are unsubstantiated or constitute overly politicised China-bashing, but that they will serve as an inflammatory torch directed at undermining, if not obliterating, China's BRI creations.

105 Lew JL et al. (2021) Independent Task Force Report No. 79, China's Belt and Road: Implications for the United States, https://www.cfr.org/report/chinas-belt-and-road-implications-for-the-united-states/download/pdf/2021-03/TFR_Belt%20and%20Road%20Initiative_03172021_SinglePages.pdf.

106 See Li and Bian (2020) on China's ISDS challenges ahead. See too, Grant Thornton, International Business Report – A bump in the road?, 1 August 2018, https://www.grantthornton.global/en/insights/articles/bump-in-the-road/.

107 See Zhao (2019).

108 Baker Mckenzie, China's Foreign Investment Law and Related Regulations Mark a New Era for Foreign Investment in China, 3 March 2021, https://www.lexology.com/library/detail.aspx?g=466b766b-9237-467f-b8d4-1bcdfedeef1a#:~:text=China%27s%20Foreign%20Investment%20Law%20and%20related%20regulations%20mark,15%2C%202019%20%28see%20our%20alert%20here%29%2C%20took%20effect.

109 See Rusmus J, Trump's 'Real Trade War': Subverting China's Technological Advance, Global Research, 22 January 2019, https://www.globalresearch.ca/trumps-real-trade-war-subverting-chinas-technological-advance/5665992.

China is likely to react to these challenges with tenacity. It will demonstrate its determination to retain its ideologically overlayered planned economy, while also accommodating a global investment order in which freedom to invest transnationally is requisite. So long as state sovereignty remains a formal beacon of the post-modern regulatory order and sovereign association remains the functional medium through which states can exercise their sovereignty, China will accommodate both its sovereignty and sovereignty by association. China is also unlikely to be seen to jettison the delineation of equality among states and their outbound investors in the new global order. It is more likely to remodel its BRL to formally disavow the liberalised directives of a past colonising West and to resist their re-incarnation along a post-colonised highway from the East. Whether that re-incarnation is no more than the echo of a colonial past, a directed pathway under China's watchful eye, or of coalescence between a centrally planned and liberalised global economy is yet to be seen and tested.

The panoramic outsider view will nevertheless portray China as imbedding its militarised economic empowerment on a controlled BIT map and along a directed BRI highway. The accusatory metaphor will be that China is re-incantating the rhetoric of Communist China in the 1950s, but with global not only domestic aspirations. Its invading warriors will be depicted as state endowed outbound investors subordinating BRI destination states as agents for the Peoples' Party.[110] The sweeping analogy will be that China's intends to disempower developing states, less through servitude attributed to the colonising West, than through its own variant of overlordship. The contrast drawn will be between China's blending of its planned domestic economy and international free trade, and the West's amalgam of domestic liberalisation and colonialism over several centuries.[111]

The image of China as an imperialist state, dictating the scope of bilateral and regional trade and investment initiatives along with its BRI, will undoubtedly be replicated, directly or otherwise, in ISDS claims. China, its outbound SOEs, and other state-sponsored investors will be portrayed as using BITs to displace the financial sovereignty of developing home states over infrastructure projects. China and its surrogates will be portrayed as patrolling its BRI, constraining foreign investors, and subjugating developing 'partner' states to it. The imagery will be of China subduing dissent over the nature, direction, and extent of travel along its ever-expanding BRI highway.[112] It will be portrayed as using IIAs to exercise licensing authority over inbound investments;[113] extending its regulatory authority

[110]Unfair competition is often identified with the unfair advantages accorded to SOEs. See, e.g. OECD (2016) State-Owned Enterprises as Global Competitors: A Challenge or an Opportunity?, p. 15.

[111]See Sornarajah (2011), p. 204; Sornarajah (2015), pp. 284–293.

[112]On the criticism that China is as engaging in unfair, extortionist and protectionist market practices, contrary to the requirements of WTO, see Office of United State Trade Representative, 'Joint Statement by the United States, European Union and Japan at MC11', 12 December 2017.

[113]See Aniodoh (2021) on how states surrender their monetary sovereignty when they sign BITs.

transnationally; and shielding itself and its outbound investors from ISDS review.[114] China will be perceived as abandoning its retreat from hard to soft law that it adopted in part to accommodate the West, by reasserting hard law to regulate both inbound and outbound foreign investment. It will be painted as using hard law as a double-edged sword, to impose rule-based imperatives on developing BRI states but not on itself.[115]

Still, China will articulate and publicise countervailing strategies. It will offset its historic BIT strategy of protecting itself by treaty from inbound investors from developed states, and by enhancing its commitment to outbound investor protections. It will seek to offset claims brought by inbound investors against it by extending treaty protections to its outbound investors from regulatory constraints imposed by treaty partner states. The incentive for it to pursue ambitious investment treaty and contract options will be to extend its multilateral Belt and Road and further cement its standing as a dominant investment superpower. China is likely to pursue these ends through alternative or supplementary measures to ISDS: such as state-to-state diplomacy; judicial and international commercial arbitration; and a multilateral investment court.[116]

Finding a functional equilibrium among these different and sometimes conflicting measures will be challenging, but not insurmountable. Few long-term instruments adopted to resolve global investment disputes have wholly upward trajectories.

Finally, China will not be alone among superpowers as a target of ISDS. ISDS proceedings constitute a two-way traffic. Just as inbound investors will proceed against China, China's outbound investors will lodge claims against foreign states for allegedly denying them investor protections substantively and in violation of the rule of law.[117]

7 Conclusion

China's future passageway along its Belt and Road includes realigning the profile attributed to it by detractors as being more an adversary than a friend of developing state partners and more of a market driver than facilitator. China's passageway is unlikely to be smooth. Alongside the economic setbacks in BRI planning it has suffering during the Pandemic are concomitant and ongoing political assaults upon its global trade and investment ambitions from the West. One assault is that China's BRI breeds supplication by foreign states and their outbound investors who travel

---

114 On China's reluctance to utilise administrative review provisions in its BITs, see Chi and Li (2021).

115 See Webb Yackee (2012) on a rule-based system that restricts the authority of states to regulate foreign investment.

116 See Sect. 7.

117 On Chinese investor claims abroad, see Berger (2019).

along it. Another assault is that the BRI is China's instrument for renewing colonialism in vulnerable investment markets, in effect, extending European colonialism into the twenty-first century.[118] That graphic depiction is of China resurrecting the assault weapons used by Western liberal states and their outbound investors to exploit the valuable assets of vulnerable states for lucrative profit.[119] A less likely but conceivable assault on China going forward is by blocs of developing countries alleging that China has besieged their fragile economies beyond their reliance on the UN General Assembly as a talking spot.[120]

Either way, the subtle economic challenge for China will be to redress the depiction of developing states being economically dependent upon it, rather than interdependent with it. China's renewed image will entail it constructing a blended vision of it as 'good neighbor, good friend and good partner', in pursuing shared not solitary gains along its BRI.[121] Building further trust will be portrayed as it seeking reciprocity of treatment for shared benefit, albeit to be sought incrementally and not instantly. The accompanying imagery will be of it establishing a viable balance between safeguarding both inbound and outbound investments and preserving financial stability in domestic markets, not limited to its own.[122] The imagery will not be of China's stoicism or sacrifice for others. It will be of mutual facilitation. However, provision for reciprocal access and treatment in China's investment treaties with developing states will need to be functional, not only formal. The functional task will be to enable foreign investors to access Chinese markets efficiently and without undue domestic regulations limiting that access.[123] Such reciprocity will ordinarily operate incrementally, as in trust building between formally sovereign states. It will also entail partner states arriving at a balance between China safeguarding its outbound investments and recipient states being able to utilise those investments to both stabilise and enrich their domestic markets.[124]

As a calculus, China's reformulation of its BRI collaborations will require that it refine narratives with state partners based on its assessment of past and prospective future costs and benefits. Central to that gains-based analysis will be how it engages in collaboration efficiently in light of its shifting geo-political objectives and changing market conditions.[125] One measure of such effectiveness is its ability to assess the economic and political risks associated with intervening market disruptions that

---

[118] See Vandevelde (2017).

[119] See Ahmed and Lambert (2021) on the evolving geopolitical and economic attributes of China's BRI in Eurasia and Africa.

[120] See Dzekashu and Anyu (2020) on the deceleration of China's BRI in Central and West Africa, and responses from the Forum on China-Africa Co-operation (FOCAC) in 2020.

[121] See Van Noort (2021) on China as a 'good neighbor, good friend and good partner' such as along its BRI in Africa.

[122] See, e.g. Bhasin and Manocha (2016) on whether and how India's BITs promote inbound investment.

[123] See Neumayer and Spess (2005).

[124] See, e.g. Bhasin and Manocha (2016) on India's BITs efforts to promote inbound investment.

[125] See Ramadhani and Noer (2022), pp. 90–103; Zhao and Tan-Mullins (2021).

impact upon the performance of BRI projects. This issue has already arisen in efforts to redress intervening supply shortages, price gyrations, and labour disruptions as consequences to the Pandemic.[126] China is well cognizant of these issues. President XI Jinping, in his open statement in June 2021, highlighted China's future commitment to openness, innovation, and sustained dialogue with IIA partner states. He enunciated further that China would finance operations 'along that [BRI] path' to protect the 'vital interests' of participating countries.[127] In place of confrontation is the imagery of China maintaining cross-border cooperation, affirming intercultural awareness and harnessing the shared benefits of BRI developments.

More subtle will be China's ability to present a level playing field to developing states that downplays the prospect of them becoming economically dependent along its Belt and Road. In place of that negative stamp attributed to unequal bargaining power will be the need for China to cultivate relationships built on the profitability to developing states of building BRI relationships along it. In place of China being perceived as exploiting those relationships, it will want to depict itself as using its capacity to exploit resources, not state partners. Its supporting rationale it will be that it will treat inbound foreign investors now as it would like their home states to treat its outbound investors in the future. In China's defence, it has undertaken to do so to in its 'New Foreign Investment Law' that came into force on 1 January 2020 which stipulates for equal treatment of foreign and domestic investors.[128]

China's political challenges in asserting its economic dominance regionally, such as in Africa where the US is seeking to re-establish beachheads, is likely to underscore competitive challenges to its BRI outreach. China's image as a global economic power is an important source of its credibility as both an inbound and an outbound investor state seeking to engage in mutually profitable ventures. However, China's image is also vulnerable to fracturing. Its internal financial difficulties, such as trade deficits, can cause investment partners to shy away from BRI investments partnerships with China, as occurred in Asia as China experienced an economic slowdown prior to the Pandemic. As a result, China's ambition to become the primary outbound investor state in the developing world will come at a high price to its domestic economy. Developing states with the strongest need for its financing are likely to be the most significant drain on its ability to support localised investment initiatives. For China to redress that reality will become a test of its functional resolve to achieve that objective, beyond prognosticating about it. It will need to do so fully cognisant that its domestic investment requirements have changed in material ways that were unthinkable 20 years ago. Once blessed with highly

[126] See Yaremko V and Franck Y, Proving Impediments Associated with Performance of the Contractual Obligations during the Spread of COVID-19. TDM, 2 June 2020, https://www.transnational-dispute-management.com/journal-advance-publication-article.asp?key=1828.

[127] See Rahman (2022). See also Jiang (2022).

[128] See Foreign Investment Law of People's Republic of China, adopted, 2nd Session, 13th National People's Congress, 15 March 2019, reproduced in English in www.npc.gov.cn/englishnpc/c23934/202012/5b80fe5055504efa93b6744f9272b3c2.shtml. That Law extends protections to foreign investors and provides for equality between foreign and domestic investors.

productive and growing workforce, China is now obliged to invest more fastidiously in domestic industries, work programs and pensions to support its elderly citizens.

These obstacles will require some modification in China's BRI ambitions. The prospect is that it will engage in a case-by-case gains-based analysis to determine whether the gains outweigh the costs of providing financial support to specific projects in developing states.[129] It will also be expected to assess with great care the aggregate gains of sustaining, or modifying its BRI program selectively and comparatively across its regional and global passageways.[130] Viewing its BRI as a composite whole, its idealised objective is to ensure that the sum of its BRI benefits are greater than the costs of its BRI parts. Should China opt for low-return investments on selected BRI partnership, that is likely to encourage it to embark on other offsetting projects that are more immediately profitable and provide it with realisable profit margins now, not later.[131]

How China will address its profitability conundrum along the BRI will depend somewhat on how it did so in prior investment cycles, but not always reliably.[132] In key respects, its past BRI successes will not ensure their successes going forward. Its ongoing use of a gains-based analysis will not always produce a dependable assessment of how total returns will compensate its outbound investors for travel along costly segments of its BRI. China's responses will be familiar in part: replanning modes and conditions for ongoing travel; modifying its construction of investment roads; and reformulating road maps to realign delivery along it. The fact that China has been playing the long BRI game for decades, traversing different stages of global economic development, is a pathway it is likely to continue navigating. The natural hurdles and combined economic and political obstructions it will encounter along the way are assuredly formidable. However, travelling on the high seas and weathering storms and tempests at different junctures, is what China has done for decades. In this author's view, it will continue to do so adeptly, but not always profitably, going forward.

References

Afzaal M (2022) Prospects for China's Belt and Road Initiative (BRI): implications, assessment and challenges. Asia Pac Bus Rev 28(1):130–139

[129] On the flexibility of the BRI rules in providing developing states with the opportunity to engage in international economic cooperation, see Li (2021).

[130] See Banga R, Impact of Government Policies and Investment Agreements on FDI Inflow, ICRIER Working Paper No 116.

[131] Zeng (2016), p. 517 on 'global governance' consisting of both regional economic integration and partnerships between states.

[132] See Hannon P and Jeong EY, China Overtakes U.S. as World's Leading Destination for Foreign Direct Investment, Wall Street Journal, 24 January 2021, https://www.wsJournalcom/articles/china-overtakes-u-s-as-worlds-leading-destination-for-foreign-direct-investment-11611511200.

Ahmed F, Lambert A (2021) The Belt and Road Initiative: geopolitical and geoeconomic aspects. Taylor & Francis, India
Akperlinova A, Jastrzebski K (2022) Reforming investor-state dispute settlement: the EU multilateral investment court perspective. J Invest Manag 11(1):1–9
Alvarez JE (2021) ISDS reform: the long view. ICSID Rev-Foreign Invest Law J 36(2):253–277
Ameyaw-Brobbey T (2021) A critical juncture? COVID-19 and the fate of the US–China struggle for supremacy. World Aff 184(3):260–293
Amineh MP (2022) China's rise and the question of hegemony and world order. In: Amineh MP (ed) The China-led Belt and Road Initiative and its reflections, 1st edn. Routledge, London, pp 36–69
Aniodoh AA (2021) Sovereign authority within the construct of bilateral investment treaties. J Afr Law 65(1):1–23
Baláž P, Zábojník S, Harvánek L (2020) FDI as a driving force of China's expansion. In: Baláž P, Zábojník S, Harvánek L (eds) China's expansion in international business: the geopolitical impact on the world economy. Palgrave Macmillan, Cham, pp 161–235
Berger A (2019) The political economy of Chinese investment treaties. In: Ka Z (ed) Handbook on the international political economy of China. Edward Elgar, Cheltenham, pp 151–168
Bhasin N, Manocha R (2016) Do bilateral investment treaties promote FDI inflows? Evidence from India. Vikalpa – J Decis Makers 41(4):275–187
Bungenberg M, Reinisch A (2020) From bilateral arbitral tribunals and investment courts to a multilateral investment court: options regarding the institutionalization of investor-state dispute settlement. Springer, Heidelberg
Buser A (2020) Recalibrating policy space in bilateral investment treaties: is there a common B (R) ICS approach? In: Congyan C, Huiping C, Yifei W (eds) The BRICS in the new international legal order on investment. Brill Nijhoff, Leiden, pp 163–203
Carmody P, Wainwright J (2022) Contradiction and restructuring in the Belt and Road Initiative: reflections on China's pause in the 'Go world'. Third World Q 43(12):2830–2851
Chaisse J (2019) China's international investment law and policy regime–identifying the three tracks. In: Chaisse J (ed) China's international investment strategy: bilateral, regional, and global law and policy. Oxford University Press, Oxford, pp 1–22
Chaisse J (2021) China's international investment policy: formation, evolution, and transformation (s). In: Chaisse J, Nottage L (eds) International investment treaties and arbitration across Asia. Brill Nijhoff, Leiden, pp 544–578
Chen W (2017) Debating the consensuses. In: Chen W (ed) The Beijing consensus? How China has changed western ideas of law and economic development. Cambridge University Press, Cambridge, pp 1–12
Chen H (2018) China's innovative ISDS mechanisms and their implications. AJIL Unbound 112: 207–211
Chen AH (2023) Law and social policy in the People's Republic of China: from communism to marketisation. In: Davy U, Chen AH (eds) Law and social policy in the global south. Routledge, London, pp 39–77
Chi M (2020) The ISDS adventure of Chinese arbitration institutions: towards a dead end or a bright future? Asia Pac Law Rev 28(2):279–296
Chi M, Li Z (2021) Administrative review provisions in Chinese investment treaties: gilding the lily? J Int Dispute Settlement 12(1):125–150
Cohen T, Schneiderman D (2017) The political economy of Chinese bilateral investment treaty policy. Chin J Comp Law 5(1):119–128
Collins D (2023) An introduction to international investment law. Cambridge University Press
Cotula L, Weng X, Ma Q, Ren P (2016) China-Africa investment treaties: do they work? IIED, London
deLisle J (2021) When rivalry goes viral: COVID-19, U.S.-China relations, and East Asia. Orbis 65(1):46–74

Deng Y (2021) How China builds the credibility of the belt and road initiative. J Contemp China 30(131):734–750
Du M (2022) Explaining China's approach to investor-state dispute settlement reform. Eur Law J. https://www.academia.edu/82421581/Explaining_Chinas_Approach_to_Investor_State_Dispute_Settlement_Reform
Dzekashu WG, Anyu JN (2020) China's Belt and Road Initiative: will it make or mar development in the Central and West Africa subregions? J Adm Gov 10(1):1936–1936
Fach Gómez K (2021) EU-China negotiations on investor state dispute settlement within the CAI framework: are we on the right track? Revista General de Derecho Europeo 55:61–71
Fan X (2020) Agree or agree to disagree: China–EU Comprehensive Agreement on Investment (CAI) negotiation and the ISDS reform. Chin J Comp Law 8(3):635–638
Fang T, Hassler J (2021) Globalization, political economy, business and society in pandemic times. In: Ghauri P, Fang T, Hassler J (eds) International business and management, vol 36. Emerald Publishing Limited, Bingley, pp 1–10
Gallagher N, Shan W (2009) Expropriation and compensation. In: Chinese investment treaties: policies and practice. Oxford University Press, Oxford
Gao H (2022) Trade and investment liberalization: the case of China. In: Bethlehem D, McRae D, Neufeld R, Van Damme I (eds) The Oxford handbook of international trade law, 2nd edn. Oxford University Press, Oxford, pp 341–373
Giest A (2017) Interpreting public interest provisions in international investment treaties. Chic J Int Law 18:321–352
Gu W (2018) China's Belt and Road Development and a new international commercial arbitration initiative in Asia. Vanderbilt J Transnatl Law 51:1305–1352
He B (2019) The domestic politics of the Belt and Road Initiative and its implications. J Contemp China 28(116):180–195
Heinberg R (2011) The end of growth: adapting to our new economic reality. New Society Publishers, Canada
Henckels C (2015) Proportionality and deference in investor-state arbitration: balancing investment protection and regulatory autonomy. Cambridge University Press, Cambridge
Henckels C (2018) Should investment treaties contain public policy exceptions. Boston Coll Law Rev 59:2825–2844
Hepburn J (2023) The past, present, and future of domestic investment laws and international economic law. World Trade Rev 22(1):18–34
Hsueh R (2011) China's regulatory state: a new strategy for globalization. Cornell University Press, Cornell
Ji X, Chaisse J (2022) Stress test for EU's Investment Court System: how will investments be protected in the comprehensive agreement on investment? Leg Issues Econ Integr 49(1): 101–124
Jiang Y (2022) Unpacking the Belt and Road Initiative: does its public diplomacy narratives match its implementation? East Asia 39:315–331
Kao PS (2021) The political economy of China's strategic layout in Europe: a case study of the Belt and Road Initiative. Chin Econ 55(4):303–316
Kinnear M (2015) ICSID and international investment treaty arbitration: progress and prospects. In: Shan W, Su J (eds) China and international investment law: twenty years of ICSID Membership. Brill Nijhoff, Leiden, pp 7–22
Laruelle M (2018) China's Belt and Road Initiative and its impact in Central Asia. The George Washington University, Central Asia Program, Washington D.C.
Lei Y, Sui S (2022) China-Pacific Island countries strategic partnership: China's strategy to reshape the regional order. East Asia 39:81–96
Li X (2021) High-quality development and institutionalization of the BRI. East Asian Aff 1(1): 2150004-1–2150004-28
Li Y, Bian C (2020) China's stance on investor-state dispute settlement: evolution, challenges, and reform options. Netherlands Int Law Rev 67:503–551

Li J, Van Assche A, Li L, Qian G (2022) Foreign direct investment along the Belt and Road: a political economy perspective. J Int Bus Stud 53(5):902–919

Liao H, Yang L, Dai S, Van Assche A (2021) Outward FDI, industrial structure upgrading and domestic employment: empirical evidence from the Chinese economy and the Belt and Road Initiative. J Asian Econ 74:101303

Liu W, Dunford M (2016) Inclusive globalization: unpacking China's Belt and Road Initiative. Area Dev Policy 1(3):323–340

Maçães B (2021) Belt and Road: a Chinese world order. Oxford University Press, Oxford

McLaughlin M (2020) State-owned enterprises and threats to national security under investment treaties. Chin J Int Law 19(2):283–327

Neumayer E, Spess L (2005) Do bilateral investment treaties increase foreign direct investment to developing countries? World Dev 33(10):1567–1585

Ning H, Qi T (2018) Multilateral Investment Court: the gap between the EU and China. Chin J Glob Gov 4(2):154–175

Parra AR (2017) The history of ICSID. Oxford University Press, Oxford

Puig S, Strezhnev A (2017) The David effect and ISDS. Eur J Int Law 28(3):731–761

Rahman ZU (2022) A comprehensive overview of China's Belt and Road Initiative and its implication for the region and beyond. J Public Aff 22(1):e2298

Ramadhani SN, Noer M (2022) China's influence on Australia's position in the South Pacific in the security sector and developing sector. J Soc Polit Sci 3(1):90–103

Rizzi C, Yu X, Tettamanti M, Ziccardi FE, Li G (2018) China's Belt and Road: the initiative and its financial focus. World Scientific, Singapore

Rooney KM (2007) ICSID and BIT arbitrations and China. J Int Arbitr 24(6):689–712

Rosenberg JM (2022) The Belt and Road Initiative: the threat of an economic cold war with China. Rowman & Littlefield, London

Rudolf M (2021) The Belt and Road Initiative, implications for the international order. World Scientific, Singapore

Sági J, Engelberth I (2018) The Belt and Road Initiative–a way forward to China's expansion. Contemp Chin Polit Econ Strateg Relat 4(1):9–37

Sangaré F (2021) International trading wars and governance: the effect of COVID-19. Bus Econ Dev 6(2):73–81

Schulhof V, van Vuuren D, Kirchherr J (2022) The Belt and Road Initiative (BRI): what will it look like in the future? Technol Forecast Soc Chang 175:121306

Shan W, Chen H (2016) China-US BIT negotiation and the emerging Chinese BIT 4.0. In: Lim CL (ed) Alternative visions of the international law on foreign investment. Cambridge University Press, Cambridge, pp 223–252

Shan W, Gallagher N (2013) China. In: Brown C (ed) Commentaries on selected model investment treaties. Oxford University Press, Oxford, pp 131–182

Shen W (2013) China and international investment law. In: Trakman LE, Ranieri NW (eds) Regionalism in international investment law. Oxford University Press, Oxford, pp 214–252

Sornarajah M (2011) Mutations of neo-liberalism in international investment. Trade Law Dev 3(1): 203–232

Sornarajah M (2015) Resistance and change in the international law on foreign investment. Cambridge University Press, Cambridge

Steinbock D (2018) U.S.-China trade war. China Q Int Strateg Stud 4(4):515–542

Tekdal V (2018) China's Belt and Road Initiative: at the crossroads of challenges and ambitions. Pac Rev 31(3):373–390

Trakman LE (2012a) Investor state arbitration or local courts: will Australia set a new trend? J World Trade 46(1):83–120

Trakman LE (2012b) The ICSID under Siege. Cornell Int Law J 45(3):603–665

Trakman LE (2014) China and foreign direct investment: does distance lend enchantment to the view? Chin J Comp Law 2(1):1–20

Trakman LE (2016) China and foreign direct investment: looking ahead. In: Liu Q, Shan W (eds) China and international commercial dispute resolution. Brill Nijhoff, Leiden, pp 129–194
Trakman LE (2017) China's regulation of foreign direct investment. In: Chaisse J, Ishikawa T, Jusoh S (eds) Asia's changing international investment regime. Springer, Singapore, pp 67–95
Trakman LE, Liu Q, Chen L (2020) Investor-state arbitration in China: a comparative perspective. In: Chen L, Janssen A (eds) Dispute resolution in China, Europe and world. Springer, Cham, pp 231–261
Vaccaro-Incisa GM (2021) China's treaty policy and practice in international investment law and arbitration: a comparative and analytical study. Brill Nijhoff, Leiden
Van Noort C (2021) China's communication of the Belt and Road Initiative: Silk Road and infrastructure narratives. Routledge, London
Vandevelde KJ (2017) The first bilateral investment treaties U.S. postwar: friendship, commerce, and navigation treaties. Oxford University Press, Oxford
Wang H, Wang L (2021) China's bilateral investment treaties. In: Chaisse J, Choukroune L, Jusoh S (eds) Handbook of international investment law and policy. Springer, Singapore, pp 1–21
Webb Yackee J (2012) Controlling the International Investment Law Agency. Harv Int Law J 53(2): 391–448
Wei S (2021) Decoding Chinese bilateral investment treaties. Cambridge University Press, Cambridge
Xi J (2014–2017) The governance of China II. Foreign Languages Press, Beijing
Zeng H (1999) Chinese foreign investment laws: recent developments towards a market economy. World Scientific and Singapore University Press, Singapore
Zeng K (2010) Multilateral versus bilateral and regional trade liberalization: explaining China's pursuit of free trade agreements (FTAs). J Contemp China 19(66):635–652
Zeng L (2016) Conceptual analysis of China's Belt and Road Initiative: a road towards a regional community of common destiny. Chin J Int Law 15:517–541
Zhao C (2018) Investor-state mediation in a China-EU bilateral investment treaty: talking about being in the right place at the right time. Chin J Int law 17:111–135
Zhao M (2019) Is a new cold war inevitable? Chinese perspectives on US–China strategic competition. Chin J Int Polit 12(3):371–394
Zhao S (2020) China's global reach: The Belt and Road Initiative (BRI) and Asian Infrastructure Investment Bank (AIIB), vol II. Routledge, London
Zhao L (2023) Modern China and international rules: reconstruction and innovation. Springer, Singapore
Zhao Y, Tan-Mullins M (2021) From the Ancient Silk Road to the Belt and Road Initiative: narratives, signalling and trust-building. Br J Polit Int Relat 23(2):280–296
Zhou J (2020) A new multilateralism? A case study of the Belt and Road Initiative. Chin J Comp Law 8(2):384–413
Zou L, Shen JH, Zhang J, Lee CC (2022) What is the rationale behind China's infrastructure investment under the Belt and Road Initiative. J Econ Surv 36(3):605–633

Leon Trakman is a Former Dean of Law at the University of New South Wales, 2002–2007, a UNSW Professor of Law (2002–2020) and a UNSW Professor (2021–). He holds both Masters' and Doctorate degrees earned at the Harvard Law School. He has served as presiding arbitrator or arbitrator in more than 140 international commercial disputes and as a mediator in over 30 disputes. He was recently appointed to the Remedies Panel established by the United States-Mexico-Canada Agreement (USMCA). Professor Trakman is the author of over 200 publications, including 11 books, on international commercial arbitration, contract, insurance, finance, insolvency, trade and investment law. He is a barrister in Australia, Canada and South Africa. His contract details are leon.trakman@trakmanassociates.com. His professional website is trakmanassociates.com.

Conflicts over Industrial and Trade Policy: Europe Between China and the United States

Carsten Hefeker

Contents

Abstract The chapter discusses the shift towards more pronounced industrial and strategic trade policies in Europe over the last years. Assessing the merits of such a policy, it is skeptical that such a policy will be successful because it is likely to be inefficient, expensive and to create conflicts with trading partners. Concerning the position of European policy in the international context, Europe should not enter into a competition over subsidies and industry location or a relocation policy that some policymakers advocate and that seems to be taking shape. Moreover, given Europe's dependence on strategic imports, a policy of decoupling and "friend-shoring", and in contrast to the United States, cannot be successful. Instead, Europe is best advised to build an independent position that stresses international cooperation and broad diversification of trading partners without pushing targeted industrial policy. Improving supply side conditions is more promising and better able to address the challenges of the demographic and environmental transition than supporting individual industries.

C. Hefeker (✉)
University of Siegen, Siegen, Germany
e-mail: carsten.hefeker@uni-siegen.de

M. Bungenberg et al. (eds.), *Asian Yearbook of International Economic Law 2023*,
Asian Yearbook of International Economic Law (2023) 2023: 53–70,
https://doi.org/10.1007/16517_2023_15, Published online: 15 March 2023

1 Introduction

The war in Ukraine has visibly divided the world. While "the West", led by the United States, imposes strong sanctions on Russia to punish it for its aggression, eight out of ten countries in the world do not. China professes "eternal" friendship with Russia while India and others call for peace and reject nuclear escalation but are unwilling to join the West in its sanctions and rather benefit from discounted prices for Russian energy. Poorer economies are affected by the fall-out from the war in terms of increasing energy and food prices but see no reason to make their situation worse by taking side in the conflict. They see the war as a European problem that should be solved there. But it is not so simple: As many observers are concerned that China may in the not too distant future make an effort to "reunite" Taiwan with the mainland, the same type of question may arise again and trade and financial conflicts between the largest economies in the world will have repercussions on all countries.

This type of conflict has been building up for a long time. The Global Financial Crisis of 2008 on the one hand yielded an impressively coordinated response. A new forum, the G-20, brought together emerging and advanced economies and a coordinated expansion in fiscal policies helped to fight a global recession. While it created optimism that international cooperation could be moved to a new level, the consequences of the crisis instead led to a backlash against globalization in many parts of the world. The negative consequences of globalization heightened economic insecurity and increasing inequality, having built up over a longer time, triggered a turn to economic nationalism and populism.[1] In the wake of the Global Financial Crisis, global trade policy consequently became increasingly restrictive, once again reinforced by Covid-19.[2]

The clear shift toward a more nationalistic trade policy became most evident with the election of Donald Trump as president of the United States and the parallel shift of Chinese policy towards a more assertive foreign and economic policy.[3] Economic policies are increasingly seen as an instrument in foreign policy, taking a subordinated role to political goals.[4] The emerging rivalry for global preeminence has created talk about a "new cold war" and prompted the Europeans to think about their own role in this. A United States no longer fully reliable and a China that is increasingly willing to use economic means to punish countries for their political "misbehavior", led the European Union to search for ways to become less vulnerable and dependent in terms of trade and financial policies. Initiatives to strengthen the role to the euro against the US-dollar and seeking alternatives to the dysfunctional

[1] Broz et al. (2021), Eichengreen (2018), Funke et al. (2016), Guriev and Papaioannou (2022), and Walter (2021).

[2] Garcia-Herrero (2022); See also the reports monitoring trade policies by Global Trade Alert, https://www.globaltradealert.org.

[3] Bergsten (2022), Doshi (2021), Economy (2021), and Rudd (2022).

[4] Baldwin (2020), Blackwill and Harris (2016), and Kamin et al. (2022).

Appellate Body at the World Trade Organization (WTO) were thus promoted by European officials.[5]

Covid-19 with its export controls for medical equipment and the collapse of global supply chains (including singular events such as the blockade of the Suez Canal) have only reinforced the awareness of vulnerabilities and consequently increased attempts to "reshore" certain industries that are deemed important in times of crises. This, at least in the European perspective, now includes as well energy, bringing together the security of supply chains with aspects of geoeconomic rivalry. Given less than full agreement among the EU members and its partners what should be done, this poses a particular challenge.

The present paper discusses the problems that have built up over the last decade from a European perspective with a particular focus on the possibilities of collaboration among "friends". It will show that the discussed revival of strategic trade and industrial policy that is pushed by the EU Commission and individual member states like Germany and France is not a very promising way to solve the issues at hand. Undeniably, Europe has to define an answer to economic nationalism, slowing economic growth and the necessary transformation of economic systems toward more environment friendly production and consumption, but the proposals that are advanced at the European level are not convincing. By focusing on certain industries and outdated concepts of desirable economic structures, Europeans risk wasting a lot of money internally, whereas externally this type of industrial policy is likely to increase tensions with international trading partners even more. Next, I turn to potential conflicts between the United States and Europe and argue that Europeans are unlikely to follow the strategy of decoupling from China to the extent the United States might want it so that industrial policy initiatives on both sides of the Atlantic may clash. Finally, I look at possible solutions what Europe can do.

2 Strategic Autonomy and European Industrial Policy

European trade and industrial policy has regained importance in recent years in response to policy changes mostly in China and the United States.[6] In 2019 the then German minister for the economy, Peter Altmaier, published his plan for a German industrial policy, followed at little later by a similar plan by the President of the

[5]European Commission (2019) Strengthening the International Role of the Euro: Results of the Consultations. Staff Working Document 600, Brussels; European Commission (2020) A New Industrial Strategy for Europe, COM (2020) 102 final, Brussels.

[6]Industrial policy is concerned with domestic economic structures whereas strategic trade policy pursues similar objectives in interaction with trading partners. In highly open economies both are strongly interconnected of course and I use the expressions interchangeably.

European Commission, Ursula von der Leyen.[7] Both papers formulated policies that would support digital and ecological technologies but should also provide a response to its trading partner to defend European economies against dumping and export subsidies with the aim to acquire or monopolize important technologies. The German paper explicitly mentioned the United States and China as strategic competitors while the Commission paper stressed the need for European autonomy. Key industries would have to be kept in Europe or recovered if lost and supply chains should be explicitly based on European partners. In both cases, significant public support should help reaching these strategic aims.

Both papers reacted to the declared Chinese strategy of subsidizing strategic sectors and acquire world leadership in them.[8] In pursuing this aim, China allegedly invests strategically to monopolize or dominate certain industries and disregards intellectual property rights, thus violating basic rules of world trade. Recurse to the World Trade Organization rules, however, is of little help because many of the contested policies are not covered by the WTO framework which, for instance, allows to address dumping issues but does not cover trade in services which becomes increasingly important. Moreover, so the argument, the WTO lost most of its impact and power to effectively regulate international trade because of institutional stalemate and the de-facto suspension of its Appellate Body.[9]

Both papers are also inspired by the shift in American trade policy due to President Trump whose administration not only pursued explicit mercantilist aims, with an intention to disrupt certain supply chains and decouple from China, but also declared a balanced current account or even a surplus as an aim of national trade policy.[10] This nationalistic turn in US trade policy, in addition to the marked shift towards increasing non-tariff barriers in international trade policy after the Global Financial Crisis,[11] were identified as needing a response.

Lastly, the ineffectiveness of the WTO, so the view, would require European countries to search for alternative mechanisms of regulating international trade to which the Commission also provided a perspective in calling for cooperation among like-minded nations to substitute for dispute settlement at the WTO. While international cooperation is mentioned, the instruments proposed are of a bilateral nature reflecting the perception that the future of international trade policy was seen as being mainly unilateral or bilateral.

The von der Leyen-Commission has continued along those lines and added, in response to Covid-19, the additional aim of ensuring supply chain security and

[7]Bundesministerium für Wirtschaft und Energie (2019) Nationale Industriestrategie 2030: Strategische Leitlinien für eine deutsche und europäische Industriepolitik. BMWi, Berlin; European Commission (2020) A New Industrial Strategy for Europe, COM (2020) 102 final, Brussels.

[8]Bergsten (2022); Doshi (2021); European Union Chamber of Commerce in China (2021) Decoupling: Severed Ties and Patchwork Globalization. European Chamber, Beijing.

[9]Baldwin (2016).

[10]Noland (2018).

[11]Evenett and Fritz (2019).

less dependency on other parts of the world.[12] Indeed, the policy target of becoming less dependent and more autonomous seems to have become increasingly ambitious over time. Internal Market Commissioner Thierry Breton advocates an industrial policy that makes Europe completely independent from foreign sources, and the French and German ministers for the economy, Bruno Le Maire and Robert Habeck[13] recently called for a Green European Industrial Policy that combines environmental aims with a targeted European industrial policy to make Europe as soon as possible less reliant on imported fossil energy. As new issues emerge, the European knee-jerk reaction seems to be a call for more extended and ambitious industrial policy and more state interventions.

3 The Strategic Use of Industrial and Trade Policy

3.1 Mercantilist Motives

One major argument for the use of trade policy is the explicit aim to shift income and economic rents between countries. By manipulating demand for imports, countries aim to improve their so-called terms of trade, which measures the relation between export and import prices.[14] The idea is simple: If an economically large country lowers the demand for foreign products, this should have an effect on the world market price of these goods. As the demand for these goods goes down, the relative net-of-tariffs price for these goods should decline thus allowing the importing country to buy relatively more imports for a given amount of exports.[15] The terms of trade have improved and the initiator of import tariffs has become relatively richer in comparison to its competitors since one unit of export goods buys more imports.

While the argument is very prominent in theory, it hinges on demanding assumptions:[16] The country has to be large, economically speaking, and thus must be able to influence its terms of trade. The country must be large in population and income to influence world market prices as well as being a substantial importer of the respective good or service. It is not clear that his applies to many countries with respect to

[12] European Commission (2021) Updating the 2020 New Industrial Strategy: Building a Stronger Single Market for Europe's Recovery, SWD (2021) 350 final, Brussels; European Commission (2021) Strategic Dependencies and Capacities, SWD (2021) 352 final, Brussels.

[13] Le Maire B and Habeck R (2022), For a European Green Industrial Policy, BMWK, Berlin, https://www.bmwk.de/Redaktion/DE/Downloads/deu-fra-gemeinsame-erklarung-zur-starkung-der-industriepolitschen-zusammenarbeit.html.

[14] Bhagwati and Johnson (1961).

[15] That is, the price at the border should go down while consumer prices increase due to tariffs. As tariffs are a purely national redistribution, the country's overall situation has improved due to relative decline of import prices at the border (net of tariffs).

[16] It is surprising that this argument still carries so much weight in trade policy discussions, given that is seems to play only a small role in reality (Ethier 2007).

many categories of goods. While the United States, China, India and the European Union may fulfill these requirements, most other countries are more likely to be at the receiving end of such policies and should have an interest to constrain such behavior.

But even larger countries only benefit if there is no retaliation by those countries that are negatively affected by their trade policy. If the United States improves its terms of trade vis-à-vis China, the latter is likely to retaliate, leading to round after round of increasing trade barriers which in the end leaves trade at a very low level, forgoing the benefits from trade and leaving both sides worse off. This, so the standard answer, is why the terms of trade argument is not a promising strategy and why international agreements like the WTO aim to protect smaller countries and avoid this self-defeating behavior by larger countries.[17]

Very popular and at first look maybe more convincing are arguments to use trade policy in order to shift production between countries. This long-standing argument comes in two variants and is the background to current policy. The first variant is concerned with the overall level of trade and production and has been behind the trade policy strategy of, for example, President Trump.[18] If production is taking place at home, so the argument goes, jobs and profits are kept at home as well. In other words, imports are bad because production is taking place abroad whereas exports are good because production is taking place at home. Selling more products to foreigners than one buys from them also means building up claims against them. This, of course, is the standard mercantilist argument which has been attacked already by Adam Smith but is surprisingly long-lived.[19] Instead, the purpose of trade, and the source of the gains from trade, is to import products that can be more efficiently produced abroad and to export those goods and services where the home country has a comparative advantage. Producing everything at home is a very inefficient way of using domestic resources and forgoes the gains from trade.

Moreover, while a deficit in terms of goods, services and primary income means that the country consumes and invests more than it produces, a surplus means that the country is a creditor to the rest of the world.[20] As long as capital imports are invested and yield higher productivity and income in the future, it is not clear why that should be problem. But being a lender to the rest of the world also entails the risk that debtors default on their obligations. A more or less balanced current account, where imports and export more or less equal, instead implies that fewer imports also mean lower exports. Preserving jobs in the import protected industry thus mirrors a loss of jobs in the export industry as constraining imports also constrains exports. And is far from clear that not more jobs are lost in the export industry than are protected in the relatively inefficient import competing industries.

[17] Bagwell and Staiger (1999).

[18] Noland (2018).

[19] Helleiner (2021).

[20] Irwin (2020).

Thus, shielding international competition and protecting and preserving industrial structures that would otherwise disappear is inefficient. Workers are kept in industries where they are not productive anymore and it implicitly keeps them from retraining and finding more productive employment in other occupations.[21] Making certain products, say steel, more expensive through tariffs will also hurt downstream industries by raising their production costs. Jobs that are protected in one industry thus implicitly lose jobs in downstream industries. In fact, in most cases the losses of jobs in other industries will be higher than the number of jobs preserved, for which the steel industry in the United States is a good example.[22]

3.2 Strategic Trade Policy

The second, and more sophisticated, variant of the argument is about the location of certain industries and is behind the political focus on the location of industrial production such as, most recently, green energy. Based on theoretical arguments developed in the 1980s,[23] the aim is to locate certain "strategic" industries at home rather than seeing them based abroad. Certain industries are identified as yielding high-value added and thus securing "good" jobs, they are considered to be "modern" and "strategic" while at the same type operating under strong economies of scale.[24] The countries which set up those industries in the first place, because of first mover advantages, are likely to dominate the respective industries in the future. This is, then, the argument and justification for government intervention to locate those industries at home. Trade policy measures (tariffs and other trade policy measures) or subsidies (industrial policy) should be used strategically to set up or attract promising industries with good, secure and high-paying jobs. If domestic and foreign firms compete about dominating a particular market, domestic government can make sure that domestic firms are successful by subsidizing their production. Being first in doing so should keep other firms from entering the market as they realize they cannot be profitable besides the incumbent.

In fact, however, many such attempts have become notorious for being very expensive and not able to create successful industries.[25] In general, the theory on

[21] It is important, however, that there be active labor market and social policies for workers to make retraining possible.

[22] Irwin (2020).

[23] Helpman and Krugman (1989) and Brander (1995).

[24] Economies of scale arise if production requires high fixed costs (mostly cost of invention) but very low marginal costs. Having made an important invention (like a software or vaccine) and setting up production, output can be produced at unit costs close to zero. Under such circumstances one or very few firms will acquire a monopolistic position and dominate the whole industry because competitors have no chance to enter the industry successfully afterwards. Only political intervention can break the first-mover advantage of the initial incumbent.

[25] Irwin (2020).

which this policy is based is not very robust. Whether subsidies and tariffs do have positive effects depends to a large extent on the number firms that compete in the domestic and foreign market, and prescriptions which instruments of support (tariffs, taxes or subsidies) should be used depends crucially on the market structure. For instance, if firms compete over prices, subsidies help domestic firms to acquire a significant market, if they compete over quantities, however, export taxes would be the appropriate instrument.[26]

As the famous conflict between Europe and the United States and their respective support for Airbus and Boeing in the production of airplanes shows, moreover, this type of competition can quickly become very expensive and acrimonious but yet ineffective. If two or more governments pursue the strategy to deter foreign rivals from the market by supporting "their" firms, policymakers may become stuck in a Prisoner's Dilemma game where both spend a lot of money but are ultimately not successful to keep rivals from entering the market. Instead, it is very likely the competing industries will continuously rely on government support. Just like in the terms of trade case, what looks like a promising strategy for a single government is very likely to fail if other governments pursue the same objectives.

There is also a political economic argument against such a policy since strategic and industrial policies are often driven by lobbying interests. Anticipating that governments may be willing to support certain sectors, firms will lobby for support and make promises of later success they may not be able to realize. They also have an incentive not to provide their best efforts in order to extract even more support as they can expect to be bailed out by the government. Policymakers in turn have an incentive to devise grand programs because they seek political support from favored industries and voters that expect higher profits, wages and more employment. Once they have agreed to support a firm or industry, however, policymaker will be under pressure to continue supporting and preserving the industry in focus even if firms are not as successful as promised. In the end, capital and labor are allocated to inefficient industries due to political reasons.

Nevertheless, while theoretically disputed strategic trade policy or industrial policy appeal to policymakers, and it is not surprising that the backlash against globalization and increasing conflicts in trade policy revived such arguments. For Europe, two developments came together that led to the revival of industrial policy. One was, magnified by the impact of the Global Financial Crisis and the European debt crisis, that globalization triggered a loss of high paying and mostly industrial jobs. Globalization, epitomized by the rise of China, and a loss of production capacities in Europe created uncertainty and resistance to international integration.[27] Combined with a crisis of public finances in many European countries, this fueled populistic sentiments and a rise of populist parties. This needed a political response and part of that was identified in protecting and bringing back investment and employment. For this, policymakers concluded, defending industrial production in

[26] Spencer and Brander (2008).

[27] Walter (2021).

Europe and, if possible, recovering once lost production lines was required. In addition, the shift in American trade policy associated with President Trump led European policymakers to realize that not only China but the United States as well would be a strategic competitor in the location of certain industries and activities.

In their respective papers mentioned above, the German government and the European Commission consequently formulated the goal to have, respectively, a share of manufacturing in GDP of 25% (Germany) and 20% (for the EU overall). While not explicitly mentioning individual sectors, it is clear that the actual numbers are lower by 2–3% for Germany and a significant 6% in the European Union, requiring that the share of manufacturing needs to be increased to achieve this goal.[28] The logic behind this target is the understanding that increases in growth and income are historically driven by industrialization. Capital intensive industrial production increases the productivity of labor and is the source of high income for employees while labor employed in agriculture and services is traditionally less productive and thus has lower income. But this logic is flawed in several respects.

First, a gradual shift towards more service-based consumption is part of increasing income levels. Relatively more income is spent on services, such as information and communication technology, consulting or recreation and mobility as people and societies become richer because these products have a higher income elasticity than industrial or agricultural products. Since this is a global trend, preserving or even increasing the European share in manufacturing requires that the process of deindustrialization in other regions of the world is even accelerated. If, as formulated in the German strategy, certain industries should be lured back to Europe, other countries would lose them and it is highly likely that this will lead to conflicts.

Second, while it is historically correct that the expansion of industry has accelerated income growth, this is no longer the case. New well-paid jobs are mainly generated in consulting, entertainment and information technology which are all part of the service sector. In fact, Zettelmeyer[29] shows that the historically observed positive correlation between the share of manufacturing and high-income levels does no longer hold. Instead, most projections expect digitalization and artificial intelligence to dominate economic progress beside robotics. Investment in this "intangible capital" takes now the major share[30] and it is the express aim of the European strategy to be leading in this field as well. A backward definition of manufacturing and arbitrary quantitative aims of industrial shares are misleading in this regard.[31]

The paper by the Commission stresses digitalization, green technology and recycling as a major future field of technology. In Germany, restructuring the automobile sector is expressly mentioned as a goal. In this, both papers are based on the perception that bureaucrats have identified the technologies of the future that

[28] Aiginger and Rodrik (2020).

[29] Zettelmeyer (2019).

[30] Baldwin (2019) and Haskel and Westlake (2017).

[31] Aiginger and Rodrik (2020).

now only need to be developed. But this thinking is flawed as well and reflects what is wrong with this type of industrial policy.

Given that the many of these technologies are characterized by a high importance of economies of scale, it is very unlikely that Europeans can become competitive in industries in which others already have dominant market positions. Industrial policy that tries to erode the dominant positions that others have already acquired is likely to be very expensive and to ultimately fail as argued above. At worst, firms are supported and kept in business with public funds that could be used more efficiently, and goods and services are produced that could be imported from more efficient and cheaper sources.

It is thus very risky if governments and their bureaucracies believe they are able to identify the future technology or industry that may come to dominate markets. However, it is rather unlikely that government or agencies have the knowledge and capability to identify the "right" industries. Committing to the support of one particular technology, as happens for instance in Germany with the focus on electrical mobility instead risks to neglect more promising future alternative technologies.[32]

Of course, nothing guarantees that private investments in high-risk technologies will be successful either but the consequences of private mistakes are different. Firms fail and jobs are lost but not public money. And the political dynamics is a different one: Declaring a certain political goal creates a dynamic which makes it very difficult for policymakers to admit defeat and pull out of the industry. Instead, there is a high danger that those industries and firms will only survive with government help. European strategies to commit to certain industries and technologies is running this risk too.

An additional factor in the European context is the probable conflict among member states where certain industries should be geographically located that are financed via common funds. This would either imply that compromises about industry location are negotiated which do not necessarily follow economic logic or that member states would compete against each other about location by subsidizing individual firms or industries even more. In particular industries that benefit from large sizes are not well suited to distribute production and head-quarters among member states due to political considerations. Competition between the member states instead would mainly benefit the larger and richer members and reinforce conflicts and asymmetries within the European Union.

In conclusion, there are not many good arguments for industrial and trade policy that aim to shift profits. Such policies are unlikely to be successful to redirect industries and profits from other countries to the home country because the expectable retaliation is likely to leave all competitors worse off. But they will in any case redistribute profits and employment within the home country. Subsidies and tariffs

[32] The German government, for instance, has committed itself that the future car industry should be based on electric vehicles; other environment friendly technologies, like artificial fuels, are not covered by its strategy.

benefit the respective industry but they hurt other industries, consumers and tax payers. Moreover, they are very often targeted at industries or particular firms that are effective at lobbying but not at inventing and producing. A more promising strategy would be to concentrate public resources on education, support of research and development in general, an efficient infrastructure, and a competitive tax system to attract and support private investment and entrepreneurial activities. Where to invest and what and how to produce, however, should not be political decisions.

3.3 *Geoeconomics*

Industrial and trade policy is increasingly also seen as part of "geoeconomics"[33] and the Russian war in Ukraine has widened the focus to the use of import and export sanctions and reinforced the discussion about strategic autonomy and restructuring of the economy for political aims. While import and export sanctions have been used for a long time in many different cases,[34] the imposition of such measures on Russia in the wake of the invasion is remarkable for the speed with which the "West" was able to implement its measures. The sanctions are covering unseen measures as well, such as blocking access to currency reserves, and they are often seen as a test-run of what might happen if a conflict with China over Taiwan becomes imminent.

There are several problems with sanctions that are related to the long-term European trade and industrial policy strategy. First, sanctions, in general, are rarely as effective as they are designed to be. It is estimated that only about a third of sanctions achieve the desired policy change in the target country.[35] Often, they have more of a symbolic character than changing the behavior of the receiving country. In fact, they may actually be counterproductive and increase the support for the regime. They may also serve as a narrative background to impose even more restrictive policies on the own population and potential opposition, as Iran and other autocratic regimes demonstrate.

But even if sanctions are successful, they need to be applied for a long time. While long-term consequences of being cut from import technology is likely to be severe, it is also clear that more ways to avoid sanctions will be found and more alternative sources will be located over time, including countries that help Russia to avoid sanctions.[36] As long as the country will be able to finance needed high-tech imports, it is likely that alternative legal and illegal sources can be found.

---

[33] Baldwin (2020), Blackwill and Harris (2016), and Kamin et al. (2022).

[34] Hufbauer et al. (2009) and Mulder (2022a).

[35] Hufbauer et al. (2009) and Mulder (2022a).

[36] The consequence of sanctions is obviously difficult to assess. For continuous estimates and reports about the impact of sanctions on Russia, see the Stanford Working Group on Sanctions (https://fsi.stanford.edu/working-group-sanctions).

Second, the Russian case is a good example for the unintended consequence of also hurting third parties. In Asia, for instance, exports to Russia fell for more than 80% for Malaysia, 69% for South-Korea and 36% for Japan while they increased for India and China. In fact, China compensated for almost all of the decline of oil export of Russia to the West, and benefited by a discount of 25–30% of its price.[37] The conflict with Russia thus may also have consequences for trading relations with other countries that are implicitly or explicitly hurt by European and US sanctions.

Europe itself may also be affected by the imposition of control of exports from the United States to China. As Garcia-Herrero[38] describes, there has been a significant tightening of licenses to American firms for exports to China in general and in particular with respect to advanced technology. This may indirectly affect European firms as they use American technology and inputs for their products and thus become indirectly subject to export controls and sanctions as well. The restriction of exports of semi-conductors technology to China, for example, is likely to have repercussions on computer and smart-phone production world wide.

Third, sanctions are an incentive to create alternative structures. The blocking of access to Russia's currency reserves held abroad has reinforced awareness of how much the international financial system depends on the US dollar. Being aware of this, Russia but also China and other countries as well have begun to diversify their currency reserves away from the US-dollar several years ago and this process will certainly be accelerated by recent events. More important from the European perspective is the American policy of excluding countries from access to the US-dollar based financial information and clearing network systems of private banks which has led to European and Chinese initiatives to create alternative networks, so far not successfully.[39] In the longer run, however, competing financial networks may arise, forcing countries and firms to use different parallel infrastructures which will certainly increase transaction costs. If the United States instead sanctions the use of alternative and parallel networks, European firms and banks may lose important business partners.

4 Decoupling and Friend-Shoring

One answer to the emerging conflict with China is the United States strategy of decoupling[40] that stresses the strategic benefit of not depending on a geopolitical rival. In the European context, the problem of depending too much on one particular

[37] Mulder (2022b).

[38] Garcia-Herrero (2022).

[39] Eichengreen (2022).

[40] Bergsten (2022); European Commission (2020b); European Union Chamber of Commerce in China (2021) Decoupling: Severed Ties and Patchwork Globalization. European Chamber, Beijing; Garcia-Herrero (2022).

adversary has become obvious in the wake of the Russian invasion, starting a discussion in how far Europeans should join the United States in this strategy against China as well. As part of this decoupling, US Secretary of the Treasury Janet Yellen more recently has advocated a policy that would focus economic relations on "friends".[41] The idea is to concentrate trade and financial flows on those nations with which one shares the same political values, such as democracy and human rights protection. This would make countries more resilient as they would not have to fear that supply chains are cut due to political conflicts. It would also cut-off competitors from access to certain products and thus reinforce and preempt geoeconomic measures.

Unfortunately, depending on the definition of what a friend is, the world of potential trading partners could become quite small. Taking the example of Germany, several studies have explored different categories of friends. Menkhoff[42] for instance has categorized countries according to their "voice and accountability" measure developed by the World Bank. This index measures as how democratic a country can be considered to be and ranges from −2.5 to 2.5 with a higher value reflecting a higher degree of political control and democracy. Taking different benchmarks, there are only 13 countries that score at least as high as Germany (not including the United States and many European states), only 88 countries that have an index as high as the lowest EU member (Bulgaria) and do not comprise Germany's main sources for energy nor its major trading partner China.

Moreover, several studies have explored how concentrated the mining, processing and refining of minerals and rare earths is[43] that are particularly important for the industries that have been identified as strategic, such as electric mobility and green energy such as wind turbines. As Leruth et al.[44] show, China dominates the supply chain for clean technologies not least because of strategic investments that not only include mining and reserves but also the refining of, for instance, rare earth. Thus, it will be difficult for European countries to implement their industrial strategy if conflicts with China arise.

Similar results can be found not only for raw materials and intermediate products. In the German case, Sandkamp[45] reports that more than 90% of its intermediate imports are sourced from other European countries whereas only 6% come from China. However, in certain areas such as smart phones and computers up to 80% come from Chinese sources. Using quantitative trade models to simulate the effects of decoupling for Europe, results predict significant economic costs of such a strategy, in particular for Germany. Simulating different scenarios about the extent

---

[41] Javorcik et al. (2022).

[42] Menkhoff (2022).

[43] Boer et al. (2021); European Commission (2021) Strategic Dependencies and Capacities, SWD (2021) 352 final, Brussels; Flach et al. (2022); Leruth et al. (2022).

[44] Leruth et al. (2022).

[45] Sandkamp (2022).

of reshoring, a complete decoupling from China could costs of up to 1% of GDP.[46] (A decoupling from Russia has about half that impact.) While losses are smaller for the European Union, as well as for the United States and China, due to the high amount of German exports as a share of GDP, it is clear that decoupling is costly for highly integrated economies.

This also explains why European countries and in particular Germany, are not enthusiastic about decoupling. Not only would a strategy for European countries therefore be almost impossible as they continue to rely on energy imports in the short to medium term but are likely to depend even in the long-run on imports of metals and rare earths that are essential for the green transition. This situation is somewhat different for the United States and it is therefore unlikely that Europe will pursue a similar strategy. In how far this will lead to conflicts between the United States and Europe about decoupling remains to be seen.

The second problem is that even "friends" can be competitors. As mentioned above with respect to strategic trade and industrial policy, Europe and the United States are in competition which may even have increased with recent decisions of the Biden administration. Since Secretary Yellen's speech the US administration passed the CHIPS and Science Act, mirrored by the European Union's Chips Act that proposes "semiconductor partnerships with like-minded countries" and the EU's Important Projects of Common European Interest (IPCEI) program that aims to promote supply chain cooperation between EU member states.[47]

In particular, the Inflation Reduction Act (IRA) that increases incentives for manufacturers to source inputs from American sources in the semiconductor, critical minerals, and battery sectors has caused consternation among European governments. While Europeans welcome the shift in policy towards environment friendly policy, they do not welcome its American focus. The program allocates US $370 billion over 9 years. Most of the money will be invested in infrastructure but around US $7.5 billion are allocated to the production of electric vehicles.[48] Firms can apply for generous subsidies to support production of electric vehicles, conditional on that inputs are sourced from US firms. (Mexico and Canada, as members of USMCA qualify as well). European policymakers are afraid that will lead European firms to redirect investments and production to the United State to benefit from these subsidies that are estimated to lower production costs by 30–40%. European officials have already declared that they consider this program as being in violation of WTO rules to exert some pressure on the Biden administration. Moreover, the Le Maire/Habeck[49] initiative can be interpreted as a reaction to this plan and the activity of lobby groups that demand a similar European program to keep production in Europe.

---

[46] Sandkamp (2022).

[47] Javorcik et al. (2022).

[48] While an impressive figure, the IRA amounts to about a tenth of a percent of American GDP annually and thus pales in comparison to many other more generous programs, including European ones.

[49] Le Maire B and Habeck R (2022), For a European Green Industrial Policy, BMWK, Berlin, https://www.bmwk.de/Redaktion/DE/Downloads/deu-fra-gemeinsame-erklarung-zur-starkung-der-industriepolitschen-zusammenarbeit.html.

Trading only with friends is hence not likely to be a realistic alternative, at least from the European side. Too many commodities need to be sourced from parts of the world where democratic, social and political rules are different and Europe will simply not be able to substitute, even at higher prices, for those sources. Trade and financial flows will continue to comprise not only Western democracies and it is therefore not to be expected that Europe will be able or willing to cut its trading ties with China and others unless it is forced to do so. An open conflict about Taiwan would likely force Europe to take a clear stance but apart from that it is rather likely that European countries will do their most to retain friendly relations with China. Especially Germany has invested a lot into its relations with China and is very reluctant to cut ties with China.[50]

Apart from these conflicts over subsidies and industrial policy, other measures by the Biden administration as well have more or less continued along the path that had been taken under the Trump administration. While the rhetoric of the current US government is less confrontational, no substantial changes in trade policy measures have been made and the government has shown no interest to revive the negotiations between the United States and the European Union about a Transatlantic Trade and Investment Partnership (TTIP) that had been cancelled by President Trump.[51]

The new US government has also continued the policy of its predecessor to block the appointment of new arbitrators to the WTO Appellate Body, a process that actually reflects a similar view of Democrats and Republicans on the WTO. As Bown and Keynes[52] show, Trump's decision to neutralize the WTO reflects a bipartisan perception that the Appellate Body has been going too far in recent years. It is hence unlikely that the US position with respect to WTO will change.

In conclusion, the European Union is unlikely to follow the American strategy of decoupling from China and this may lead to more conflicts between the United States and Europe about access to important technologies. Competition about industrial policy and the location of certain industries have further potential for conflicts and a combination of these factors could lead to a clash between them. While conflicts about trade and industrial trade are not new, they are likely to become larger since more issues are involved. Unfortunately, the parties cannot expect that the WTO will help to solve them.

[50] In fact, German firms still continue to invest in China. The chemical producer BASF for instance has just decided to move part of its production from Germany to Zhanjiang in China for cost reasons.

[51] The interest of the European side in pursuing TTIP was low at the time as well. Given the acrimonious debate about TTIP at the time of negotiation (Irwin 2020), it is not sure that a renewed attempt, even under a changed name, will find more support on the European side now. In fact, although provisionally in force since 2017, the similar CETA agreement between Canada and the European Union has still not been ratified by all member states.

[52] Bown and Keynes (2020).

5 Policy Conclusions

Europeans have been struggling with adjusting to changes in international economic policy for a while. Since at least the Trump shock, it has become increasingly clear that the world economy is turning towards a more nationalistic trade policy. Individual countries, like Germany and France try to define their position, and the European Commission is trying to do the same for the Union. The problem is that they do not know what they are preparing for.

The European response so far with its focus on strategic and industrial policy is not convincing. Committing to a particular mix of green or other industries, defining certain technologies that should be used, focusing on the size of enterprises by creating national or European champions, all assumes to be able to know what future technologies and which firms will be successful. Of course, Europe must not be naïve and adapt to Chinese and US policy but it should not make the mistake to concentrate on numerical targets concerning sectoral shares, focusing on certain types of firms (national champions), defining and supporting certain sectors, or even particular technologies.[53] All of this is likely to create additional incentives for lobbying and, because of information and knowledge problems, lead to inefficient outcomes. The European Commission instead is right when it demands more and better education and universities, more innovation, migration of highly qualified individuals, and more venture-capital oriented capital markets. Creating an attractive place for European and external investment by improving supply side conditions is more likely to be successful in the long run, even if less attractive politically. Recent proposals, however, seem to point in the direction of more direct interventions.

The European response to other countries on the other hand faces a high degree of uncertainty. Europe and the United States are at the moment united against Russia and they certainly do not share the same political philosophy with China, but concerning economic relations with China it is already apparent that the United States and Europe are not likely to follow the same strategy. Europe should therefore continue to diversify its trading relations.

First, as conflicts are likely to increase and as uncertainty will increase as well, countries should be prepared that even more or less reliable partners will fail sometimes. Covid-19 has demonstrated that even close trading ties within the European Union were suddenly subject to export controls and that even a common market with full mobility of labor experienced borders being closed again. Diversification will not only help to become less vulnerable and exposed with respect to individual trading partners but having alternative options also increases the relative bargaining position with potential adversaries if alternative sources exist.

Second, it is also advisable for individual firms, countries and the European Union to create redundancies in their trading relations. Not only should sources be diversified but there should also be more sources than strictly needed at a given point in time. This would create a necessary if costly safety net. Redundancies by

[53] Aiginger and Rodrik (2020).

definition imply that more is contracted than strictly necessary and this will be costly. It will require warehousing of commodities and goods and maybe even eventual destruction of some of them. An alternative and maybe more efficient way of creating safety nets would be to buy options for the delivery of certain goods or inputs that can be exercised or not.

Third, because it is unlikely that multilateralism on a global scale under the umbrella of the WTO can be revived in an effective way, Europe should seek closer integration with trading partners in Latin America, Africa and Asia to become less dependent on China but also to become less dependent on the United States if for different reasons. Reviving and closing negotiations that have stalled or been put on hold should have priority but the European Commission should also actively initiate and pursue further integration agreements. In the long run, this should also include becoming more open to migration which would help to address Europe's demographic problem and hopefully keep it innovative as well.

References

Aiginger K, Rodrik D (2020) Rebirth of industrial policy and an agenda for the twenty-first century. J Ind Compet Trade 20:189–207

Bagwell K, Staiger RW (1999) An economic theory of GATT. Am Econ Rev 89:215–248

Baldwin R (2016) The World Trade Organization and the future of multilateralism. J Econ Perspect 30:95–116

Baldwin R (2019) The globotics upheaval: globalization, robotics and the future of work. Oxford University Press, Oxford

Baldwin DA (2020) Economic statecraft, New edn. Princeton University Press, Princeton

Bergsten CF (2022) The United States vs. China: the quest for global economic leadership. Polity Press, Oxford

Bhagwati J, Johnson HG (1961) A generalized theory of the effects of tariffs on the terms of trade. Oxf Econ Papers 13:225–253

Blackwill RD, Harris JM (2016) War by other means. Harvard University Press, Cambridge

Boer L, Pescatori A, Stuermer M (2021) Energy transition metals. IMF working paper 21/243

Bown CP, Keynes S (2020) Why Trump shot the Sheriffs: the end of WTO Dispute Settlement 1.0. Peterson Institute for International Economics working paper 20(4)

Brander JA (1995) Strategic trade policy. In: Grossman G, Rogoff K (eds) Handbook of international economics, vol 3. Elsevier, Amsterdam, pp 1395–1455

Broz JL, Frieden J, Weymouth S (2021) Populism in place: the economic geography of the globalization backlash. Int Organ 75:464–494

Doshi R (2021) The long game: China's grand strategy to displace American order. Oxford University Press, Oxford

Economy EC (2021) The world according to China. Wiley, New York

Eichengreen B (2018) The populist temptation: economic grievance and political reaction in the modern era. Oxford University Press, Oxford

Eichengreen B (2022) Sanctions, SWIFT, and China's cross-border interbank payments system. Center for Strategic and International Studies Brief

Ethier WJ (2007) The theory of trade policy and trade agreements: a critique. Eur J Polit Econ 23: 605–623

Evenett S, Fritz J (2019) Going it alone? Trade policy after three years of populism. Global trade alert report 25, Centre for Economic Policy Research, London

Flach L, Gourevich I, Grandum L, Scheckenhofer L, Teti F (2022) How dependent is Germany on raw material imports? An analysis of inputs to produce key technologies. Econpol Policy Brief 43
Funke M, Schularick M, Trebesch C (2016) Going to extremes: politics after financial crises, 1870–2014. Eur Econ Rev 88:227–260
Garcia-Herrero A (2022) Slowbalisation in the context of US-China decoupling. Intereconomics 57(6):352–358
Guriev S, Papaioannou E (2022) The political economy of populism. J Econ Lit 60:753–832
Haskel J, Westlake S (2017) Capitalism without capital: the rise of the intangible economy. Princeton University Press, Princeton
Helleiner E (2021) The neomercantilists: a global intellectual history. Cornell University Press, Ithaca
Helpman E, Krugman P (1989) Trade policy and market structure. MIT Press, Cambridge
Hufbauer GC, Schott JJ, Elliott KA (2009) Economic sanctions reconsidered, 3rd edn. Peterson Institute of International Economics, Washington
Irwin DA (2020) Free trade under fire. Princeton University Press, Princeton
Javorcik BS, Kitzmueller L, Schweiger H, Yildirim MA (2022) Economic costs of friend-shoring. EBRD working paper 274
Kamin K, Bernoth K, Dombrowski J, Felbermayr G, Fratzscher M, Hoffmann M, Horn S, Neuhoff K, Poitiers NF, Rieth M, Sandkamp A, Weil P, Wolff G, Zachmann G (2022) Instruments of a strategic foreign economic policy. Institute for the World Economy, Kiel
Leruth L, Mazarei A, Regibeau P, Renneboog L (2022) Green energy depends on critical minerals. Who controls the supply chains? Peterson Institute for International Economics working paper 22-12
Menkhoff L (2022) Kleine Welt: Wenn Deutschland nur mit Demokratien handelt. Wirtschaftsdienst 102:439–444
Mulder N (2022a) The economic weapon: the rise of sanctions as a tool of modern war. Yale University Press, Yale
Mulder N (2022b) Economic sanctions in East Asia: disruption and adaptation. Hinrich Foundation Report
Noland M (2018) US trade policy in the Trump administration. Asian Econ Policy Rev 13:262–278
Rudd K (2022) The world according to Xi Jinping: what China's ideologue in chief really believes. Foreign Aff 101(6):8–21
Sandkamp A (2022) Reshoring by decree? The effects of decoupling Europe from global value chains. Intereconomics 57(6):359–362
Spencer B, Brander J (2008) Strategic trade policy. In: Durlauf S, Blume L (eds) The new Palgrave dictionary of economics. Palgrave Macmillan, Basingstoke
Walter S (2021) The backlash against globalization. Annu Rev Polit Sci 24:421–442
Zettelmeyer J (2019) The return of economic nationalism in Germany. Peterson Institute for International Economics, Policy Brief 19-4

Carsten Hefeker is professor of economic policy at the University of Siegen in Germany and a research fellow of CESifo. He specializes in international economics as well as political economy and institutional economics.

Future Unready: Does the WTO Need to Bolster Its Security Exceptions?

Shailja Singh

Contents

Abstract The WTO's security exceptions turned 75 in 2022. The world today faces many challenges that could only be described as science fiction in 1947. This raises questions regarding the modern-day relevance of these exceptions. This paper examines the security exceptions in light of the historical context and the prevailing jurisprudence. In particular, it examines the two urgent challenges of cybersecurity and energy security from the lens of WTO security exceptions to identify the lacunae in their existing interpretation in specific fact scenarios. It highlights certain ambiguities in these exceptions that render them ill-equipped to address the two issues effectively. Hence, it argues that it is critical that the WTO updates these exceptions to make them future-ready. While the current impasse at the WTO makes it unlikely that such an agreement would be arrived at, especially in the short term, it would be in the interest of the membership that future dispute panels and the Appellate Body

Views expressed are personal.

S. Singh (✉)
Centre for WTO Studies, Indian Institute of Foreign Trade, New Delhi, India
e-mail: shailja@iift.edu

M. Bungenberg et al. (eds.), *Asian Yearbook of International Economic Law 2023*,
Asian Yearbook of International Economic Law (2023) 2023: 71–96,
https://doi.org/10.1007/16517_2023_14, Published online: 3 March 2023

(once restored) adopts a more expansive interpretation of these exceptions, with the requisite checks and balances.

1 National Security and International Trade: An Introduction

The geopolitical developments in 2022 have, once again, turned the spotlight toward national security in international law and international relations. Or perhaps it would be more accurate to state that national security never really left the global centre-stage. Russia's war against Ukraine has merely exposed the fragility of global peace. Close international links through trade – long referred to as the harbinger of world peace and stability have not been successful in preventing Russia's escalations.[1] In fact, along expected lines, international trade has been severely impacted due to the war.[2] Western nations have responded with an array of trade sanctions against Russia for its incursions, in particular on its petroleum and natural piped gas exports.[3] In the unlikely event of a WTO dispute brought by Russia, sanctioning countries will rely upon the WTO's "Security Exceptions" to justify any potential inconsistencies with their multilateral trade commitments.

These are, however, not the only recent instances where security exceptions have been called or sought to be called into action. In 2020 and 2021, the Covid-19 pandemic brought out sharp debates regarding the recourse to these exceptions for deviating from WTO commitments to tackle and control the pandemic.[4] Before that,

[1]Martin et al. (2008); McDonald (2004); Nicholas S, If Goods Don't Cross Borders, Foundation for Economic Foundation, 26 October 2010, https://fee.org/resources/if-goods-dont-cross-borders/ (accessed 25 November 2022); Adorney J, Want Peace, Promote Free Trade, Hinrich Foundation, 10 September 2020, https://www.hinrichfoundation.com/research/tradevistas/sustainable/trade-and-peace/ (accessed 25 November 2022). *Cf.* Soll J, One of the Most Famous Ideas in Economics is Wrong – History Shows That Free Trade Can't Buy World Peace, Politico, 10 May 2022, https://www.politico.com/news/magazine/2022/10/05/free-markets-dont-buy-peace-00060236 (accessed 25 November 2022).

[2]Kryvetska O, Russia's Aggression Against Ukraine: Global Trade Implications After 7 Months of War IISD, 26 September 2022, https://www.iisd.org/articles/policy-analysis/russia-ukraine-trade-implications#:~:text=The%20war%2C%20waged%20in%20the,by%20the%20COVID%2D19%20pandemic (accessed 25 November 2022); US Congressional Research Service, Russia's 2022 War Against Ukraine: Global Economic Effects, May 12, 2022, https://crsreports.congress.gov/product/pdf/IF/IF12104 (accessed 25 November 2022); WTO (2022), The Crisis in Ukraine Implications of the War for Global Trade and Development, https://www.wto.org/english/res_e/booksp_e/imparctukraine422_e.pdf (accessed 25 November 2022).

[3]BBC News, What Are the Sanctions on Russia and Are They Hurting its Economy?, 30 September 2022, https://www.bbc.com/news/world-europe-60125659 (accessed 25 November 2022).

[4]See Abbott F (2020), The TRIPS Agreement Article 73 Security Exceptions and the COVID-19 Pandemic, South Centre, Geneva, Research Paper, No. 116, https://www.southcentre.int/wp-content/uploads/2020/08/RP-116.pdf (accessed 25 November 2022); Chieng (2021); Oke (2021).

in 2018, the United States, under its former President Donald Trump, had unilaterally increased tariffs on its steel and aluminium imports on the ground of national security against some of its closest allies leading to an array of WTO disputes[5] and raising questions regarding the potential abuse of the exceptions.[6] In parallel, there have been several restrictive cybersecurity-related trade measures – particularly relating to 5G equipment and Chinese apps that have been introduced on the ground of cybersecurity.[7]

All these instances illustrate that there has been constant testing of the limits of security exceptions in recent years. Apart from the immediate triggers of the pandemic and Russia's war on Ukraine, the shifting global geopolitical dynamics have also been an important determinator of how countries, particularly the United States, perceive and resort to these exceptions. As Anthea Roberts et al. note, we are now witnessing the transition from the post-Cold War Neoliberal Order to a new Geoeconomic Order.[8] This has been driven largely by the rise of China in the world order and the consequent trade wars with the United States. While the two issues of trade and security had largely followed independent trajectories, particularly in the post-Cold war world – the shift to a Geoeconomic Order has led to an increasing "securitisation of economic policy and economisation of strategic policy".[9] It is no secret that both the United States and China have hegemonic ambitions, with the former being the reigning (albeit, declining) hegemon and China, the strategic rival, fast catching up.[10] Today, China has not just surpassed the United States to become the world's largest economy, but it has also displaced the US to become the biggest trading partner of most nations.[11] This has been attributed as the key driver of the United States' turn to protectionism in trade, illustrating the fear of a declining

[5] For the list of disputes, see WTO News Item, Panels established to review US steel and aluminium tariffs, countermeasures on US imports, 21 November 2018, https://www.wto.org/english/news_e/news18_e/dsb_19nov18_e.htm (accessed 25 November 2022).

[6] Nagy (2019).

[7] Friis and Lysne (2021); see also Channel E2E – A CyberRisk Alliance Resource, Huawei Banned and Permitted in Which Countries? List and FAQs, 5 December 2022, https://www.channele2e.com/business/enterprise/huawei-banned-in-which-countries/ (accessed 25 November 2022); India Today, Full List of Chinese Apps Banned in India so Far, 21 August, 2022, https://www.indiatoday.in/technology/news/story/bgmi-garena-free-fire-tiktok-and-more-banned-in-india-check-the-full-list-1990048-2022-08-19 (accessed 25 November 2022).

[8] Roberts et al. (2019), p. 655.

[9] Roberts et al. (2019), p. 655.

[10] Modabadze (2020); Strobl J and Heiko B (2021), Storms Ahead – The Future Geoeconomic World Order, Raffeisen Bank International, https://www.bruegel.org/sites/default/files/wp-content/uploads/2021/10/Storms-Ahead_AGH_chp6.pdf (accessed 29 December 2022); Kim (2019), pp. 30–40.

[11] Graham Allison et al. (2022), The Great Economic Rivalry: China vs. the US, Belfer Center for Science and International Affairs, Harvard Kennedy School, https://www.belfercenter.org/sites/default/files/files/publication/GreatEconomicRivalry_Final_2.pdf (accessed 26 December 2022).

hegemony.[12] Against this context, the US decision to rely on national security for increasing tariffs on steel and aluminium imports is hardly surprising.

As per Heath, we live in times of new security threats, new actors, new vulnerabilities, new temporalities, and new politics in the economic order.[13] In this new world, how do the WTO's security exceptions fare? Are they adequate to deal with these emerging aspects that impact the international trading system? Moreover, are the security exceptions best placed to deal with some of these issues? The present chapter attempts to examine the exceptions in this context. For brevity, the focus here is on two of, what this author considers, the biggest challenges at present, namely cybersecurity and energy security. While energy security has always been important for national development, the Russian war on Ukraine and the climate change crisis have added a layer of urgency to it. In a similar vein, reliance on technology and the internet for connectivity, particularly in international trade, has heightened the risks posed to cyberspace, adding to the national security considerations of states.

To better understand the interface of these challenges with the WTO security exceptions, this chapter adopts the following structure. First, it introduces these exceptions in light of the prevailing jurisprudence. This is followed by a discussion on the two specific challenges of cybersecurity and energy security to evaluate how they fare *vis-à-vis* the stated exceptions. This is followed by a possible path forward at the WTO, leading to the chapter's conclusion.

2 WTO's Security Exceptions

2.1 Introduction

For almost seventy years since the adoption of GATT in 1947, the GATT Contracting Parties, and later the WTO Members had largely exercised self-restraint when invoking the security exceptions. In fact, till recently, very few formal disputes were launched under the GATT and the WTO challenging national security measures.[14] This changed in 2016 when Ukraine launched a formal dispute against Russia regarding the latter's restrictions on traffic in transit originating from Ukraine to third countries through Russia. The outcome of the dispute process resulted in the adoption of the first WTO panel report interpreting the security exceptions.[15] This has been elaborated further in the subsection below.

---

[12] Kim (2019), p. 31.

[13] Heath (2020).

[14] Schloemann and Ohloff (1999), p. 432.

[15] Panel Report, *Russia – Measures Concerning Traffic in Transit*, WT/DS512/R and Add.1, adopted 26 April 2019, DSR 2019:VIII, p. 4301 (hereinafter: Panel Report, *Russia - Traffic in Transit*).

The security exceptions under GATT 1994 can be found in Article XXI, which has also served as the template for the corresponding exceptions in GATS (Article XIV*bis*) and the TRIPS Agreement (Article 73). These are the only three instances of explicit exceptions on national security grounds in the multilateral trade agreements at the WTO. Since the language is similar in all three, for the sake of reference, the text of GATT Article XXI (b) and (c) are reproduced below:

> *Security Exceptions under GATT Article XXI*
>
> Nothing in this Agreement shall be construed
>
> (b) to prevent any contracting party from taking any action *which it considers necessary* for the *protection of its essential security interests*
>
> (i) relating to fissionable materials or the materials from which they are derived;
> (ii) relating to the traffic in arms, ammunition and implements of war and to such traffic in other goods and materials as is carried on directly or indirectly for the purpose of supplying a military establishment;
> (iii) *taken in time of war or other emergency in international relations*; or (*Emphasis supplied*)
>
> (c) to prevent any contracting party from taking any action in pursuance of its obligations under the United Nations Charter for the maintenance of international peace and security.

Article XXI(b) contains the operative part detailing when the security exceptions can be invoked. Three issues of interpretation in this paragraph have rankled governments and scholars alike for several decades.[16] First, how self-judging is the phrase "which it considers necessary"? Second, what really are the "essential security interests", and finally in sub-paragraph (iii) when does "other emergency in international relations" exist? While these issues have been resolved at the level of the WTO panel for the time being (unless there are modifications by the Appellate Body, once restored, in the future), the political sensitivity around this provision continues to exist. The drafters of the GATT were very well aware of the need to make the exception a balanced one to avoid any abuse. In fact, during one of the initial discussions during the 1947 Geneva Session, the delegate from the United States had stated:

> I think there must be some latitude here for security measures. It is really a question of balance. We have got to have some exceptions. We cannot make it too tight, because we cannot prohibit measures which are needed purely for security reasons. On the other hand, we cannot make it so broad that, under the guise of security, countries will put on measures which really have a commercial purpose.[17]

Any future reform of the security exceptions should also try to maintain this very delicate balance. However, the author admits that it would be an oversimplification

---

[16] See Singh S (2012), WTO Compatibility of United States' Secondary Sanctions Relating to Petroleum Transactions with Iran, Centre for WTO Studies, Working Paper CWS/WP/200/1, https://wtocentre.iift.ac.in/workingpaper/Iran%20Sanctions.pdf (accessed 25 November 2022); Alford (2011); Schill and Briese (2009).

[17] United Nations Economic and Social Council, Verbatim Report, Second Session of the Preparatory Meeting of the United Nations Conference on Trade and Employment, 24 July 1947, E/PC/T/A/PV/33, 21.

to conclude that the above statement captures the whole gamut of views that existed domestically within the United States on this issue. As is well documented now, while the US Department of State was concerned with the potential abuse of the security exceptions, the officials from the Army, Navy, and War Departments wanted to retain complete control over how the exception was interpreted and deployed.[18] To balance these different positions, the US negotiators had agreed to a compromise language that had certain factual elements, such as "taken in time of war or other emergency in international relations".[19]

2.2 Existing Jurisprudence

Recent panel reports have examined the invocation of the security exceptions at the WTO. This includes an examination under GATT 1994 (*Russia – Traffic in Transit*)[20] and the TRIPS Agreement (*Saudi Arabia — Protection of IPR*).[21] While the panel report in *Russia – Traffic in Transit* was adopted by the Dispute Settlement Body (DSB), the report in *Saudi Arabia – Protection of IPR* was never adopted, with Qatar notifying the DSB of its intention to terminate the dispute in April 2022. These have now been followed by a series of 4 related panel reports on security exceptions in complaints brought by China, Norway, Switzerland, and Turkey against the United States tariffs on steel and aluminium imports, which also examines the GATT exception.[22] Interestingly, the panels in the four *United States – Steel and Aluminium* disputes make minimal reference to the two prior panel rulings, deciding instead to examine the self-judging issue and the interpretation of the term "emergency in international relations" in a more independent manner. The findings in these disputes are, however, not much different from the preceding two panel reports.

As mentioned above, GATT Article XXI, GATS Article XIV*bis*, and TRIPS Article 73 contain the WTO security exceptions. There are no direct dispute findings

---

[18] Pinchis-Paulsen (2020).

[19] Pinchis-Paulsen (2020), p. 192.

[20] Panel Report, *Russia – Traffic in Transit*, WT/DS512/R and Add.1, adopted 26 April 2019, DSR 2019:VIII, p. 4301.

[21] Panel Report, *Saudi Arabia – Measures Concerning the Protection of Intellectual Property Rights*, WT/DS567/R and Add.1, circulated to Members on 16 June 2020, dispute terminated while appeal pending (hereinafter: Panel Report, *Saudi Arabia – Protection of IPR*).

[22] Panel Report, *United States — Certain Measures on Steel and Aluminium Products (China)*, WT/DS544/R, circulated on 9 December 2022 (hereinafter: Panel Report, *US – Steel and Aluminium (China)*); Panel Report, *United States — Certain Measures on Steel and Aluminium Products (Norway)*, WT/DS552/R, circulated on 9 December 2022; Panel Report, *United States — Certain Measures on Steel and Aluminium Products (Switzerland)*, WT/DS556/R, circulated on 9 December 2022; *United States — Certain Measures on Steel and Aluminium Products (Türkiye)*, WT/DS564/R, circulated on 9 December 2022.

yet for the corresponding GATS exceptions under Article XIV*bis*. The exceptions, *inter alia*, provide that nothing in the three agreements shall be construed to prevent a WTO Member from taking any action "which it considers necessary" for the protection of its "essential security interests". This is followed by a list of three scenarios where these exceptions are available. It is crucial to note that the WTO panel in *Russia – Traffic in Transit* had laid down a scheme of general interpretation and analytical framework for the exceptions, and the same was transposed to the examination in *Saudi Arabia – Protection of IPR*[23] based on the fact that the parties (Saudi Arabia and Qatar) and multiple third parties (Brazil, Canada, the European Union, Japan, and Russia) in that dispute agreed with the approach. Both these disputes examined paragraph (b)(iii) of the exceptions.

Self-Judging (or not)

Before the panel reports were released, there was much divergence on the "self-judging" aspect of the exceptions among legal scholars as well as Members.[24] This was on account of the use of the phrase "which it considers necessary" in the text of paragraph (b). The positions varied from perceiving the whole exception as non-justiciable to the self-judging aspect being restricted to only certain elements in the chapeau of paragraph (b). The panels in both *Russia – Traffic in Transit* and *Saudi Arabia – Protection of IPR* have held that the elements listed in sub-paragraphs (i) to (iii) are subject to an objective assessment. Moreover, despite the self-judging element in paragraph (b), Members' ability to successfully invoke the security exception was tempered by other considerations such as articulation of "essential security interests", meeting the requirement of good faith, etc. Since both these disputes dealt with sub-paragraph (b)(iii), the key findings are highlighted below.

The *US – Steel and Aluminium (China)* panel report undertook a fresh assessment of the self-judging aspect of the security exceptions. A primary argument put forth by the US was based on the text and the grammatical structure of the exceptions, arguing that the phrase "which it considers" qualifies all the terms that follow the word "action" in the provision as a single relative clause.[25] The panel examined the United States submission as per Article 3.2 of the WTO's Dispute Settlement Understanding (DSU) and the customary rules of interpretation of public international law. According to the panel, neither the grammatical construction led to a definitive conclusion, nor the grammatical references cited by the US indicated any categorical rule in favour of its position. In fact, the US acknowledged that the drafters deviated from typical English usage in Article XXI(b), indicating the

[23] Panel Report, *Saudi Arabia - Protection of IPR*, para. 7.243.

[24] See Ranjan (2020); Balan (2019); Gustavo and Duque (2019); Yoo and Ahn (2016); Hao (2020); Singh S (2012), WTO Compatibility of United States' Secondary Sanctions Relating to Petroleum Transactions with Iran, Centre for WTO Studies, Working Paper CWS/WP/200/1, https://wtocentre.iift.ac.in/workingpaper/Iran%20Sanctions.pdf (accessed 25 November 2022).

[25] Panel Report, *US – Steel and Aluminium (China)*, para. 7.106.

drawback associated with a purely grammatical analysis.[26] The panel, thus, relied on the context provided in the DSU and the object and purpose of the WTO Agreement to conclude that the rules are intended to strike a balance between the rights and obligations of the Members.[27] With respect to, *inter alia*, the negotiating history and the internal documents of the US delegation to the ITO, the panel concluded that these did not provide any clear guidance on the issue.[28] In conclusion, the panel rejected the US argument on the security exceptions being completely self-judging, concluding that the conditions and circumstances mentioned in Article XXI are to be met for a successful invocation.

2.2.1 Existence of "War or Other Emergency in International Relations"

The panel in *Russia – Traffic in Transit* concluded that the circumstance in sub-paragraph (iii) is an "objective fact" that is "amenable to objective determination.[29] The panel also found that the term "emergency in international relations" refers generally,

> to a situation of armed conflict, or latent armed conflict, or of heightened tension or crisis, or of general instability engulfing or surrounding a state.[30]

Such situations, in the panel's view, "give rise to particular types of interests for the Member in question, i.e. defence or military interests, or maintenance of law and public order interests". For the panel, while "political" and "economic" conflicts could sometimes be considered "urgent" and "serious" in a political sense, such conflicts will not be "emergenc[ies] in international relations within the meaning of subparagraph (iii) "unless they give rise to defence and military interests, or maintenance of law and public order interests".[31]

In *Saudi Arabia – Protection of IPR*, the panel went a step further to also state that one Member's severance of all diplomatic, consular, and economic ties with another Member could be regarded as "the ultimate State expression of the existence of an emergency in international relations".[32] The panel in the *US – Steel and Aluminium (China)* dispute also agreed that the term "war" informs the meaning of "emergency in international relations".[33] The US argued that the global excess capacity in steel

---

[26] Panel Report, *US – Steel and Aluminium (China)*, paras. 7.119–7.121.

[27] Panel Report, *US – Steel and Aluminium (China)*, paras. 7.123–7.126.

[28] Panel Report, *US – Steel and Aluminium (China)*, para. 7.127.

[29] Panel Report, *Russia - Traffic in Transit*, para. 7.71; Panel Report, *Saudi Arabia - Protection of IPR*, para. 7.244.

[30] Panel Report, *Russia – Traffic in Transit*, para. 7.76.

[31] Panel Report, *Russia - Traffic in Transit*, paras. 7.75–7.76; Panel Report, *Saudi Arabia - Protection of IPR*, para. 7.245.

[32] Panel Report, *Saudi Arabia - Protection of IPR*, paras. 7.259, 7.262.

[33] Panel Report, *US – Steel and Aluminium (China)*, para. 7.139.

and aluminium led to excess imports resulting in the weakening of the domestic economy, consequently impairing national security. The panel concluded that these factors did not have commensurate relevance or weight to conclude that there was an emergency in international relations.[34]

2.2.2 "Taken in Time of"

The panel in *Russia – Traffic in Transit* examined the introductory phrase "taken in time of" in subparagraph (iii) and noted that it connects the "action: referred to in the chapeau of paragraph (b) to the phrase "emergency in international relations" in subparagraph (iii). In the panel's view, this introductory phrase "require[s] that the action be taken *during* the war or other emergency in international relations." The connection between these two elements constitutes a "chronological concurrence [that] is also an objective fact, amenable to objective determination.[35] The panel in *US – Steel and Aluminium (China)* also found that there is a temporal link between the action taken by a Member and the emergency in international relations.[36]

2.2.3 Articulation of Relevant "Essential Security Interests"

The panel in *Russia – Traffic in Transit* concluded it would be required to assess whether a respondent has sufficiently articulated its "essential security interests" in the sense of the chapeau of paragraph (b). The panel noted that essential security interests is evidently a narrower concept than "security interests" with the former generally concerning 'those interests relating to the quintessential functions of the state, namely, the protection of its territory and its population from external threats, and the maintenance of law and public order internally.[37] For the panel,

> "[t]he specific interests that are considered directly relevant to the protection of a state from such external or internal threats will depend on the particular situation and perceptions of the state in question, and can be expected to vary with changing circumstances". For these reasons, the panel considered that "it is left, in general, to every Member to define what it considers to be its essential security interests."[38]

The Panel in *Saudi Arabia – Protection of IP* recalled that in *Russia – Traffic in Transit*, the standard applied to the invoking Member was whether the articulation of

[34] Panel Report, *US – Steel and Aluminium (China)*, para. 7.142–7.144.

[35] Panel Report, *Russia - Traffic in Transit*, paras. 7.70, 7.71; Panel Report, *Saudi Arabia - Protection of IPR*, para. 7.247.

[36] Panel Report, *US – Steel and Aluminium (China)*, para. 7.140.

[37] Panel Report, *Russia - Traffic in Transit*, para. 7.130; Panel Report, *Saudi Arabia - Protection of IPR*, para. 7.249.

[38] Panel Report, *Russia - Traffic in Transit*, para. 7.131; Panel Report, *Saudi Arabia - Protection of IPR*, para. 7.249.

its essential security interests was "minimally satisfactory" in the circumstances. The requirement that an invoking Member articulates its "essential security interests" sufficiently to enable an assessment of whether the challenged measures are related to those interests is not a particularly onerous one and is appropriately subject to limited review by a panel. [39]

2.2.4 The Good Faith Test

The panel in *Russia – Traffic in Transit* had noted that a Member is not "free to elevate any concern to that of an 'essential security interest''; rather, "the discretion of a Member to designate particular concerns as 'essential security interests' is limited by its obligation to interpret and apply Article XXI(b)(iii) of the GATT 1994 in good faith.[40] For the panel, this "obligation of good faith requires that Members not use the security exception as a means to circumvent their WTO obligations."[41] The panel concluded that "[i]t is therefore incumbent on the invoking Member to articulate the essential security interests said to arise from the emergency in international relations sufficiently enough to demonstrate veracity."[42]

2.2.5 Connection Between Measures and the "Essential Security Interests"

The panel in *Russia – Traffic in Transit* considered the "obligation of good faith" to apply not only to the respondent's articulation of "its essential security interests", but also to the connection between the measures at issue and those interests. Thus, the term "which it considers necessary" for the protection of its essential security interests is not unfettered in its scope. This obligation, for the panel, is "crystallized in demanding that the measures at issue meet a minimum requirement of plausibility in relation to the proffered essential security interests".[43] Specifically, a panel must determine "whether the measures are so remote from, or unrelated to, the ... emergency that it is implausible that [the respondent] implemented the measures for the protection of its essential security interests arising out of the emergency".[44]

---

[39] Panel Report, *Saudi Arabia - Protection of IPR*, para. 7.281.

[40] Panel Report, *Russia - Traffic in Transit*, para. 7.132; Panel Report, *Saudi Arabia - Protection of IPR* para. 7.250.

[41] Panel Report, *Russia - Traffic in Transit*, para. 7.133; Panel Report, *Saudi Arabia - Protection of IPR* para. 7.250.

[42] Panel Report, *Russia - Traffic in Transit*, para. 7.134; Panel Report, *Saudi Arabia - Protection of IPR* para. 7.250.

[43] Panel Report, *Russia - Traffic in Transit*, para. 7.138; Panel Report, *Saudi Arabia - Protection of IPR* para. 7.252.

[44] Panel Report, *Russia - Traffic in Transit*, paras. 7.139 and 7.134; Panel Report, *Saudi Arabia - Protection of IPR*, para. 7.252.

3 Cybersecurity

3.1 Background

Cybersecurity risks can pose grave threats to nations with newer forms of cyber warfare[45] techniques emerging every day. While interconnectedness over the internet comes with inherent vulnerabilities that may be difficult to completely overcome – instances of synchronised across-the-border cyber-attacks have become a periodical occurrence[46] – thrusting cybersecurity as one of the high-priority policy goals of governments across the world. A vast majority of countries now have some form of national cybersecurity policy in place.[47] Although the definition of cybersecurity may vary, the understanding of the concept appears to be universal, which is protecting networks, devices, and data from unauthorised use to ensure integrity, among other things.[48] There are multiple reasons why cybersecurity breaches are attempted. These include attempts to damage or limit critical cybersecurity infrastructure; gain unauthorised access to sensitive information; or gain unauthorized access to cyber resources such as nuclear plants, communications, utility companies, etc.[49]

High-profile cyber warfare attempts have been making international headlines for several years now. In fact, as per the Centre for Strategic and International Studies, there have been more than 100 significant cyber incidents in 2022.[50] Global geo-politics seems to foreshadow most of these attacks. For instance, recent Russia's war on Ukraine has led to several allegations of state-sponsored

[45] There is no universally accepted definition of cyber warfare. It is broadly understood to mean actions by a nation-country to penetrate another country's computers or networks for the purposes of causing disruption or damage, Clarke and Knake (2012).

[46] See Centre for Strategic and International Studies (2022), *List of Significant Cyber Incidents since 2006*, https://www.csis.org/programs/strategic-technologies-program/significant-cyber-incidents (accessed 25 November 2022); See also Huang K et al. (2018), Interactions between Cybersecurity and International Trade: A Systematic Framework, Cybersecurity Interdisciplinary Systems Laboratory (CISL), MIT Sloan School of Management, Working Paper CISL# 2018-13, https://web.mit.edu/smadnick/www/wp/2018-13.pdf (accessed 25 November 2022).

[47] International Telecommunications Union (ITU), National Cybersecurity Strategies Repository, https://www.itu.int/en/ITU-D/Cybersecurity/Pages/National-Strategies-repository.aspx (accessed 25 November 2022).

[48] See United States Cybersecurity and Infrastructure Security Agency, *What is cybersecurity*, https://www.cisa.gov/uscert/ncas/tips/ST04-001 (accessed 25 November 2022); For a more detailed definition, see the ITU definition (referring to ITU-T X.1205, https://www.itu.int/en/ITU-T/studygroups/com17/Pages/cybersecurity.aspx (accessed 25 November 2022).

[49] Sima J (2011), *Cybersecurity:* The Next threat to National Security, US Defense Technical Informational Centre, available at https://apps.dtic.mil/sti/citations/ADA601238 (accessed 25 November 2022).

[50] See Centre for Strategic and International Studies (2022), List of Significant Cyber Incidents since 2006, https://www.csis.org/programs/strategic-technologies-program/significant-cyber-incidents (accessed 25 November 2022).

cybersecurity breaches. A European Parliament report mentions, for instance, the Russian attack on KA-SAT satellite that provides broadband internet across Europe, a cyber attack on a border control station to prevent Ukrainian refugees from entering Romania, and an attack on Ukrainian digital infrastructure blocking access to financial services and energy.[51] For its part, Russia too has accused the United States of a massive campaign of "cyber aggression" that has targeted its media, critical infrastructure, and life support systems since the start of the Ukraine invasion.[52] While several of these attacks are an extension of the tit-for-tat tactics in international relations to cyberspace, the very nature of the domain makes it difficult to trace the exact source of the attacker. In 2021, Australia accused China of "malicious cyber activities" within its territories which were rejected as "groundless" by China.[53]

There have also been instances when governments have responded to cybersecurity threats with trade measures. However, not all maybe WTO-inconsistent. These include restricting access to or flow of data across borders on grounds of privacy or otherwise, introducing of cybersecurity standards and related certifications, etc.[54] Other examples include the ban on Huawei 5G equipment by the United States, Canada, Sweden, and others. Similarly, in June 2020, the Government of India issued a Press Release (the first of few) banning 59 mobile applications (apps) "which are prejudicial to the sovereignty and integrity of India, defence of India, security of state and public order".[55] The apps were ostensibly Chinese in origin and the ban was preceded by a violent conflict at the India-China border in Ladakh, which led to the death of 20 Indian soldiers.[56] China could potentially claim a violation of the market access (modes 1 and 3) and most-favoured nation commitments under Articles XVI and II of the GATS respectively (the former determined by the services classification of the apps and India's related sectoral commitments).

---

[51] European Parliament, Briefing – Russia's War on Ukraine: Timeline of Cyber-attacks, European Parliament Research Service, June 2022, https://www.europarl.europa.eu/RegData/etudes/BRIE/2022/733549/EPRS_BRI(2022)733549_EN.pdf (accessed 25 November 2022).

[52] Reuters, Russia accuses U.S. of massive 'cyber aggression', 30 March 2022 at https://www.reuters.com/world/russia-warns-us-consequences-cyber-aggression-2022-03-29/ (accessed 25 November 2022).

[53] The Guardian, Australia joins allies in accusing China of 'malicious cyber activities', 20 July 2021, https://www.theguardian.com/world/2021/jul/19/australia-joins-allies-in-accusing-china-of-malicious-cyber-activities (accessed 25 November 2022).

[54] See Meltzer J and Kerry C, Cybersecurity and Digital Trade: Getting it Right, Brookings, 18 September 2019, https://www.brookings.edu/research/cybersecurity-and-digital-trade-getting-it-right/ (accessed 25 November 2022).

[55] Ministry of Electronics and IT, Government Bans 59 mobile apps which are prejudicial to sovereignty and integrity of India, defence of India, security of state and public order, 29 June 2020, https://pib.gov.in/PressReleseDetailm.aspx?PRID=1635206 (accessed 25 November 2022).

[56] The Hindu, Indian Army says 20 soldiers killed in clash with Chinese troops in the Galwan area, 16 June 2020, https://www.thehindu.com/news/national/indian-army-says-20-soldiers-killed-in-clash-with-chinese-troops-in-the-galwan-area/article61668218.ece (accessed 25 November 2022).

In the event of a potential WTO dispute, these instances would need to meet the requirements of the WTO security exceptions.

3.2 *Interface with International Trade Law and WTO Security Exceptions*

3.2.1 Cybersecurity and the WTO

As discussed above, cybersecurity is a recognised security concern globally. Although the first cybersecurity incident was reported in the 1960s,[57] international trade rules have not directly addressed this issue until very recently. The WTO Agreements do not mention the term cybersecurity anywhere. This, of course, in no way implies that cybersecurity measures do not interact with international trade rules. For instance, the Annual Report by the Director General on the 'Overview of Developments in the International Trading Environment' released at the WTO Trade Policy Review Body on 22nd November 2022 notes that, to date, more than 70 cybersecurity-related TBT measures have been notified to the TBT Committee, 70% of which were in the last three years.[58] Beyond the TBT Agreement, cybersecurity-related measures would continue to be subject to the commitments under GATT, GATS and the TRIPS Agreement, depending upon their nature.

Interestingly, in the case of free trade agreements (FTAs) and digital economy partnership agreements too, only 47 of the 379 agreements reviewed in the TAPED dataset include provisions on cybersecurity.[59] Even among the agreements where such stand-alone provisions are found, they are only soft in nature and typically focus on cooperation.[60] Certain agreements, however, do expand on the scope of the security exceptions to include within the scope of essential security interests the

[57] Chadd K (2020), The History of Cybersecurity, Avast https://blog.avast.com/history-of-cybersecurity-avast (accessed 27 November 2022).

[58] WTO, Annual Report of the Director General, Overview of Developments in the International Trading Environment (mid-October 2021 to mid-October 2022), WT/TPR/OV/25, 22 November 2022.

[59] See Mira B et al., TAPED: Trade Agreements Provisions on Electronic Commerce and Data, https://unilu.ch/taped (accessed 25 November 2022).

[60] See Mira B et al., Codebook, TAPED: Trade Agreements Provisions on Electronic Commerce and Data (Version June 2022), https://unilu.ch/taped, p. 18 (accessed 25 November 2022). For instance, The Comprehensive and Progressive Agreement for Trans-Pacific Partnership (CPTPP) in Article 14.16 of the Electronic Commerce chapter merely provides that the parties "recognise the importance of" building capabilities of their relevant national entities and using existing collaboration mechanism to cooperate to identify and mitigate cybersecurity threats. The Regional Comprehensive Economic Partnership Agreement (RCEP) in Article 12.13 also contains a similar provision, with minor changes. The US-Mexico-Canada Agreement (USMCA) goes a step further and provides that the parties shall endeavour to employ, and encourage parties to, inter alia, use risk-based approaches to identify and protect against cybersecurity threats (Article 19.15).

protection of critical public infrastructures, such as communication, power, and water infrastructures, from deliberate attempts intended to disable or degrade such infrastructures.[61] While this approach may address cybersecurity issues relating to certain types of critical infrastructure, it is ineffective in addressing other kinds of cybersecurity threats. Nevertheless, this may serve as a good starting point for future reforms.

3.2.2 Interface with WTO National Security Exceptions in Select Fact Scenarios

The overarching question here is to what extent can cybersecurity measures be covered under the security exceptions contained in GATT 1994, GATS, and the TRIPS Agreement? Needless to add not all cybersecurity breaches are a question of national security. Some are just plain and simple instances of transnational cybercrime or cyber fraud.[62] The water gets a bit murkier when the attacks upon the networks, devices, and data of another country are carried out by another state or are state-sponsored. Several scenarios are possible in this context which is examined below. Please note that not all the elements of the security exceptions are discussed in each example.

State-Sponsored Cyber Warfare Against Military/Critical Infrastructure

In the first scenario, the hypothetical cyber-attack could be a clear case of state-sponsored cyber warfare against the military infrastructure or the critical infrastructure[63] of another country. As per the prevailing WTO jurisprudence discussed above, essential security interests pertain to the quintessential functions of the state, namely, the protection of its territory and its population from external threats, and the

[61] Article 6.13, India-Singapore Comprehensive Economic Cooperation Agreement (applies to the Investment chapter); Article 13, Agreement on Trade in Goods of the Framework Agreement on Comprehensive Economic Co-Operation Between China and ASEAN (applies to the whole Agreement). See Garcia-Santaolalla N (2020), A Proposal to Reform "Security-Emergency" Exceptions in Trade, unescap.org/sites/default/files/57%20Final-Nadia%20Garcia-Mexico_0.pdf (accessed 28 December 2022).

[62] See Interpol, Cybercrimes cross borders and evolve rapidly, https://www.interpol.int/en/Crimes/Cybercrime; United Nations Office on Drugs and Crime, Global Programme on Cybercrime, https://www.unodc.org/unodc/es/cybercrime/global-programme-cybercrime.html (both accessed 25 November 2022).

[63] The United States Cybersecurity and Infrastructure Security Agency describes "critical infrastructure" in the American context to mean "the physical and cyber systems and assets that are so vital to the United States that their incapacity or destruction would have a debilitating impact on our physical or economic security or public health or safety", at https://www.cisa.gov/infrastructure-security#:~:text=Critical%20infrastructure%20describes%20the%20physical,or%20public%20health%20or%20safety (accessed 27 November 2022).

maintenance of law and public order internally.[64] A WTO Member when invoking the exception under Article XXI(b) (and the corresponding GATS and TRIPS Agreements exceptions) enjoys a certain degree of leeway due to the self-judging language and only has to articulate its interests in a minimally satisfactory manner and in good faith. Thus, subject to the conditions under sub-paragraphs (i) to (iii) being satisfied, the scenario shared above would broadly appear to fulfil the understanding of the panel with respect to essential security interests (provided the articulation and good faith tests are met).

Further, in case the WTO Member facing the cyber-attack decides to take WTO-inconsistent trade measures in response, to meet the test of good faith - it would be required to satisfy that its response is not merely to circumvent its obligations.[65] This has a basis in both Article 31(1) (i.e. a treaty shall be interpreted in good faith) and Article 26 (i.e. every treaty must be performed in good faith) of the Vienna Convention on the Law of Treaties. As Peng notes, it is widely agreed that good faith includes the general elements of reasonableness as well as honesty.[66] This raises interesting questions. Would an attack on only the public websites of the critical infrastructure or military infrastructure suppliers threaten a country's essential security measures? Especially if it's not impacting the use or deployment of the critical or military infrastructure *per se*, but merely hampering the public information services provided on these sites. Perhaps not, if we go by the definition of the high-threshold definition of essential security interests laid down in *Russia – Traffic in Transit*.

Cyber-Attacks by Non-state Actors

In the second scenario, the cyber-attacks could be carried out by non-state entities when it may be disputable or unclear whether they are acting at the behest of another state. For instance, Anonymous,[67] the international activist and hacktivist collective, has carried out several cyber-attacks against Russia since the start of the Ukraine war. This includes leaks of emails from the Belurasian weapons manufacturer Tetraedr which provides logistical support to Russia.[68] Again from the perspective of the country invoking the WTO security exceptions, a threshold issue that arises here is can the targeted country justify a measure under the exception even in cases where there is no clear evidence of it being sponsored by a particular state. It is pertinent to note that the language of WTO security exceptions is drafted from the

64 Panel Report, *Russia - Traffic in Transit*, para. 7.130; Panel Report, *Saudi Arabia - Protection of IPR*, para. 7.249.

65 Panel Report, *Russia - Traffic in Transit*, para. 7.133.

66 Peng (2015), p. 467.

67 See https://twitter.com/YourAnonNews? (accessed 25 November 2022).

68 CNBC, Global hacking group Anonymous launches 'cyber war' against Russia, March 1, 2022, https://www.cnbc.com/2022/03/01/how-is-anonymous-attacking-russia-disabling-and-hacking-websites-.html (accessed 25 November 2022).

perspective of the country in need of protecting its essential security interests and does not focus on the source of the threat (i.e. state-sponsored or otherwise).

However, as noted in the WTO panel jurisprudence, there needs to be a connection between the essential security interests and the countermeasure in question. Very often than not, these countermeasures are targeted towards a particular country deemed/found to be the origin of the said threat. Here, the critical overarching issue of attribution of the action of the non-state actor to the state arises. While there has been much discussion regarding this issue in public international law,[69] in the context of the WTO, the literature has only rarely touched upon the security exception invocation.[70] As noted by Ranjan, countries could opt for a strict or lenient standard of attribution.[71] In the case of the strict test, it needs to demonstrate that the state had effective control over the military or paramilitary operations.[72] This could be extended to cybersecurity threats as well. Another approach as proposed by Margulies is to modify the rules of state responsibility for cybersecurity by introducing a virtual control test which puts the burden on the state to demonstrate that it was not responsible for the cyber threat.[73] Lastly, in such scenarios, while it may be easier to meet the good faith requirement for "essential security interests", it may be more onerous to demonstrate the existence of an emergency in international relations, as elaborated below.

Cyber-Attacks on a Private Player or Players

In the third scenario, cyber-attacks could target a country's prominent private player or players causing substantial economic loss or disruption. An example of this could be the North Korean hacking of Sony Pictures servers as a response to the satirical movie "The Interview" which showed the assassination of North Korean Supreme Leader Kim Jung-un. The United States alleged that this was part of a larger state-sponsored campaign that led to a loss of USD 1.3 billion from banks and other businesses.[74] While the US does not appear to have responded to this with a trade measure, it is an open question whether such a response could have met the requirements of the WTO Security Exceptions. Although the Members have a lot of leeway in determining their essential security interests, whether a one-off attack on a domestic private player in the entertainment industry or as it was later revealed, a coordinated attack on a number of businesses, would have met the requirements as

[69] See Brunnee and Toope (2018); Trapp (2007).

[70] Ranjan (2020); *Cf.* Vidigal (2017); Miranda (2010); Villalpando (2002).

[71] Ranjan (2020), p. 662.

[72] See Military and Paramilitary Activities in and Against Nicaragua (Nicaragua v. United States) (Merits) [1986] ICJ Rep 14, pp. 109–115; Ranjan (2020), p. 662.

[73] Margulies (2013). For a critique of this approach see Tran (2018).

[74] Horn, John, Fallout Continues for Sony's North Korean Satire, 'The Interview', February 17, 2021, https://laist.com/news/sony-north-korea-satire-interview-cyberattack-indictment (accessed 25 November 2022).

articulated by the panel in *Russia – Traffic in Transit* remains to be seen. It could, perhaps, if it led to a potential law and order situation. However, as the panel succinctly stated, not all security measures can be elevated to "essential" ones.

A Cybersecurity Emergency in International Relations?

Aside from the scenarios discussed above, one of the biggest challenges for the country involving the security exceptions that would arise in all cases when invoking the GATT Article XXI(b)(iii) relates to demonstrating they were "taken in time of war or other emergency in international relations". As discussed earlier, the panel in *Russia – Traffic in Transit* has clarified that this requirement is an objective fact subject to an objective determination. The panel in *US- Steel and Aluminium (China)* also noted that emergency in international relations took colour from the preceding word "war" and refers to a certain gravity or severity and international tensions that are of a critical or serious nature in terms of their impact on the conduct of international relations".[75] Hence, while cyber warfare when there is an active military conflict or a heightened tension or crisis may be an unambiguous case of an emergency in international relations, it is still unclear if cyber-attacks by themselves could constitute such an emergency in international relations.[76]

4 Energy Security

4.1 Background

Energy is the engine that drives the world's economy, making it especially critical to international trade. From traditional manufacturing to new-age cloud computing – all forms of economic activities relevant to international trade rely on some underlying form of energy – making it an essential component of global development.[77] Thus, the subject of energy security is critical for every nation, despite there being no universal definition of the term. The International Energy Agency (IEA) defines it as the "uninterrupted availability of energy sources at an affordable price".[78] The United Nations in the World Assessment Report of 2000 also explains energy security to mean the availability of energy at all times in various forms, in sufficient

[75] Panel Report, *US – Steel and Aluminium (China)*, para 7.147.

[76] Mishra (2020), p. 58.

[77] See Beare M (2018), The Importance of Energy Security, Oxford Policy Management, https://www.opml.co.uk/blog/importance-energy-security (accessed 25 November 2022).

[78] See https://www.iea.org/areas-of-work/ensuring-energy-security (accessed 25 November 2022). The IEA is an intergovernmental organisation comprising of 31 countries as members, established under the OECD framework in 1974.

quantities, and at affordable prices.[79] Energy security comprises both long-term and short-term aspects. While long-term energy security addresses the need for "timely investments" to supply energy taking into account economic development and environmental concerns, short-term energy security addresses the ability to manage sudden disruptions to the supply and demand of energy.[80] The world in 2022 is facing challenges on both accounts.

Energy security, particularly long-term, has gained special significance in the light of climate change challenges which impacts the types of energy resources that can or should be used to prevent a climate catastrophe. According to a multi-agency report from the World Meteorological Organisation released in October 2022, the supply of electricity from clean energy sources "must double within the next eight years to limit the global temperature rise.[81] Given the urgent need to move to renewable energy sources, "green energy security" is perceived to be the viable way forward for the world.[82] At the same time, Russia's war on Ukraine has caused extreme disruption to the international trade in energy products, particularly in oil and piped natural gas. Russia has drastically cut down its export of piped natural gas to the EU after the Ukraine invasion, with its October 2022 exports being 80% lower compared to 2021.[83] The EU, in turn, has announced a ban on imports of Russian oil brought from the sea from December 2022 and the ban on all refined oil products from Russia in February 2023.[84] The US has also announced the ban on all Russian oil, liquefied natural gas, and coal[85]

---

[79] United Nations Development Programme (2020), World Energy Assessment: Energy and the Challenge of Sustainability, https://www.undp.org/sites/g/files/zskgke326/files/publications/World%20Energy%20Assessment-2000.pdf (accessed 25 November 2022).

[80] United Nations Development Programme (2020), World Energy Assessment: Energy and the Challenge of Sustainability, https://www.undp.org/sites/g/files/zskgke326/files/publications/World%20Energy%20Assessment-2000.pdf (accessed 25 November 2022).

[81] World Meteorological Organisation, Climate change puts energy security at risk, 11 October 2022, https://public.wmo.int/en/media/press-release/climate-change-puts-energy-security-risk (accessed 25 November 2022).

[82] Skorupska N, Green energy security is achievable immediately - there's no need to wait, 5 April 2022, https://www.businessgreen.com/opinion/4047775/green-energy-security-achievable-immediately-wait (accessed 25 November 2022); See also Rutherford (2020).

[83] International Energy Agency, Frequently Asked Questions, Have Russian oil and gas exports continued to flow since the start of its invasion of Ukraine?, 16 November 2022, https://www.iea.org/articles/frequently-asked-questions-on-energy-security (accessed 25 November 2022).

[84] BBC News, What are the sanctions on Russia and are they hurting its economy?, 30 September 2022, https://www.bbc.com/news/world-europe-60125659 (accessed 25 November 2022).

The EU has adopted 8 packages of sanctions against Russia (not just limited to energy products) since the start of the Ukraine War till 26 November 2022. See https://www.consilium.europa.eu/en/policies/sanctions/restrictive-measures-against-russia-over-ukraine/sanctions-against-russia-explained/ for details. It has been reported that the EU is preparing for a ninth package of sanctions against Russia. See https://www.reuters.com/world/europe/eu-preparing-9th-russia-sanctions-package-von-der-leyen-says-2022-11-24/ (last accessed 25 November 2022).

[85] See, The White House, Fact Sheet: United States Bans Imports of Russian Oil, Liquefied Natural Gas, and Coal, March 8, 2022, https://www.whitehouse.gov/briefing-room/statements-

Cornell describes the nexus between energy security and national security at three levels.[86] At the primary level, energy is essential to keep the military running, at the secondary level, energy is essential for the critical infrastructure (from communication to transportation), and lastly, at the tertiary level, energy prices need to be reasonable for the public at large.[87] Against this background, this subsection will examine how the ground of energy security fares when invoking the national security exceptions under the WTO agreements. It is noteworthy that the thrust here is not just on the trade in energy products but rather the reliance on energy security as a ground for national security (which could include, for instance, trade in equipment that may be required to produce energy as well).

4.2 Interface with International Trade Law and the Security Exceptions

4.2.1 Energy Security and the WTO

Energy security is not a term found in WTO Agreements. Indeed, as scholars have previously noted, despite the GATT 1947 covering the international trade in goods generally, it was not very apparent if energy trade *per se* was covered by the trade rules. Marhold has attributed this to a misunderstanding that the GATT negotiators had a "gentleman's agreement" to keep the petrol trade outside GATT 1947.[88] As Lamy has noted, when the GATT was negotiated "opening trade in energy was not a political priority".[89] However, the 1970s oil crisis prompted countries such as the United States to include the issue of export restrictions on oil as one of the agenda items during the Tokyo Round of Multilateral Trade Negotiations between 1973–79.[90] A subsequent attempt was made to address issues like dual pricing through the Negotiating Group on Natural Resources-Based Products during the

releases/2022/03/08/fact-sheet-united-states-bans-imports-of-russian-oil-liquefied-natural-gas-and-coal/ (accessed 25 November 2022).

[86] Cornell (2009).

[87] Cornell (2009), pp. 64–65; See also, Mitchell J (2002), Renewing Energy Security, The Royal Institute of International Affairs, https://www.chathamhouse.org/sites/default/files/public/Research/Energy,%20Environment%20and%20Development/renewing_energy_security_mitchell_july_2002.pdf (accessed 25 November 2022).

[88] For details regarding factors that contributed to this misunderstanding see Marhold (2021), pp. 36–39; See also UNCTAD (2000), Trade Agreements, Petroleum and Energy Policies. UNCTAD/ITCD/TSB/9, https://unctad.org/system/files/official-document/itcdtsb9_en.pdf (accessed 25 November 2022).

[89] Lamy P. (2007), Doha Round Will Benefit Energy Trade, https://www.wto.org/english/news_e/sppl_e/sppl80_e.htm (accessed 25 November 2022).

[90] See also UNCTAD (2000), Trade Agreements, Petroleum and Energy Policies, UNCTAD/ITCD/TSB/9, https://unctad.org/system/files/official-document/itcdtsb9_en.pdf, p. 15.

Uruguay round of Trade Negotiations between 1986–94.[91] This attempt, too, was unsuccessful. Nevertheless, it should be noted that tariffs on energy products such as crude oil have been incorporated in the schedule of commitments of the GATT Contracting Parties since 1947.[92]

In sum, WTO rules continue to apply to energy trade. Hence, any deviation would require justification under one of the exceptions under the WTO Agreements. It is essential to note two points at this juncture. First, energy is no longer just limited to fossil fuel sources. Hence, the scope extends to green/renewable energy sources too like nuclear, solar, wind, hydel power etc. Second, as the definition indicates, the concept of "energy security" is broader in scope than energy trade. It includes, for instance, trade in solar cells and modules, which are used in the production of electricity from solar energy, since it is an essential component towards the attainment of energy security.

The WTO has witnessed several disputes relating to energy in the last few years. This includes the *Canada – Renewable Energy* and *Canada - Feed in Tariff*;[93] *India – Solar Cells*;[94] *US – Renewable Energy*[95] and *EU – Energy Package*.[96] Except for the last dispute, all the previous ones listed dealt with green energy. Although in none of these disputes, Article XXI was resorted to by the defendant, in *India – Solar Cells*, India had relied on GATT Article XX (d) and (j) of the General Exceptions[97] to state the domestic content requirement imposed by it in the production of electricity from solar cells and modules was aimed towards attaining energy security domestically, by reducing reliance on imports. The Appellate Body had rejected India's defense under Article XX, stating it had failed to fulfil the conditions therein. It remains to be seen if such an attempt would succeed under GATT Article XXI, given the latter appears to be less stringent compared to Article XX, on account of certain flexibilities in determining the essential security interests. The FTA exception dealing with critical infrastructure discussed in the context of

[91] Marhold (2021), pp. 47–48.

[92] Marhold (2021), pp. 39–42.

[93] Appellate Body Reports, *Canada – Certain Measures Affecting the Renewable Energy Generation Sector/Canada – Measures Relating to the Feed-in Tariff Program*, WT/DS412/AB/R/WT/DS426/AB/R, adopted 24 May 2013, DSR 2013:I, p. 7.

[94] Appellate Body Report, *India – Certain Measures Relating to Solar Cells and Solar Modules*, WT/DS456/AB/R and Add.1, adopted 14 October 2016, DSR 2016:IV, p. 1827.

[95] Panel Report, *United States – Certain Measures Relating to the Renewable Energy Sector*, WT/DS510/R and Add.1, circulated to WTO Members 27 June 2019, appealed on 15 August 2019.

[96] Panel Report, *European Union and its member States – Certain Measures Relating to the Energy Sector*, WT/DS476/R and Add.1, circulated to WTO Members 10 August 2018, appealed on 21 September 2018.

[97] GATT Article XX(d) broadly provides an exemption in cases where the measure is necessary to secure compliance with laws or regulations which are not inconsistent with the provisions of this Agreement. GATT Article XX(j) is available when a measure is essential to the acquisition or distribution of products in general or local short supply. Additionally, the requirements of Article XX's chapeau is to be met for a successful invocation.

cybersecurity could also potentially be resorted to for energy security-related aspects of such infrastructure.

4.2.2 Interface with WTO National Security Exceptions in Select Fact Scenarios

There are several possibilities where security exceptions may be called into the picture for meeting energy security targets, as discussed below. Please note that not all the elements of the security exceptions are discussed in each example.

Primary and Secondary Energy Security and National Security

In Cornell's description of the interface between energy security and national security discussed above, the interface could take place at the primary (i.e. military) or secondary (i.e. critical infrastructure) levels. In the first scenario, can a WTO Member rely upon energy security as a ground for national security to introduce WTO-inconsistent measures under GATT Article XX(b)(iii) and the other corresponding Agreements? The rationale for such measures could be to attain domestic energy security by cutting down reliance on imports for the military and critical infrastructure. This is not very different from the arguments presented by former United States President Trump's administration for imposing tariffs on imports of steel and aluminium from certain countries.[98] In fact, India had presented a similar argument for self-reliance on energy, but in the context of Article XX of GATT 1994. A successful invocation of the security exceptions under this scenario would, once again, in the case of Article XXI(b) chapeau be dependent on the articulation of essential security measures and the principle of good faith. Thus, so long, as the invoking country can demonstrate that its WTO inconsistent trade measures were not introduced to circumvent its obligations and they do deal with "essential" security interests, there may be a possibility of meeting the chapeau requirements. However, such a case has yet to be brought to WTO's dispute settlement proceedings.

Green Energy Security and National Security

Given the compulsions of the current times, is green energy security placed on a higher pedestal compared to plain and simple energy security on account of climate change? In this scenario, could countries claim that there exists an "emergency in

---

[98] United States Congressional Research Service, Section 232 of the Trade Expansion Act of 1962, April 1, 2022, https://crsreports.congress.gov/product/pdf/IF/IF10667 (accessed 26 November 2022).

international relations" on account of climate change urgencies, hence satisfying the requirements under Article XXI(b)(iii) and other corresponding WTO exceptions. The *Russia – Traffic in Transit* panel has defined emergency in international relations to be closely related to 'war' and hence, according to the panel, it is to be understood as a situation of armed conflict, or latent armed conflict, or of heightened tension or crisis, or of general instability engulfing or surrounding a state.[99] Therefore, prima facie, in its narrowest sense, it appears to be difficult to classify climate change exigencies as an emergency in international relations.

Nevertheless, notwithstanding the panel finding, the impact of climate change can be devastating for countries across the globe, for some more than others. For instance, take the case of Tuvalu, a series of nine small coral atolls in the Pacific Ocean. Tuvalu, along with other small vulnerable islands is likely to be unliveable in the next three decades due to climate change.[100] In its submission on the possible security implications of climate change to be included in the report of the UN Secretary-General to the UN General Assembly 64th Session, it identifies the loss of territory/sovereignty, disease/pandemic, conflict/unrest, food insecurity, water, and resource scarcity as the possible implication of climate change for the small nation.[101] What happens with Tuvalu and other similarly placed WTO Members, should they attempt to bypass their WTO commitments for green energy security? As discussed earlier, the panel has found essential security interests to be related to the quintessential functions of the state, namely, the protection of its territory and its population from external threats, and the maintenance of law and public order internally.[102] This appears to directly deal with the situation Tuvalu is foreseeing on account of climate change. Further, a more liberal interpretation of the panel's reading could support a finding of emergency in international relations, since it would lead to a general instability engulfing or surrounding a state. Nevertheless, we are yet to receive a more expansive interpretation from the WTO's panel/Appellate Body to date.

Lastly, even in cases that are not so extreme, could green energy security be looked at as a dimension of economic security (in light of the need to reduce reliance on fossil fuels), and hence a part of national security? As noted by Rutherford, in the prevailing literature, economic security has been argued to be part of national security.[103] However, whether it can qualify as an "essential security interest" in the context of WTO security exceptions appears to be unlikely in light of the understanding adopted by the WTO panels. This could be overcome if future

[99] Panel Report, *Russia – Traffic in Transit,* para. 7.76.

[100] Franks (2021), p. 531.

[101] Tuvalu's Views on the Possible Security Implications of Climate Change to be included in the report of the UN Secretary General to the UN General Assembly 64th Session (2009), https://www.un.org/esa/dsd/resources/res_pdfs/ga-64/cc-inputs/Tuvalu_CCIS.pdf (accessed 27 November 2022).

[102] Panel Report, *Russia - Traffic in Transit*, para. 7.130; Panel Report, *Saudi Arabia - Protection of IPR,* para. 7.249.

[103] Rutherford (2020), p. 129.

panels/Appellate Body adopted a more contemporaneous interpretation of the term.[104]

5 Conclusion and the Way Forward

The WTO's security exceptions are based on a text finalised in 1947 when several of the new-world challenges were not part of the discourse. In fact, they were very much science fiction. Cybersecurity and energy security are just two of these new tests to the multilateral trading system. The WTO has, to date, failed to address these issues in a head-on manner, with no targeted multilateral negotiations on these issues on the horizon. This brings us to the existing arsenal available in the WTO Members' kitty. This chapter has examined the WTO's security exceptions and their availability in different scenarios relating to cybersecurity and energy security. What it has found is that there are several ambiguities pertaining to how these exceptions would apply in specific instances.

While we now have the benefit of WTO panel reports since these disputes dealt with the traditional notion of national security, and by extension, essential security interests, they are not particularly useful in the present context. Nevertheless, these reports did an excellent job of adopting a balanced approach toward the interpretation of the self-judging security exception. What is perhaps needed is a more evolutionary approach of interpretation towards cybersecurity and energy security, at least till such time more focussed trade rules are agreed upon. The WTO's Appellate Body (though now defunct) is no stranger to this approach. In the *US-Shrimp Turtle* dispute, the Appellate Body adopted an evolutionary interpretation for "exhaustible natural resources" to include living resources, in the context of Article XX(g) of GATT 1994 on General Exceptions.[105] The expanded provision on security exceptions pertaining to critical infrastructure in certain FTAs could also serve as a template to build upon the exceptions in the future. However, until the Appellate Body is resurrected, such an interpretation may be difficult, particularly in the context of national security which requires delicate balancing. Of course, nothing stops the WTO Membership (at least in theory) from adopting an authoritative interpretation under Article IX: 2 of the Marrakesh Agreement with respect to the security exceptions. While the decision to adopt an interpretation only requires a three-fourths majority, the political reality of the day makes it unlikely that such an attempt would be made. The detractors of this approach may perceive this to be an unnecessary expansion of the security exceptions. However, given the changing times – an expansive approach may not be undesirable, provided it has sufficient checks and balances to prevent misuse and abuse.

[104] Rutherford (2020), p. 129.

[105] Appellate Body Report, United States – Import Prohibition of Certain Shrimp and Shrimp Products, WT/DS58/AB/R, adopted 6 November 1998, DSR 1998:VII, p. 2755.

References

Alford R (2011) The self-judging WTO security exception. Utah Law Rev 3:697–759

Balan GD (2019) On fissionable cows and the limits to the WTO security exceptions. Glob Trade Cust J 14(1):2–10

Brunnee J, Toope SJ (2018) Self-defense against non-state actors: are porwerful states but unwilling to change international law. Int Comp Law Q 67(2):263–286

Chieng D (2021) Supply chains, COVID-19 and the GATT security exception: legal limits of 'pandemic exceptionalism'. Aust Year Book Int Law Online 39(1):13–31

Clarke RA, Knake RK (2012) Trial runs. In: Cyber war: the next threat to national security and what to do about it, 1st Ecco paperback edition. HarperCollins Publishers, New York, pp 1–32

Cornell P (2009) Energy and the three levels of national security: differentiating energy concerns within a national security context. Connections 8(4):63–80

Franks S (2021) Exploring climate security to Article XXI of the GATT. Wash Univ Global Stud Law Rev 20(2):523–531

Friis K, Lysne O (2021) Huawei, 5G and Security: technological limitations and political responses. Dev Change 52:1174–1195

Gustavo A, Duque G (2019) Interpreting WTO rules in times of contestation (Part 2): a proposed interpretation of Article XXI(b)ii–iii of the GATT 1994 in the light of the Vienna Convention of the Law of the Treaties. Glob Trade Cust J 14(1):31–44

Hao W (2020) A harmonized interpretation of freedom of transit in the fragmented international legal system: applying Article 31(3)(c) of the Vienna Convention on the Law of Treaties to the Russia – Traffic in Transit dispute. J World Trade 54(3):397–416

Heath BJ (2020) The new national security challenge to the economic order. Yale Law J 129:1020–1098

Kim MH (2019) A real driver of US–China trade conflict - the Sino–US competition for global hegemony and its implications for the future. Int Trade Polit Dev 3(1):30–40

Margulies P (2013) Sovereignty and cyber attacks: technology's challenge to the law of State responsibility. Melb J Int Law 14:496–519

Marhold A (2021) Energy's place in international trade law history. In: Energy in international trade law: concepts, regulation and changing markets. Cambridge University Press, Cambridge, pp 35–65

Martin P, Meyer T, Thoenig M (2008) Make trade not war? Rev Econ Stud 75(3):865–900

McDonald P (2004) Peace through trade or free trade? J Conflict Resolut 48(4):547–572

Miranda J (2010) Causal link and non-attribution as interpreted in WTO trade remedy disputes. J World Trade 44(4):729–762

Mishra N (2020) The trade: (cyber)security dilemma and its impact on global cybersecurity governance. J World Trade 54(4):567–590

Modabadze V (2020) US-China rivalry for global hegemony. J Liberty Int Aff 6(2):167–173

Nagy C (2019) World trade, imperial fantasies and protectionism: can you really have your cake and eat it too? Indiana J Glob Leg Stud 26(1):87–132

Oke E (2021) COVID-19, pandemics, and the national security exception in the TRIPS Agreement. J Intell Prop Inf Technol Electron Commerce Law 12(3):397–407

Peng S (2015) Cybersecurity threats and the WTO national security exceptions. J Int Econ Law 18(2):449–478

Pinchis-Paulsen M (2020) Trade multilateralism and U.S. national security: the making of the GATT security exceptions. Mich J Int Law 41(1):109–193

Ranjan P (2020) National security exception in the General Agreement on Tariffs and Trade (GATT) and India–Pakistan trade. J World Trade 54(4):643–666

Roberts A, Moraes H, Ferguson V (2019) Toward a geoeconomic order in international trade and investment. J Int Econ Law 22(4):655–676

Rutherford A (2020) The applicability of the law of the WTO to green energy security. In: Energy security and green energy national policies and the law of the WTO. Springer Nature, Cham, pp 103–139
Schill S, Briese R (2009) If the state considers': self-judging clauses in international dispute settlement (2009). In: Bogdandy A, Wolfrum R (eds) Max Planck Yearbook of United Nations Law, vol 13. Brill Nijhof, Leiden, pp 61–140
Schloemann H, Ohloff S (1999) Constitutionalization' and dispute settlement in the WTO: national security as an issue of competence. Am J Int Law 93(2):424–451
Tran D (2018) The law of attribution: rules for attributing the source of a cyber-attack. Yale J Law Technol 20:376–441
Trapp KN (2007) Back to basics: necessity, proportionality and the right of self-defense against non-state terrorist actors. Int Comp Law Q 56(1):141–156
Vidigal G (2017) Attribution in the WTO: the limits of 'sufficient government involvement'. J Int Trade Arbitr Law 6:133–160
Villalpando S (2002) Attribution of conduct to the State: how the rules of state responsibility may be applied within the WTO dispute settlement system. J Int Econ Law 5(2):393–420
Yoo JY, Ahn D (2016) Security exceptions in the WTO system: bridge or bottle-neck for trade and security? J Int Econ Law 19(2):417–444

Shailja Singh is a Legal Consultant (Associate Professor) at the Centre for WTO Studies, Indian Institute of Foreign Trade, New Delhi. She is a lawyer and trade policy adviser with over a decade of experience in international economic law; and is part of the Government of India's trade negotiations, policy and dispute teams. She has also worked at the Advisory Centre on WTO Law (ACWL), Geneva, Switzerland on a special secondment. Shailja has acted as a Legal Counsel to the Government of India in several WTO disputes. She participates in the FTA negotiations on behalf of India as a designated Sector Expert for E-Commerce, SPS and TBT chapters. In this capacity, she has participated in the RCEP negotiations (2016–19), and in India's FTA negotiations with the UAE, UK and Australia (2021–22). Shailja is part of the Centre's core team for training programmes on international trade issues and is the faculty coordinator for the Joint Academy on International Trade Law and Policy, a one-month summer school jointly organized with the World Trade Institute, Bern. Shailja is a gold medallist from the W.B. National University of Juridical Sciences, Kolkata and she completed her masters from the University of Cambridge.

Uzbekistan Investment Law and Policy: Challenges and Opportunities

Said Saidakhrarovich Gulyamov and Otabek Sadievich Narziev

Contents

Abstract The paper aims to introduce Uzbekistan's experience in designing its foreign investment law and policy, especially in the last 5 years. It gives some insights into the investment environment of Uzbekistan, provides the analyses of main influencing factors, and novelty in the recent legislation in the sphere. The paper also provides an analysis of the challenges and opportunities of foreign investment law and policy of Uzbekistan.

The findings of the study will benefit both local investors who are interested in assessing investment opportunities in Uzbekistan. The complexities of the evolution of investment opportunities in emerging markets have been studied before. The problems associated with transparency, foreign exchange volatility, and liquidity impact pricing and valuation across countries and regions. The overall business climate in Uzbekistan can be described as stable, but with a potential for rapid growth in the event of more radical reforms towards the market.

S. S. Gulyamov
Council of Young Scientists of the Academy of Sciences of the Republic of Uzbekistan, Tashkent, Uzbekistan

O. S. Narziev (✉)
Department of Private International Law, Tashkent State University of Law, Tashkent, Uzbekistan
e-mail: otabeknarziev@tsul.uz

M. Bungenberg et al. (eds.), *Asian Yearbook of International Economic Law 2023*, Asian Yearbook of International Economic Law (2023) 2023: 97–104,
https://doi.org/10.1007/16517_2023_17, Published online: 22 April 2023

1 Introduction

Uzbekistan is a Central Asian nation with a rich cultural heritage and a diverse natural landscape. It is also home to a rapidly growing economy, with a GDP that has increased by an average of 8% per year over the past decade.[1] In 2022, the country made relatively substantial progress, with the GDP amounting to about US $70 billion and real GDP growth increasing by 5.8%, being among the few countries in the world with positive economic growth.[2] There is a solid share of investment policy and reforms implemented by the government in recent years in achieving such continuous economic growth. The investment climate in any country depends primarily on its political stability. The same factor allows foreign investors to invest in another country based on long-term contracts. Such an environment allows for the implementation of long-term investment plans. The main feature of the investment climate in Uzbekistan is that it is the most stable country in Central Asia.

Investment climate implies the existence of several factors that foreign investors usually consider before they decide to invest in the country.[3] Generally, these factors include political, economic, social, and legal factors. Political factors include the following: foreign investment policy; the degree of state intervention in the economy; compliance of the country with international agreements; stability of the political situation; effective and transparent functioning of the state apparatus; the compatibility of tax, currency, price, a monetary policy with foreign investment policy; the environmental situation and the scope of the government's environmental health policy.

Other essential factors that affect the positive investment decision of the foreign investor are economic factors. The economic factors include the following: customs procedure, inflation rate, tax regime and benefits, resources (natural, raw material, human), demand and supply for certain goods, competition level, currency conversion and national exchange rate stability, bank interest rates, foreign economic relations of the country, geographical and territorial location of the country (natural disasters, sea and land routes, climatic conditions, etc.)

Investment climate effectiveness also depends on the social factors that usually foreign investors consider as one essential. Social factors include the following: the socio-economic situation of the country and its diversity; ideological views of the population and their diversity; attitudes towards different nationalities in the country; literacy level of the population; level of the skilled and experienced workforce; the attitude of the population to innovations and the level of their acceptance in the country.

Giving due attention to the essence of all the above-mentioned factors and considering the expertise of the authors, this paper mainly considers legal factors and their implications for improving the foreign investment policy of Uzbekistan.

[1] Anderson and Tomotsune (2022).

[2] The World Bank in Uzbekistan, https://www.worldbank.org/en/country/uzbekistan/overview.

[3] Rustambekov and Isakulov (2019).

Legal factors usually imply the robustness of the legal framework for investment activities; the degree of robustness of the legal framework that directly supports investment activities; normative bases of investment activity (laws, regulations, decrees, decisions, instructions, etc.); the legal, economic and organisational conditions of foreign investment in the territory of Uzbekistan are reflected in several laws and regulations.

2 Latest Legal Reforms in the Foreign Investment Regulation

Uzbekistan has implemented several reforms in recent years to attract foreign investment and encourage economic development. These reforms mainly consist of enacting special laws and by-law acts on improving investment regulation, liberalisation of administrative procedures, and providing additional preferences for foreign investors. A new Investment Law[4] and Law on PPP[5] in 2019 could serve as a solid base for improving the foreign investment environment in Uzbekistan.

The law 'On Investments and Investment Activities' (hereinafter new Investment Law) consolidates several previous legislative acts relating to foreign investments, investor rights and obligations, and investment activity in Uzbekistan. In part, the Law serves as a unified document that combines the main provisions of the laws 'On Foreign Investments', 'On Investment Activities' and 'On Guarantees and Measures to Protect the Rights of Foreign Investors', which all lost their validity since coming into force of the new Investment Law.[6] The new Investment Law provides several benefits to investors, including tax breaks, land leases at reduced rates, and access to financing. It also includes provisions to protect the rights of investors and ensure a fair and transparent business environment. This Law introduced several novelties that were not in the previous editions. Namely, previous laws did not distinguish between foreign and domestic investors, while the new Investment Law provides clear definitions of domestic and foreign investors. The law also introduced additional requirements for the contents of the investment agreements on compulsory including to such agreements anti-corruption and anti-monopoly clauses.

Another main legal act—Law on Public-Private Partnerships also provides new opportunities for foreign investors to participate in large projects, with tenders. Since 2018, foreign bidders have signed PPP agreements to implement several fossil fuel and renewable energy projects. The Government wants to attract investments for

[4]Law on Investments and Investment Activity of Uzbekistan, https://investmentpolicy.unctad.org/investment-laws/laws/328/uzbekistan-the-law-on-investments-and-investment-activity.

[5]Law on Public-Private Partnership of Uzbekistan, http://old.lex.uz/docs/4329272.

[6]Rustambekov and Isakulov (2021).

$14 billion on a PPP basis to the energy, transport, healthcare, education, ecology, utilities, water management, and other sectors in 2022–2026.[7]

To sum up the latest reforms in investment regulation provide a wide range of guarantees for foreign investors, including protection against discrimination, protection from harm caused by the retroactive implementation of legislation, protection from interference by the state in the economic activity of foreign investors, and protection from any changes in legislation that worsens foreign investment conditions.

Despite the huge scale of reforms, enactment of several laws, and establishment of a special regulatory body, there are still several challenges that could be seen in Uzbekistan's foreign investment policy.

3 Challenges and Opportunities

One of the main challenges is improving the investment attractiveness of Uzbekistan, along with the harmonisation of legal and regulatory documents with international standards. The investment attractiveness of the country, along with legal and political factors, depends on the level of development of management in the country and the responsibility of managers for the project and the company. There is no methodological basis for ensuring the participation of Uzbekistan in key indexes of the investment climate of the country as widely used in world practice, such as Genuine saving (GS), and The Global Competitiveness Index (GCI). Uzbekistan's participation in these indices allows investors to identify the country's ability to achieve sustainable economic growth, and to assess technology, government institutions, and macroeconomic status.[8] According to recent studies, Uzbekistan needs to take systemic measures on ensuring a favourable investment climate, its necessary elements, and, first of all, legal protection of business; improving the conditions for the activities of investors, business entities (registration, licensing, financing, etc.); and improving the quality of project management with the participation of foreign capital.[9] The task can be started by strengthening the legal mechanisms for the protection of the rights and interests of business entities, and ensuring their guarantees, clarifying the regulatory functions of authorised bodies.

As shown by the experience of developed countries, to raise the attractiveness of foreign capital, especially in the form of foreign direct investment (FDI), along with the introduction of incentive measures and protection of foreign investors, it is necessary to increase the investment attractiveness of each enterprise and the industry as a whole. To this end, based on innovative approaches, Uzbekistan has

---

[7] International Trade Administration, Uzbekistan country commercial guide. July 8, 2022, https://www.trade.gov/country-commercial-guides/uzbekistan-market-opportunities.

[8] Mustafakulov (2019).

[9] Nadirkhanov (2021).

adopted comprehensive long-term development programs in the field of pharmaceuticals, textiles, leather and footwear, cotton, silk, and other processing industries. Improving the business climate and its environment, protecting interests, and guaranteeing business are other basic issues that every foreign investor finds important. As practice has shown, a favourable investment climate includes many conditions, the most important of which is the entrepreneur's belief in the future and confidence in protecting his business. Legal protection of the investor, and private property, ensuring economic security and protecting the interests of the entrepreneur, both domestic and foreign ones, subsequently became a reliable foundation for the emerging new 'framework conditions' for business. The creation of a competitive environment and equal conditions for business, a continuation of the course of reforms aimed at the development of transparency, and simplification of procedures for business have become the urgent tasks of developing the market environment in Uzbekistan. The investment climate cannot be considered a favourable one, if some significant conditions are not provided, such as the operation of all the necessary market structures—stock exchanges and the provision of business entities with the necessary raw materials and materials, improvement of insurance services, and the tax sector. The development of corporate governance and the quality of management not only increases the efficiency of the joint-stock company or industry but also improves their capitalisation, as well as their investment attractiveness.

For a long time foreign investors, among the unfavourable factors of the investment climate, noted the lack of currency conversion and shortcomings in the banking system of the republic. It is no coincidence that several decisions have been adopted and are being implemented in the republic to radically improve the situation in this important area. Since September 2017, when a Presidential Decree on the liberalisation of foreign exchange policy was adopted and a lot of work is being done to create conditions for increasing the efficiency of the banking sector, ensuring financial stability, reducing the state share in this sector, increasing the availability and quality of financial services. Since 2020, national investment programs began to be developed for the next 3 years (instead of 1 year), which gives them greater stability, and prospects for investors. In the formation of investment programs large infrastructure projects have become the main object of investment, because, they contain high internal multipliers and give impetus to stimulate the economy.

Uzbekistan is actively developing new and complex forms of investment project implementation like public-private partnerships and production-sharing agreements. In addition to the traditional and long-term practice of focusing on foreign capital in general, Uzbekistan is giving priority to increasing the volume and improving the quality of attracted foreign direct investment. Uzbekistan's experience in attracting foreign capital, especially in the FDI form, demonstrates the relationship between the country's rating and the volume and quality of attracted foreign capital. On the other hand, Uzbekistan should itself seek to influence the process of large-scale restructuring of its national economy through systemic information, organisational, and diplomatic work in this direction. This regard raises the other important issue that directly shows the effectiveness and transparency of the countries' investment policy. As some researches show, the applied form of national statistics on foreign investments does not contribute to the growth of the investment attractiveness of the republic.[10] This is the necessity of improvement of national statistics on foreign investment that in most cases become divergent from the international ratings. Complete, accurate, and timely statistics lead to an increase in the international rating of Uzbekistan as a host country, and a high rating itself attracts new investment flows. Moreover, complete, accurate, and timely statistics can become a guarantee of high-quality projects and management decisions.

4 Conclusion

The state of the investment climate requires a created legal framework and its foundations, a quality structure of legislation, and compliance. The level of modern economic development of the country, as well as the growth rate of ongoing investment activity, will depend on the investment climate. It is necessary to create the existing conditions for attracting foreign investment in the economy of the republic, foreign investment can be made in the economy of the country only when the economic, political, social, and legal conditions exist. One of the important aspects of creating a favourable investment climate is the legal and regulatory framework, which should protect and guarantee the property interests of each potential investor, as well as ensure the understanding and clarity of the existing investment mechanism in the country. In this paper, we tried to address this issue from the perspective of the Uzbekistan experience.

References

Anderson M, Tomotsune (2022) Uzbekistan preparation of the investment guidebook of Uzbekistan and information gathering and surveys regarding investment promotion activities. Japan International Cooperation Agency (JICA). https://openjicareport.jica.go.jp/pdf/1000047739.pdf

Mustafakulov S (2019) Improvement of the investment climate in Uzbekistan, Religación. Revista de Ciencias Sociales y Humanidades 4(19):85–92

Nadirkhanov U (2021) Increasing the investment attractiveness of the Republic of Uzbekistan: results, problems, prospects. J Contemp Issues Bus Gov 27(2):4030–4036

Rustambekov I, Isakulov A (2019) Business environment and investment climate in the Republic of Uzbekistan. Int J Adv Res, 7, 1282–1285. https://doi.org/10.21474/IJAR01/8951

Rustambekov I, Isakulov A (2021) Uzbekistan in 2020: Foreign Direct Investment and Investor-State Dispute Resolution. Int Aca J Law; 2(1), 52–57

[10] Nadirkhanov (2021).

Said Saidakhrarovich Gulyamov is the Chairman of the Council of Young Scientists of the Academy of Sciences of the Republic of Uzbekistan.

Otabek Sadievich Narziev is a Professor of the Department of Private International Law at the Tashkent State University of Law.

Environmental Regulation and International Investment Law in South Asia

Pushkar Anand

Contents

Abstract The adoption of policies by host states aimed at general environmental regulation, and climate change mitigation through the transition to renewable energy, has opened the floodgates of disputes between foreign investors and host states. The number of ISDS cases challenging such measures has substantially increased in the last few years. Such cases have the potential of introducing

---

This article is an updated version of the paper presented in the 5th SIEL Biennial Global Conference held at the University of Witwatersrand, Johannesburg, South Africa, from 7 to 9th July 2016. I am thankful to the anonymous reviewers, and Prof. Prabhash Ranjan for their comments on the paper. Views and errors are my own.

P. Anand (✉)
Macquarie Law School, Macquarie University, Sydney, NSW, Australia

Faculty of Law, University of Delhi, New Delhi, India
e-mail: pushkar.anand@hdr.mq.edu.au

M. Bungenberg et al. (eds.), *Asian Yearbook of International Economic Law 2023*,
Asian Yearbook of International Economic Law (2023) 2023: 105–132,
https://doi.org/10.1007/16517_2023_13, Published online: 4 March 2023

regulatory chill especially in developing and least developed countries. Against this backdrop, this paper attempts to study the interaction of international investment law and environmental regulation in South Asia. The integration of South Asian countries with the global economy and the legal framework supporting it, has resulted in sizeable foreign investment directed to these countries, protected by a large number of investment treaties based on the older generation, capital-exporting models with scant support for environmental regulation, and may create an obstacle in the adoption of policies aimed at climate change mitigation, and general environmental protection and preservation.

1 Introduction

Environmental protection and the advancement of climate goals are the core components of sustainable development and are no longer a marginal consideration.[1] The transition from a brown to a green economy is in motion, says Viñuales, and 'its fine print, including the regulatory and litigation risks it entails, is taking an increasingly recognizable shape'.[2] This transition is reflected in the attempts at the international, regional, and national levels to revisit international investment law (IIL). The backlash against IIL has led the way to contestation, reimagining, and redesigning its content.[3] While the Working Group-III of the United Nations Commissions on International Trade Law (UNCITRAL) is deliberating reforms of investor-state dispute settlement (ISDS),[4] there is an increasing demand to situate and overhaul the substantive content of IIL within the backdrop of sustainable development,[5] apparent by increasing references to sustainable development, and environmental concerns in the new generation of investment treaties.[6]

Another facet of this transition is the swelling ISDS caseload involving environmental issues. ISDS has been used by foreign investors to challenge the environment-related measures taken by the host states.[7] For instance, a spate of ISDS cases challenging changes in renewable energy policies in Spain, and other European states has prompted the reform of the Energy Charter Treaty (ECT) and

[1] See, Viñuales (2012).

[2] See, Viñuales (2012), p. 1.

[3] See, Perrone (2021).

[4] See, https://uncitral.un.org/en/working_groups/3/investor-state.

[5] See, UNCTIRAL ISDS Working Group III, Possible reform of Investor-State dispute settlement (ISDS) Submission from the Government of South Africa, A/CN.9/WG.III/WP.176 (17 July 2019), para 19 https://undocs.org/en/A/CN.9/WG.III/WP.176.

[6] See Viñuales (2012); The term 'investment treaties' refers to standalone Bilateral Investment Treaties (BIT), Free Trade Agreement (FTA) investment chapters, and all three terms have used throughout the chapter as per the requirement.

[7] See, Viñuales (2012), who has complied a dataset of 117 cases with 'environmental components' between 1970 and 2015.

also led to the exit of various states from the ECT.[8] Similarly, ISDS cases have been filed by investors in the fossil fuel sector against states opting to phase out the use of coal for energy generation in line with their commitment under the Paris Agreement 2015.[9]

Such ISDS cases have the capacity to derail or delay the transition to a green economy by instilling a regulatory chill i.e., the prospect of an impending ISDS claim forcing the host states to either abandon the regulatory measures or to dilute it in a manner making it ineffective.[10] In an empirical study conducted in the context of tobacco-related public health measures, Moehlecke confirms the presence of a chilling effect resulting from the ISDS across developed and developing countries.[11] The chilling effect is more pronounced for developing countries. The study confirms the argument that the regulatory autonomy of developing states is more restricted owing to the obligations under the IIL and the ISDS.[12] It is therefore important for developing countries to have sufficient regulatory space in their investment treaties so that they can freely adopt measures for protecting the environment including those necessary for climate change mitigation.

This paper aims at studying the capacity of the states in South Asia to adopt such measures under their investment treaties.[13] Given that most of the states in the region fall in the lower middle-income group, and are either developing or least developed, foreign investment plays a significant role in their development. Owing to the greater economic integration of South Asia with the global economy since the 1980s,[14] the volume of foreign direct investment (FDI) has increased over the last decade and lifted the living standards of millions in the region.[15] However, increased FDI in the region also has a flip side to it – empirical research shows that FDI and energy consumption patterns in South Asia have an adverse impact on the environment.[16] Simultaneously, foreign investment is essential for the states in the region to achieve their climate change mitigation goals.[17] Given the fact that global integration is not

[8] See, Brauch MD (2022) The Agreement in Principle on ECT "Modernization": A Botched Reform Attempt that Undermines Climate Action, CCSI, 17 October 2022, https://ccsi.columbia.edu/news/agreement-principle-ect-modernization-botched-reform-attempt-undermines-climate-action.

[9] See, *RWE v. Netherlands,* ICSID Case No. ARB/21/4; Also see, Salvatore LD (2021) Investor-State Disputes in Fossil Fuel Industry, IISD, December 2021, https://www.iisd.org/system/files/2022-01/investor%E2%80%93state-disputes-fossil-fuel-industry.pdf.

[10] See, Tienharra (2018).

[11] See, Moehlecke (2020).

[12] See, Moehlecke (2020), p. 10.

[13] South Asia here refers to the region comprising of 8 countries which are the member of SAARC – Afghanistan, Bangladesh, Bhutan, India, Maldives, Nepal, Pakistan and Sri Lanka.

[14] See, Sahoo (2014).

[15] Sahoo (2014), p. 8.

[16] See, Sabir et al. (2020).

[17] Triyana M, (Claire) Li Y (2022) Green Energy Can Accelerate Sustainable Growth Across South Asia, World Bank Blogs, 19 October 2022, https://blogs.worldbank.org/endpovertyinsouthasia/green-energy-can-accelerate-sustainable-growth-across-south-asia.

only economic but also legal as the South Asian states have signed a sizeable number of investment treaties, it creates a potential situation of conflict between investment protection obligations and the environmental and climate change-related measures that these states may adopt.

While other regions like Southeast Asia,[18] have attracted considerable scholarly attention in IIL scholarship, South Asia as a region has failed to draw similar attention with certain exceptions.[19] This is partly because of the apparent inactivity of most of the South Asian states when the entire international community is witnessing and participating in the rapidly 'shifting landscape' of IIL.[20] Except for India,[21] the position of other South Asian states on investment treaties presumably remains unchanged. However, this does not mean that there is no discussion or deliberation within these countries.[22] Even, India has not yet made any statement explaining its position on the ongoing ISDS reforms at UNCITRAL. Notwithstanding the fact that investment treaties are not solely responsible for attracting foreign investments, South Asian states do not seem to be entirely rejectionist, and continue to engage with IIL. Therefore, it is important to study the investment treaties of these states in order to understand whether they offer sufficient policy space for taking environmental measures, including climate change mitigation efforts. Section 2 discusses the global context of the debate surrounding environmental concerns in IIL. Section 3 analyzes the relationship between foreign investment and the environment in South Asia providing a rationale for studying the investment treaties of the region; Sect. 4 then analyzes environmental provisions (EPs) in the investment treaties; Sect. 5 traces new developments in South Asia, and Sect. 6 concludes suggesting pathways for states in the region.

[18] For instance, on ASEAN BITs see, Cho and Kurtz (2016); Chaisse and Jusoh (2016).

[19] See, Sinha (2017); Ranjan and Anand (2017, 2018).

[20] Roberts A (2017) The Shifting Landscape of Investor-State Arbitration: Loyalists, Reformists, Revolutionaries and Undecideds. EJIL *Talk*, 15 June 2017, https://www.ejiltalk.org/the-shifting-landscape-of-investor-state-arbitration-loyalists-reformists-revolutionaries-and-undecideds/.

[21] India after being hit by several ISDS cases (more than 20) has recently come up with a new Model Text for BITs. See, Model Text for the Indian Bilateral Investment Treaty 2016 (2016 Indian Model BIT), http://indiainbusiness.nic.in/newdesign/upload/Model_BIT.pdf. For a comprehensive analysis of the 2016 Model Indian BIT, see, Ranjan and Anand (2017).

[22] On Pakistan see: Ghouri and Mahmood (2012); Poulsen LS and Vis-Dunbar D (2009) Reflections on Pakistan's Investment Treaty Programme after 50 years: an interview with former Attorney General of Pakistan, Makhdoom Ali Khan. Investment Treaty News, 16 March 2009, https://www.iisd.org/itn/2009/03/16/pakistans-standstill-in-investment-treaty-making-an-interview-with-the-former-attorney-general-of-pakistan-makhdoom-ali-khan/; On Sri Lanka see, Pathirana (2016); On Bangladesh, Shuvo A (2017) More bilateral treaties for better investment deal? New Age, 24 May 2017, http://www.newagebd.net/print/article/16168; Ahmad M (2017) Bilateral Investment Treaties under the scanner, The Financial Express, 1 June 2017, http://www.thefinancialexpress-bd.com/2017/06/01/72376/Bilateral-investment-treaties-under-the-scanner/print.

2 Environment, Climate Change, and ISDS: Recent Trends

While environmental issues have figured in investment arbitrations since the 1970s, the intersection between the two fields has become more prominent after 2012.[23] Of the total 117 cases identified by Viñuales until 2017, more than half have been filed after 2012.[24] These disputes arise out of states' regulatory measures relating to extractive industry, waste, water, environmental degradation and remediation, conservation, environmental permitting, etc.[25] While it is difficult to analyze all environment-related cases, two ISDS events are worth discussing here. First, the challenge posed to the renewable energy transition through ISDS cases brought under the Energy Charter Treaty (ECT). Second, the interpretative mistake committed by the arbitral tribunal in the case of *Eco Oro Mineral v. Colombia.*[26]

2.1 ISDS Cases Threatening Clean Energy Transition

In the early 2000s, a number of European states introduced various incentives for attracting investments in the renewable energy sector. For instance, Spain adopted laws guaranteeing *inter alia* a fixed feed-in tariff to renewable energy investors. However, due to the financial strain on the economy caused among other things, by the payment of incentives, Spain abolished the fixed feed-in-tariff.[27] These changes prompted the investors to file a spate of ISDS cases totaling more than 50, under the ECT alleging violation of fair and equitable treatment standard due to frustration of investor's legitimate expectations.[28] These cases have resulted in an inconsistent interpretation of legitimate expectations, especially the question of whether a general legislation can give rise to legitimate expectations.[29]

For instance, the tribunal in *Charanne v. Spain*[30] held that a general regulation even though directed to a limited group of investors would not be considered a specific commitment as it "would constitute an excessive limitation on power of

[23] Viñuales (2012).

[24] Viñuales (2012).

[25] Viñuales (2012).

[26] *Eco Oro Minerals v. Colombia,* ICSID Case No. ARB/16/41.

[27] Pang HH (2022) The Role of Investor-State Arbitration in Promoting Climate Change Mitigation: From "Shield" to "Sword" Through Renewable Energy Disputes. Working Paper, EUI AEL, 2022/05, European Society of International Law Paper, https://cadmus.eui.eu/handle/1814/74450.

[28] UNCTAD, Spain, https://investmentpolicy.unctad.org/investment-dispute-settlement/country/197/spain.

[29] Schmidl M (2021) The Renewable Energy Saga from Charanne v. Spain to The PV Investors v. Spain: Trying to See the Wood for the Trees, Kluwer Arbitration Blog, 21 February 2021, http://arbitrationblog.kluwerarbitration.com/2021/02/01/the-renewable-energy-saga-from-charanne-v-spain-to-the-pv-investors-v-spain-trying-to-see-the-wood-for-the-trees/.

[30] *Charanne and Construction Investments v. Spain,* SCC Case No. V 062/2012.

states to regulate the economy in accordance with the public interest."[31] While the tribunal in *Masdar v. Spain*[32] evaded this question altogether, other tribunals held that generally applicable legislation may reflect specific commitment creating legitimate expectations that regulatory changes could frustrate.[33]

Such inconsistent interpretation of legitimate expectations and FET poses a challenge in bridging the gap between IIL and climate change goals. More generally, such cases may increase the cost of the energy transition for climate change adaptation. With technological advancement, the cost of renewable energy production will decline, and the host States should have the flexibility of adopting necessary regulatory changes to benefit from such developments, rather than 'extending unsustainable regulatory frameworks that socialize the risks arising from the energy transition.'[34]

Additionally, ISDS cases such as *RWE v. Netherlands,*[35] and *Uniper v. Netherlands*[36] under ECT, where the Dutch government's decision to ban the use of coal for electricity generation by 2030 in compliance with its Paris Agreement commitments has been challenged, present another battle frontier in the clean energy transition.[37] These claims directly pit ISDS against the goals of climate change. According to Tienhaara and Cotulla, 75 percent of the foreign-owned coal power plants which should be retired early in accordance with the Paris Agreement are covered by at least a treaty with ISDS, thus exposing the regulatory measures related to their phasing out to risk.[38] Amidst these developments, the ECT reform process was also initiated in 2017 to modernize it and make it compatible with the climate change goals under Paris Agreement and the SDGs. The recently published draft of the Agreement in Principle on ECT modernization has *inter alia* introduced a flexibility mechanism allowing State parties to individually deny investment protection to fossil fuel investors.[39] However, this approach will be effective only if all or at least majority of the parties use this flexibility to phase out fossil fuel invest-

[31] *Charanne and Construction Investments v. Spain*, SCC Case No. V 062/2012, para 493.

[32] *Masdar v. Spain,* ICSID Case No. ARB/14/1.

[33] For instance, see *Novenergia v. Spain,* SCC Case No. 063/2015, Final Award, 15 February 2018, para 666–667; *Cube v. Spain*, ICSID Case No. ARB/15/20, Award, 26 July 2019, para 401; *9REN v. Spain*, ICSID Case No. ARB/15/15, Award, 31May 2019, para 257, 294.

[34] UNCTAD, Treaty Based Investor-State Dispute Settlement Cases and Climate Action, Issue 4, September 2022, https://unctad.org/system/files/official-document/diaepcbinf2022d7_en.pdf.

[35] *RWE v. Netherlands,* ICSID Case No. ARB/21/4.

[36] *Uniper v. Netherlands,* ICSID Case No. ARB/21/22.

[37] See also, *Rockhopper Italia v. Italian Republic*, ICSID Case No. ARB/17/14; *Lone Pine Resources v. Canada,* ICSID Case No. UNCT/15/2; *Westmoreland Mining Holdings v. Canada,* ICSID Case No. UNCT/20/3.

[38] Tienhaara and Cotula (2020).

[39] Brauch MD (2022) The Agreement in Principle on ECT "Modernization": A Botched Reform Attempt that Undermines Climate Action, CCSI, 17 October 2022, https://ccsi.columbia.edu/news/agreement-principle-ect-modernization-botched-reform-attempt-undermines-climate-action.

ments.[40] The reform of ECT appears to be a missed opportunity, seemingly apparent after the withdrawal of Spain, the Netherlands, and Poland, and a recent proposal of EU for a collective and coordinate exit from the ECT.

2.2 *Exceptional Interpretation of the General Exceptions Clause*

Apart from challenging climate change goals, ISDS has also been used by foreign investors to contest other environmental measures such as regulatory action aimed at the conservation of ecologically sensitive areas. The recently decided *Eco Oro Minerals v Colombia* is a case in point. In this case, the arbitral tribunal has set an exceptional example of how to not interpret general exceptions provision. General exception clauses, and environmental carve-outs securing the right to regulate, are important policy tools that states have increasingly adopted to balance environmental and other public policy concerns with investment protection in the newer generation of investment treaties.[41] Alshner and Hui find that while such general public policy exceptions have progressively been adopted, they have either not been raised by the respondents, or have been interpreted by arbitral tribunals in such a manner that makes them ineffective.[42]

The tribunal in *Eco Oro* did precisely the latter. The claimant, a Canadian gold mining company challenged the mining ban imposed by the Colombian government to protect *páramos* – high-altitude wetlands rich in biodiversity.[43] While the tribunal rejected the claims of indirect expropriation holding that ban was a *bona fide* exercise of the police powers 'to protect a legitimate public welfare objective, namely the protection of environment,' it held Colombia liable to pay compensation for the breach of minimum standards of treatment clause of Canada-Colombia free trade agreement (FTA). Interestingly, when Colombia invoked the general exception clause given in article 2201(3) of the FTA, the tribunal held that while the 'State cannot be prohibited from adopting or enforcing an environmental measure in accordance with Article 2201(3), [the tribunal] cannot accept.…. that in such circumstance the payment of compensation is not required.'[44] The reasoning of the tribunal is severely problematic. As rightly pointed out by Heath, the tribunal erred

[40] Brauch MD (2022) The Agreement in Principle on ECT "Modernization": A Botched Reform Attempt that Undermines Climate Action, CCSI, 17 October 2022, https://ccsi.columbia.edu/news/agreement-principle-ect-modernization-botched-reform-attempt-undermines-climate-action.

[41] See, Alshner and Hui (2018).

[42] See, Alshner and Hui (2018).

[43] *Eco Oro Minerals v. Colombia,* ICSID Case No. ARB/16/41.

[44] *Eco Oro Minerals v. Colombia,* ICSID Case No. ARB/16/41, Decision on Jurisdiction, Liability and Directions on Quantum, 9 September 2021, para 836.

in 'identifying the source of the compensation obligation' and in that process obliterated the rationale for the existence of the general exceptions clause.[45] The interpretation adopted by the tribunal in *Eco Oro* has exposed the problems associated with 'policy exceptionalism' i.e., relying on exceptions and carve-outs for preserving domestic regulatory space.[46] It is in light of these developments that this paper will analyze South Asian states' interaction with the environment and IIL.

3 Foreign Investments and Environment in South Asia

There are various instances in South Asian states where the regulation of foreign investment may translate into an ISDS case. Such cases may arise out of general regulation for the protection and preservation of the environment, or measures taken specifically to meet climate change goals.

In Bangladesh, for instance, the drilling activity undertaken by Niko Resources, a Canadian company, led to explosions causing damage to the gas field and the local environment. The incident led to a contract-based ICSID arbitration between Niko Resources and Bangladesh, where Niko Resources has been held liable to compensate for the damages caused to the local environment.[47] In another instance within Bangladesh, the construction of a coal-fired thermal power plant, in the vicinity of Sundarbans with substantial Indian investments, has met with local opposition due to its high potential of ravaging the ecosystem of Sundarbans – the world's largest tidal halophytic mangroves and a UNESCO world heritage site. Nevertheless, the Bangladesh government has continued with the construction of the thermal plant. Any future environmental regulation by the Bangladeshi government adversely affecting the investment has the potential of translating into an ISDS dispute under the India-Bangladesh BIT.[48]

In Sri Lanka, the 1.4-billion-dollar Chinese investment – the 'Colombo Port City Project' initiated in 2014 continues to face opposition due to alleged adverse environmental impacts. It is claimed that the activities such as 'extensive mining, reclamation of land, dredging shall alter the ocean current patterns in the regions putting the local marine ecosystem at risk.'[49] However, the Sri Lankan government has continued with the project. Most recently in 2018, India's largest copper

---

[45] Heath JB (2021) Eco Oro and the twilight of policy exceptionalism, IISD, 20 December 2021, https://www.iisd.org/itn/en/2021/12/20/eco-oro-and-the-twilight-of-policy-exceptionalism/.

[46] Heath JB (2021) Eco Oro and the twilight of policy exceptionalism, IISD, 20 December 2021, https://www.iisd.org/itn/en/2021/12/20/eco-oro-and-the-twilight-of-policy-exceptionalism/.

[47] *Niko Resources v. Bangladesh*, ICSID Case Nos. ARB/10/11 and ARB/10/18.

[48] See, Ranjan P, Anand P (2016) Regulating the Rampal Power Project could mean trouble under India-Bangladesh BIT, The Wire, 11 October 2016, https://thewire.in/environment/rampal-power-project-india-bangladesh-bit.

[49] Patrick A (2016) Revival of Colombo Port City Project: Implications for India. National Maritime Foundation, http://www.maritimeindia.org/View%20Profile/636131464409108056.pdf.

smelting plant owned by Sterlite Copper, a part of the multinational Vedanta Group, was permanently shut down by the Tamil Nadu government on the ground of flouting environmental norms, and damaging the health of the locals. Sterlite challenged the closure of the plant, which was upheld by the Madras High Court.[50] Presently the case is pending before the Indian Supreme Court. If the Supreme Court upholds the decision to shut down the copper plant, Vedanta Group based in the United Kingdom may file an investment claim under the India-UK BIT alleging indirect expropriation and violation of FET.

South Asian states are heavily dependent on fossil fuels for their energy needs. The energy sector in South Asia is the largest contributor to greenhouse emissions.[51] The shift to renewable, and low-carbon energy is the key to achieving sustainable development goals in low-income countries. The participation of the private parties through investment in the renewable energy sector has been recognized as important for the transition to sustainable energy consumption.[52] South Asian states have huge renewable energy potential and the sector is attracting considerable foreign investment. India for instance, attracted around 1.6 billion USD of investment in 2021–2022.[53] Similarly, Sri Lanka and Bangladesh are attracting major foreign investments in solar and wind energy.[54] Pakistan has recently decided against establishing any new coal-fired plant, and is now looking forward to Chinese investment in renewable energy.[55] However, this transition has to be done carefully. Tienhaara and Cotulla find that India and Pakistan have ten each, and Bangladesh has eleven foreign-owned coal-fired thermal plants.[56] For India 70 percent of such plants are protected by at least one BIT with ISDS mechanism; for Bangladesh, such coverage is 91 percent, and for Pakistan, 100 percent,[57] thus exposing these states to the risk of *RWE* and *Uniper-type* ISDS cases.

Additionally, there are possibilities of ISDS disputes of the kind initiated against Spain due to changes in renewable energy policies relating to incentives such as feed-in-tariff. In India, for instance, in 2019 the government of Andhra Pradesh

---

[50] *Vedanta Limited and Ors v. State of Tamil Nadu and Ors.*, Madras High Court, Judgment, 18 August 2020, https://www.livelaw.in/pdf_upload/pdf_upload-380108.pdf.

[51] Triyana M, (Claire) Li Y (2022) Green Energy Can Accelerate Sustainable Growth Across South Asia, World Bank Blogs, 19 October 2022, https://blogs.worldbank.org/endpovertyinsouthasia/green-energy-can-accelerate-sustainable-growth-across-south-asia.

[52] Article 6(4), Article 6(8), Paris Agreement to the United Nations Framework Convention on Climate Change, 2015.

[53] Garg V (2022) Renewable energy investment surges in India, IIEFA, 9 June 2022, https://ieefa.org/resources/renewable-energy-investment-surges-india.

[54] Sri Lanka eyes over $1 bn in FDI, The Economic Times, 3 June 2022 https://economictimes.indiatimes.com/news/international/business/sri-lanka-eyes-over-1-bn-in-fdi-including-from-adani-group/articleshow/91983308.cms?from=mdr.

[55] Analysis: China's shifting energy investments in Pakistan, from coal to renewables, Dawn, 23 November 2022, https://www.dawn.com/news/1722458.

[56] Tienhaara and Cotula (2020), p. 29.

[57] Tienhaara and Cotula (2020), p. 29.

ordered the cancellation of power purchase agreements (PPAs) entered into between various solar and wind energy companies, and the state power distribution companies (DISCOMs), asking for the tariff renegotiation on the ground that DISCOMs were facing financial strain.[58] This measure triggered a reaction from the Japanese ambassador to India asking the state government to reconsider its position, given the fact that Japanese investors have sizeable foreign investments in the renewable sector in Andhra Pradesh. The foreign investors also threatened the Indian government with arbitration.[59] The measure was challenged domestically and the Andhra Pradesh High Court ruled in favour of the renewable energy companies asking the DISCOMs and the government to honour the terms of the PPAs.[60] In an ISDS case of this kind, foreign investors may argue that the domestic regulation is not only inconsistent with the investment protection obligations under the investment treaty but also against their climate change mitigation obligations under the international environmental agreements, to strengthen their claim.[61]

As the South Asian countries develop further and adopt measures and policies aimed at stringent environmental protection, and climate change mitigation, it is possible that they may be subject to ISDS claims, as is reflected by the trend globally. Accordingly, the following section analyzes whether the South Asian states have sufficient regulatory space to adopt measures relating to environmental concerns.

4 Investment Treaties of South Asian States and Environmental Protection

The section maps and analyzes all the investment treaties (including the treaties which are not in force, and the treaties terminated yet operational due to sunset clause) of India, Pakistan, Bangladesh, Sri Lanka, Nepal, and Afghanistan.[62] This

[58] Clean energy project cancellations: Andhra faces global arbitration threat, Business Standard, 20 November 2019, https://www.business-standard.com/article/companies/andhra-scraps-clean-energy-projects-financiers-threaten-legal-action-119111901521_1.html.

[59] Clean energy project cancellations: Andhra faces global arbitration threat, Business Standard, 20 November 2019, https://www.business-standard.com/article/companies/andhra-scraps-clean-energy-projects-financiers-threaten-legal-action-119111901521_1.html.

[60] *Walwhan Renewable Energy Limited v. State of Andhra Pradesh & Ors.*, Writ Appeal No. 383 of 2019, High Court of Andhra Pradesh, 15 March 2022.

[61] Pang HH (2022) The Role of Investor-State Arbitration in Promoting Climate Change Mitigation: From "Shield" to "Sword" Through Renewable Energy Disputes. Working Paper, EUI AEL, 2022/05, European Society of International Law Paper, https://cadmus.eui.eu/handle/1814/74450.

[62] The chapter does not include Bhutan and Maldives, as Bhutan has not signed any BIT, and as Maldives' only BIT with UAE is not available in the public domain.

chapter categorizes the environmental provisions (EPs) based on the location where they are found in a BIT.[63] Of all the Indian BITs of India studied for mapping, only 32 BITs have some sort of EPs. For, Pakistan, out of 43 BITs only three BITs have EPs. Bangladesh has only two BITs out of 21 BITs studied, which have EPs. Sri Lanka has two, and Nepal has only one BIT having an EP.

4.1 EPs as Part of the Preamble

The preamble of any treaty is an important interpretative tool that forms a part of the overall context in which such a treaty is to be interpreted.[64] In the past, ISDS tribunals have relied on preambles referring to 'protection of investments' as the object and purpose of the treaty, to adopt an interpretation prioritizing investment protection.[65] Therefore, the use of language reflecting a commitment to protect the environment in the preamble broadens the context by including environmental protection, and sustainable development as one of the objects of the treaty. This, in turn, is capable of preventing an interpretation of the BIT that focusses only on the rights of the investor.

Of all the investment treaties of the South Asian states, only the India-Trinidad and Tobago BIT and the Bangladesh-Turkey (2012) BIT specifically mention the protection of the environment as an objective in their preamble. The India-Trinidad BIT in its preamble states that objectives of fostering, and protecting investments *'can be achieved without relaxing health, safety and environmental measures of general application.'*[66] An identical expression is found in the Bangladesh-Turkey (2012) BIT.[67] However, the recent Indian BITs signed with Brazil, Belarus, Kyrgyzstan, and Taiwan after the adoption of the 2016 Model BIT have included 'promotion of sustainable development' as one of the objectives of BIT in the preamble. Such preambular statements regarding environmental concerns have been referred to as non-operational EPs, as they do not create any substantive rights and obligations on the parties, despite being an integral part of the treaty.[68]

---

[63] See, Gordon K and Pohl J (2011) Environmental Concerns in International Investment Agreements: A Survey. OECD Working Papers on International Investment, 2011/01, https://www.oecd.org/daf/inv/investment-policy/WP-2011_1.pdf. The report formulated a seven-pronged typology based on the 'purposes' which the EPs in the BITs served. A similar study in context of the Chinese BITs uses a typology which is based on the location of these provisions, See, Chi (2015).

[64] Article 31(2), Vienna Convention on Law of Treaties 1969.

[65] *SGS v. Philippines,* ICSID Case No. ARB/02/6, Decision on Jurisdiction, 29 January 2004.

[66] Preamble, India-Trinidad and Tobago BIT.

[67] Preamble, Bangladesh-Turkey BIT (2012) – "*Being convinced that these objectives can be achieved without relaxing health, safety and environmental measures of general application as well as internationally recognized labor rights*".

[68] See, Chi (2015).

4.2 EPs as General Exceptions

As already pointed out, general exceptions clauses or non-precluded measures (NPM) clauses in investment treaties allow the host states to take regulatory measures aimed at protecting public policy objectives such as health, environment, labour rights, etc., which would otherwise be a violation of the obligations under the treaty.[69] The scope of an NPM clause depends on the permissible objectives,[70] the nexus requirement links,[71] and other conditions as reflected by the language of such provision.[72] The investment treaties generally contain two kinds of NPM provisions – first, modelled on the Article XX of the General Agreement on Tariffs and Trade (GATT); second, which are BIT specific and do not follow any specific model.

4.2.1 General Exception Clauses Modelled on Article XX of GATT

A small number of investment treaties of the South Asian countries are modelled on Article XX of GATT. Such provisions contain a number of permissible objectives, a nexus requirement, and a chapeau. The permissible objective relates to important public policy concerns such as the protection of public health, the environment, public morals, etc., for which the state can deviate from its treaty obligations. The nexus requirement establishes a causal relationship between the regulatory measures adopted and the permissible objective.

If regulatory measures fall under any of the listed exceptions under Article XX, it has to then satisfy the requirements of the chapeau which imposes two conditions – the measures should not be applied in a manner so as to constitute a means of arbitrary or unjustifiable discrimination against the foreign investors,[73] or it should not constitute a disguised restriction on investments of investors of a Party in the territory of the other Party. For instance, Article 10.18 of the India-Korea FTA investment chapter provides:

> Subject to the requirement that such measures are not applied in a manner which would constitute a means of arbitrary or unjustifiable discrimination between states where like conditions prevail, or a disguised restriction on investors and investments, nothing in this Chapter shall be construed to prevent the adoption or enforcement by any party of measures:
>
> ....
>
> b) necessary to protect human, animal or plant life or health, or the environment;

[69] For, an analysis of NPM clauses in the BITs of South Asia, see Sinha (2017).

[70] Sinha (2017).

[71] Sinha (2017).

[72] Sinha (2017).

[73] With respect to this requirement, the India-Korea FTA, India-Singapore FTA, ASEAN-Investment Agreement, and the Sri Lanka – Singapore FTA restrict it to situations where 'like conditions' prevail. The India-Colombia BIT does have any such limitation related to 'like conditions.'

....

e) necessary to conserve exhaustible natural resources if the measures are made effective in conjunction with restriction on domestic production or consumption.

In the above mentioned treaty provision, conserving exhaustible natural resources is a permissible objective. 'Necessary' represents the nexus requirement. Such clauses provide wide regulatory latitude to the host state for the protection of the environment, as well as the conservation of exhaustible natural resources. However, such measures need to satisfy the stricter test of necessity and steer clear of acting as arbitrary discrimination between investments of different states, or a disguised restriction on investments. The FTA investment chapters of Singapore and Korea with India, the ASEAN-India Investment Agreement and the India-Colombia BIT, and the investment chapter of the Sri Lanka-Singapore FTA, all five of them contain a comprehensive general exception clause based on Article XX of GATT.

However, unlike Article 10.18.1(b) of the India-Korea FTA, and Article 13.5 (c) of the India-Colombia BIT, the India-Singapore FTA investment chapter and the ASEAN-India Investment Agreement do not mention 'environment' in any of their permissible objectives. The relatively recent Sri Lanka-Singapore FTA also does not expressly refer to 'environment' in Article 10.23 (b), and (d), but the footnotes to both these clauses explain the parties' understanding that measures referred aforesaid clauses include environmental measures 'necessary to protect human, animal, plant life or health', and 'relating to the conservation of living and non-living exhaustible natural resources.'

Further, unlike India-Korea FTA which uses only 'necessary' as a nexus requirement for all permissible objectives, India-Colombia BIT uses a less strict 'relating to' as a nexus requirement for the 'protection of environment, and conservation of natural resources.'[74] Similarly, the ASEAN-India Investment Agreement, India-Singapore FTA, and Sri Lanka-Singapore FTA use 'relating to' for the conservation of natural resources.[75]

Further, while India-Korea FTA, India-Singapore FTA, Sri Lanka-Singapore FTA, and ASEAN-India investment agreement include a requirement of 'like conditions' in the chapeau, the India-Colombia BIT does not have any such requirement. Importantly after the adoption of the 2016 model BIT, the investment treaties signed by India do not contain clauses modelled exactly on article XX of GATT.

4.2.2 General Exceptions Clauses Not Modelled on Article XX of GATT

BITs also contain general exception clauses that are not based on Article XX of GATT. Such general exception clauses can further be categorized into two types, first those which refer to 'environmental protection' directly as a permissible objective, and second those that do not.

---

[74] Article 13.5(c), India-Colombia BIT.

[75] Article 21.1(e), ASEAN-India Investment Agreement; Article 6.11 (e), India-Singapore FTA.

Clauses Directly Referring to Environmental Protection

A rather small group of relatively recent investment treaties, such as FTA investment chapters of India with Korea, and Singapore, the India-Colombia BIT, and the BITs of Turkey with Pakistan and Bangladesh signed in 2012, use the term 'environment' expressly and provide a broad base for environmental regulation. For instance, Article 5.1 of the Bangladesh-Turkey BIT (2012) provides:

> Nothing in this Agreement shall be construed to prevent a Contracting Party from adopting, maintaining, or enforcing any non-discriminatory legal measures:
>
> (a) designed and applied for the protection of human, animal or plant life or health, or the environment;
> (b) related to the conservation of living or non-living exhaustible natural resources.

Pakistan-Turkey BIT (2012) contains an identical clause.[76] India-Singapore FTA investment chapter permits the regulatory bodies of the host State 'to adopt, maintain and enforce any measures on a non-discriminatory basis,' and judicial bodies 'to take any measure' to meet environmental concerns, provided that such measures are consistent with the rest of the investment chapter.[77] India-Korea FTA investment chapter has a similar provision without the requirement of non-discrimination.[78] Further, while the India-Singapore FTA investment chapter makes the regulatory measures subject to its consistency 'only with the investment chapter' of the FTA, the India-Korea FTA investment chapter requires such measures to be consistent with 'the entire FTA' i.e., not only the investment chapter but the entire agreement including that on trade, intellectual property, etc.[79] This increases the threshold for justification in any ISDS case for the host State. It is also doubtful whether an ISDS tribunal constituted under the investment chapter of the FTA would have the jurisdiction to decide the compliance of the regulatory measure in question with the other chapters of the FTA.

Interestingly, Article 4.2 of Bangladesh-Turkey BIT (2012) also provides the host States with the right 'to exercise all legal measures in case any loss, destruction or damage occurs to. . .the environment' due to the investments of the investors.[80] The right of the host States in this case apparently, shall be triggered only when some environmental loss or damage occurs. This provision, arguably, can act as the legal basis for bringing counter-claims as a legal measure against the investors in an arbitration, where investors have caused damage to the environment by their activities. The right of the host state to take all legal measures can be interpreted as including the right to invoke a counterclaim in case of environmental damage.

[76] Article 5.1, Pakistan-Turkey BIT (2012).

[77] Article 6.10, India-Singapore FTA.

[78] Article 10.16, India-Korea FTA.

[79] Article 10.16.1, India-Korea FTA.

[80] Article 4.2, Bangladesh-Turkey BIT (2012).

Clauses Not Referring to the Environment Directly

Most of the BITs of the South Asian states have NPM clauses that do not directly refer to the term 'environment', nonetheless are relevant in the context of environmental protection. For instance, the Pakistan-Mauritius BIT allows the parties to apply prohibitions or restrictions which are '*directed to the protection of...the protection of public health or the prevention of diseases and pests in animals or plants*.'[81]

The majority of the BITs of the South Asian states fall in this category.[82] Further, most of the Indian BITs use similar formulations of the permissible objectives for which states can derogate from their obligations subject to certain general conditions of good faith and non-discrimination.[83] Interestingly, India-Bosnia BIT also explains 'non-discriminatory' treatment as '*giving the same treatment to all investors in the like situations*,'[84] thus setting the threshold a bit higher for the states to invoke the exception. Such an explanation is not present in any other BITs of India or of any other South Asian state. Some Indian BITs also confine the scope of application of the exception only in the '*circumstances of extreme emergency*' which substantially limits the opportunity for the host state to invoke the exception.[85] On the other hand, Pakistan – Singapore BIT allows the host states to apply prohibitions or restrictions of any kind which is directed to 'prevention of diseases and pest in animals and plants'[86] without any conditions of 'non-discrimination' or 'good faith' etc. Similar is the case with Sri Lanka – China BIT which allows the States to apply prohibitions or restrictions or take any action that is directed to the 'prevention of diseases and pests in animals.'[87]

[81] Article 12, Pakistan – Mauritius BIT.

[82] Article 12, India-Bosnia BIT; Article 12, India-Czech BIT; Article 12, India-France BIT; Article 10.2, India-Korea BIT; Article 10.2, India-Malaysia BIT; Article 11.3, India-Mauritius BIT; Article 12, India-Netherlands BIT; Article 3.3, India-Russia BIT; Article 13.2, India-Spain BIT; Article 12, India-Italy BIT; Article 12, India-Germany BIT; Article 12.2, India-Denmark BIT; Article 12, India-BLEU BIT; Article 15, India-Australia BIT; Article 14, India-Kuwait BIT; Article 13, India-Senegal BIT; ASEAN-India Investment Agreement; Article 12, Pakistan-Mauritius BIT; Article 11, Pakistan-Singapore BIT; Article 11, Sri Lanka-China BIT; Article 5.1, Bangladesh-Turkey BIT (2012).

[83] India-Bosnia BIT; India-Czech BIT; India-France BIT; India-Malaysia BIT; India-Mauritius BIT; India-Netherlands BIT; India-Spain BIT; India-Italy BIT; India-Russia BIT; India-Denmark BIT; India-Australia BIT; India-Kuwait BIT; India-Germany BIT; India-BLEU BIT; India-Senegal BIT.

[84] Article 12 of the India-Bosnia BIT.

[85] Article 12, India-Bosnia BIT; Such formulation is also present in the following BITs: India-Czech BIT; India-France BIT; India-India-Malaysia BIT; India-Spain BIT; India-Denmark BIT; India-Kuwait BIT.

[86] Article 11, Pakistan-Singapore BIT.

[87] Article 11, Sri-Lanka-China BIT.

General Exception Clauses Post-2016 Model Indian BIT

Article 32.1 of the 2016 model Indian BIT provides the following general exceptions clause:

> Nothing in this Treaty shall be construed to prevent the adoption or enforcement by a Party of measures of general applicability applied on a non-discriminatory basis that are necessary to:
>
> ...
>
> (ii) protect human, animal or plant life or health;
>
> ...
>
> (iv) protect and conserve the environment, including all living and non-living natural resources;
>
> ...

This provision enables the host state to take non-discriminatory regulatory measures which are necessary to protect and conserve the environment irrespective of whether such measures are inconsistent with the obligations under the BIT. Interestingly, a footnote in the BIT makes it clear that in considering whether a measure is "*necessary*", the tribunal *shall take into account whether there was no less restrictive alternative measure reasonably available to a Party.* Therefore, in a way, the model BIT clearly has adopted the approach of the tribunal in *Continental Casualty v. Argentina*[88] by providing an explanation in the text of the BIT itself.[89] This is important as it eliminates any chance of different interpretations by the tribunal, given the widely diverse views regarding the interpretation of 'necessary'.[90] This instills clarity and eliminates arbitral discretion, something which is absent in the previous investment treaties of South Asian states which use 'necessary' as a nexus requirement.

Important to note that while structurally Article 32.1 appears modelled on article XX of GATT, it is different as it does not contain the twin conditions present in the chapeau of GATT article XX type clause such as the one in India-Colombia BIT. The absence of these conditions affords greater regulatory power to the host state, which arguably could also be abused, and will be subject to lesser scrutiny by the arbitral tribunals in an ISDS case.[91] Similar provisions are present in the newer BITs which India has signed with Belarus,[92] Kyrgyzstan,[93] Taiwan,[94] and Brazil.[95]

[88] *Continental Casualty v. Argentina,* ICSID Case No. ARB/03/9.

[89] Ranjan (2020).

[90] See, Kurtz (2010).

[91] See, Ranjan (2022).

[92] Article 32.1, India-Belarus BIT.

[93] Article 32.1, India-Kyrgyzstan BIT.

[94] Article 31.1, India-Taiwan BIT.

[95] Article 23, India-Brazil BIT.

Interestingly, the India-Brazil BIT also has a separate '*provision on investment and environment, labor affairs and health*.'[96] It enables the host state to adopt measures to ensure that investment activity is undertaken in accordance with its environmental law. However, such measures must not constitute 'means of arbitrary or unjustifiable discrimination or a disguised restriction.'[97]

4.3 EPs as an Exception to National Treatment, Expropriation, and Performance Requirement

Some investment treaties contain exceptions to specific substantive obligations such as national treatment (NT), most-favoured nation treatment, or fair and equitable treatment. Such exception is different from the general exceptions clause which is applicable to the entire treaty. The study of the investment treaties of South Asian states reveals that EPs are present in form of exceptions to NT, expropriation, and performance requirement clause.

4.3.1 Exception to National Treatment

The NT provision in the ASEAN-India Investment Agreement has an environment-related exception, which provides that the '*extension of financial assistance or measures taken by the host State in favour of its investors and their investments in pursuit of legitimate public purpose including the protection of health, safety, the environment shall not be considered as a violation of national treatment obligations*.'[98]

Such an exception is helpful in allowing the host state to pursue climate change mitigation objectives. It allows the state to incentivize or provide financial assistance to its domestic firms for adapting to cleaner technology leading to reduction in carbon emissions. Even if the host state does not extend such incentives or assistance to foreign investors in the same sector, it will not amount to a violation of the NT obligation. Unfortunately, none of the other investment treaties of the South Asian states has such an exception.

Interestingly, while the ASEAN-India investment agreement directly carves an exception from the NT obligation, the 2016 model Indian BIT adopts an indirect route. Article 4 of the 2016 Model BIT prohibits the host states from according more favourable treatment to its domestic investors compared to foreign investors in 'like circumstances.' However, a footnote explains that for determining the likeness of circumstances for foreign and domestic investors/investments, a totality of

[96] Article 22.1, India-Brazil BIT.
[97] Article 22.1, India-Brazil BIT.
[98] Article 3.5, ASEAN-India Investment Agreement.

circumstances has to be taken into consideration, which includes 'the actual and potential impact of the investment on third persons, local community, or the environment.'

This means that a host state can decide to treat domestic and foreign investors differently on the ground that foreign investor despite operating in the same sector has a greater adverse impact on the environment. For instance, a state can provide more incentives or subsidies to a domestic firm using clean energy for manufacturing products, in comparison to foreign investors relying on traditional energy sources for production. If such a regulatory measure is challenged in ISDS, the differential impact on the environment will become an important factor pointing to non-likeness and hence shielding the host state's regulatory measure. The ASEAN-India Investment Agreement also lists certain factors for determining the likeness of circumstance but does not include 'impact on environment' as determining factor. In any case, a clear and direct exception provides greater regulatory autonomy to protect and preserve the environment.

4.3.2 Exceptions to Expropriation Clause

Several investment treaties of South Asian states have environmental exceptions in the expropriation provision – fifteen Indian BITs have EPs as an exception to expropriation, Pakistan, Bangladesh, and Nepal have one BIT each having an exception to expropriation in favour of environmental regulation by the host state. However, there are variations in the language of such provisions. For example, Article 4(3) of the India-Saudi Arabia BIT, provides:

> This article shall not be construed to prevent a Contracting Party from taking a regulatory action, for the public benefit of that Contracting Party on a non-discriminatory basis, to protect legitimate public welfare objectives, such as health, safety, and the environment.

Such exceptions are present in the BITs of India with Nepal and Colombia, and the BITs of Turkey with Bangladesh and Pakistan.[99] Some BITs, on the other hand, have interpretive annexes explaining how the provision related to expropriation should be interpreted. Such annexes also contain environmental exceptions. For example, para 3 of annexure A of the Indian-Jordan BIT provides:

> Except in rare circumstances, non-discriminatory regulatory actions by a Party that are designed and applied to protect legitimate public welfare objectives including health, safety and the environment concerns do not constitute expropriation or nationalization.

Similar exceptions, excluding environment-related measures from the purview of expropriation except in 'rare circumstances' exist in interpretative Annexes of

[99] See Article 6.2(c), India-Colombia BIT; Article 5.2(c), India-Nepal BIT; Article 6.2, Bangladesh-Turkey BIT (2012); Article 6.2, Pakistan-Turkey BIT (2012).

several BITs.[100] Such provisions are significant as they will protect the host states even when their regulatory measure aimed at protecting the environment leads to substantial deprivation of the investment.[101] For instance, if the dispute relating to the closure of Sterlite Copper pursuant to the order of the Tamil Nadu government in India on the ground of adversely impacting the environment, were to translate into an ISDS dispute, such an exception could become a tangible defense for the host state against investor's claim of indirect expropriation. Simultaneously, however, the interpretation of such an exception would also require giving meaning to the term 'except in rare circumstance' as found in most of the Indian BITs. The meaning of the term 'except in rare circumstances' is explained in only two investment treaties, first India-Brunei BIT, which explains 'rare circumstances' as situations 'when a measure or series of measures is so severe in the light of the purpose that they cannot be reasonably be viewed as having been adopted and applied in good faith;'[102] and second, India-Korea FTA investment chapter, according to which 'rare circumstance' implies that 'a measure or series of measures is extremely severe or disproportionate in light of its purpose or effect.'

In other words, an arbitral tribunal would have to compare the impact of the regulatory measure with the purpose or object such measure seeks to achieve – which makes it somewhat akin to a proportionality review.[103] Similar meaning arguably can be given to 'rare circumstances' in the BITs where it has not been defined. Additionally, there are certain interpretative annexes[104] that do not contain 'rare circumstance' limitations.

Interestingly, the India-Japan FTA investment chapter[105] does not specifically recognize measures taken to protect the environment as an exception to the expropriation. It provides that 'objectives of the government action, including whether such action is taken for legitimate public objectives such as. . .protecting and preserving environment' shall be taken into consideration while deciding in a fact-based inquiry whether a given action or series of actions amounts to indirect expropriation.[106] In other words, an environmental regulatory measure becomes a factor that has to be considered by the tribunal under the India-Japan FTA investment chapter, for determining whether indirect expropriation has occurred.

Lastly, some BITs state that the actions and awards by the judicial bodies of a host state addressing environment-related issues shall be immune from the claim of

[100] See, Para 3, Annex, India-Iceland BIT; Para 3, Annex, India-Syria BIT; Clause II(d), Protocol, India-Brunei BIT; Para 3, Annexure 5.1, India-Senegal BIT; Para 3, Annexure, India-Mozambique BIT; Ad Article 5(4)(c), Protocol, India-Latvia BIT; Para 3, Annex, India-Lithuania BIT; Para 3, Protocol, India-Slovenia BIT; Para 3(b), Annex 10-A, Ch 10, India-Korea CEPA.

[101] See Ranjan (2022).

[102] Article 5, India-Brunei BIT.

[103] See, Ranjan (2022).

[104] See, Para 3, Annex, India-Trinidad BIT; Para 4, Annex 10-1, Ch 10, India-Malaysia FTA.

[105] Annex 10, Ch 8, India-Japan FTA.

[106] See, Annex 10, India-Japan FTA.

expropriation. For example, Para 4 of Annex A to the India-Jordan BIT provides that, '*actions and awards by judicial bodies of a Party that are designed, applied or issued in public interest including those designed to address health, safety and environmental concerns do not constitute expropriation or nationalization.*' The effect of this provision is to exclude such judicial awards and decisions which are issued in furtherance of the promotion of environmental objectives, which may have an adverse impact on foreign investments and therefore may be susceptible to expropriation claims. Many other BITs have similar provisions.[107]

Further, the 2016 model India BIT under Article 5.5 also creates a specific exception to the expropriation provision. It makes non-discriminatory regulatory measures taken by a host state or measures or awards taken by the judicial body of the host state, designed and applied to protect the environment, immune to the claim of expropriation. All the Indian BITs signed post-adoption of the model BIT contain an identical clause.[108]

4.3.3 Exceptions to Performance Requirement

Performance requirements are 'stipulations, imposed on investors, requiring them to meet certain specified goals with respect to their operations in the host country.'[109] Alternatively, PRs are measures that require foreign investors to act in a certain way or to achieve certain economic or non-economic goals within the host state.[110]

The BITs of India with Kuwait[111] and the United Arab Emirates,[112] both contain an exception with respect to the environmental protection in the performance requirement provisions. The India-Kuwait BIT specifically mentions 'environment' related measures as an exception to the performance requirement obligations under Article 4 which provides:

> Once established investment shall not be subjected in the host Contracting State to additional performance requirements which may hinder or restrict their expansion or maintenance or adversely affect or be considered as detrimental to their viability, unless such requirements

[107] See, Article 5.2(d), India-Nepal BIT; Para 4, Protocol to India-Slovenia BIT; Article 6.2(d), India-Colombia BIT; Para 4, Annex, India-Lithuania BIT; Para 4, Annexure, India-Mozambique BIT; Para 4, Annex 5.1, India-Senegal BIT; Para 4, Annex, India-Syria BIT; Para 4, Annex, India-Iceland BIT; Para 4, Annex, India-Trinidad BIT.

[108] Article 6.4, India-Brazil BIT; Article 5.5, India-Kyrgyzstan BIT; Article 5.5, India-Belarus BIT; Article 5.5, India-Taiwan BIT.

[109] UNCTAD (2003) Foreign Direct Investment and Performance Requirements: New Evidence from Selected Countries. http://unctad.org/en/docs/iteiia20037_en.pdf.

[110] Nikiema SH (2014) Performance Requirements in Investment Treaties. IISD, https://www.iisd.org/system/files/publications/best-practices-performance-requirements-investment-treaties-en.pdf.

[111] Article 4.4, India-Kuwait BIT.

[112] Article 4.3, India-UAE BIT.

> are deemed vital for reasons of public order, public health or environmental concerns and are enforced by law of general application.[113]

Accordingly, in the post-establishment stage, the general obligation of the state is not to impose any performance requirement which may be detrimental to the viability of the investment. However, if considered important for the purpose of promoting or protecting the environment, additional performance requirements may be imposed on the investment. This exception provides the host state with policy space to impose a requirement for achieving health and environmental goals. For instance, the host state may stipulate that a foreign investor will have to procure a certain portion of its energy requirement from renewable sources. Even if the cost of renewable energy is higher in comparison to that of non-renewable sources, and might be a burden for the investors, such a requirement will not be a violation of the treaty obligations as it contributes to the climate change goals by reducing the carbon emissions.

4.4 EPs as 'Non-Lowering of Environmental Standards' Clause

A few investment treaties in South Asia restrict the host states from relaxing their environmental measures to attract investment. In other words, rather than creating a right for either investor or state, it requires the host state to refrain from relaxing environmental norms to attract foreign investment. It has often been argued, and in some cases empirically tested that relaxed environmental standards attract more foreign investment. For instance, Xing and Kolstad, find that laxity of environmental regulation in the host country was a 'significant determinant' for outward US FDI from heavily polluting industries.[114] Similarly, a recent study in the context of India finds that the strength of environmental governance does not necessarily affect the decisions relating to FDI.[115]

Further, in the context of South Asia generally, based on the positive linkage between the FDI and CO_2 emissions, it has been argued that the pollution haven hypothesis (i.e., that the firms will try to avoid the cost of strict environmental regulations by shifting productions in regions with lower environmental standards) holds true for this region.[116] There is a general perception among the states that lowering the environmental standards would attract more FDI. A few investment treaties in this region aim to counter this race to the bottom in terms of environmental measures for attracting FDI.

For instance, article 99 of the India-Japan FTA investment chapter provides – *Each Party recognises that it is inappropriate to encourage investment activities in*

---

[113] Article 4.4, India-Kuwait BIT.

[114] Xing and Kolstad (2002).

[115] Kathuria (2018).

[116] Musah et al. (2022).

its Area of investors of the other Party by relaxing its environmental measures. To this effect each Party should not waive or otherwise derogate from such environmental measures as an encouragement for establishment, acquisition or expansion of investments in its Area. It is pertinent to note that the India-Korea FTA investment chapter[117] has a similar provision under article 10.16.2 except for one addition that '*if a Party considers that the other Party has offered such an encouragement, it may request consultations with the other Party and the Parties shall consult with a view to avoiding any such encouragement.*' In other words, India-Korea FTA provides a mechanism for the implementation of this provision in case there is a derogation.

Bangladesh-Turkey (2012) BIT has a similar provision requiring the host state to refrain from waiving or derogating from its environmental policies as an encouragement to attract environment, however without any implementation procedure.[118]

Similarly, Article 2(2) of the Bangladesh-Denmark BIT states that 'investment objective should be achieved without relaxing health, safety and environmental measures of general application.' Interestingly, the second line of Article 2(2) gives an enforceable right of adequate and effective compensation to the host State if it suffers destruction or damage in respect of the environment. This compensation has to be accorded under the laws and regulations of the host or if necessary, under international law. By referring to compensation payable under international law, this provision indirectly opens an avenue for counter-claims by the host State in the event an ISDS case is brought under this BIT. Further, Article 22.2 of the India-Brazil BIT contains a 'non-lowering of standards' provision similar to the one present India-Korea FTA with a consultation mechanism.

4.5 Environmental Regulation in Absence of EPs: Police Powers Doctrine

A vast majority of the treaties of South Asian states do not contain any EP. In such cases, the states may rely on the police powers doctrine to shield their environmental regulation from the claims of expropriation. The doctrine of police powers entails that a *bona fide*, non-discriminatory measure taken for public purpose does not amount to indirect expropriation, and there is no obligation to compensate. While the exact scope and content of the police powers are far from settled,[119] the *Methanex v. United States* provides most articulate content of the doctrine: "*as a matter of general international law, a non-discriminatory regulation for a public purpose, which is enacted in accordance with due process and, which affects, inter*

[117] Article 10.16.2, India-Korea FTA.

[118] Article 4.1, Bangladesh-Turkey BIT (2012).

[119] See, Ranjan and Anand (2017).

alios, a foreign investor or investment is not deemed expropriatory and compensable unless specific commitments had been given by the regulating government."[120] Despite the debate as to whether the police power doctrine amounts to customary international law or the general principle of international law,[121] the fact remains that the doctrine is increasingly being accepted and acted upon in the arbitral jurisprudence relating to the environment and public health.[122] Most recently, the tribunal in *Eco Oro v. Colombia,* held that the ban on gold and silver mining in the Santurban *páramo* does not amount to indirect expropriation as it was a valid exercise of the police powers of the state aimed at the preservation of the environment.[123]

5 New Developments in South Asia

As d'Aspremont and Köppen put it, IIL is facing two main forms of contestations, first directed toward the reform of the universal IIL regime by making adjustments in the rules to strike a proper balance between the rights and obligations of both the foreign investors and the host states, which they refer as an attempt towards 'global reform' and second, reflected in the attempts of individual States or regions to emancipate themselves from the existing universal IIL regime to which they have hitherto been subjected to and have had sour experiences, characterized as the attempts of 'regional emancipation'.[124] Certain regions from the third world, such as Latin America, and Africa have been proactive in mounting a resistance to the extant IIL regime and re-imagining the contents of IIL. Unfortunately, South Asia lags behind in this movement. The only outlier in the region seems to be India. India has the greatest number of ISDS cases filed against it compared to other states in the region. India's experience with ISDS prompted it to revise its investment treaty programme and adopt a new model BIT in 2016. Importantly, while other states such as Pakistan, Bangladesh, and Sri Lanka have all been at the receiving end of the ISDS, they are yet to launch a full-fledged overhauling of their investment treaty programme. There are two new innovations by the 2016 model BIT. First, the inclusion of a soft investor obligation provision. Second, a slight experiment with the ISDS clause. We look at both these features in the following sections.

[120] *Methanex v. United States,* (2005) 44 ILM 1345, Final Award of the Tribunal on Jurisdiction and Merits, Part IV, Chapter D, Page 4.

[121] See, Kurtz (2014); Titi (2018).

[122] See, *Philip Morris v. Uruguay*, ICSID Case No. ARB/10/7; *Chemtura v. Canada,* NAFTA (2010).

[123] *Eco Oro Minerals v. Colombia,* ICSID Case No. ARB/16/41.

[124] See, D'Aspremont and Köppen (2017).

5.1 Inclusion of Investor Obligations

One of the main reasons for the backlash against the IIL is the asymmetrical rights and obligations of the investors and the host states, wherein the investors are the recipient of rights enforceable under international law without any corresponding international obligations. However, the newer generation of investment treaties is attempting to address this asymmetry by including provisions imposing some kind of obligations on the investors under the BITs. While only a few BITs include mandatory and enforceable investor obligations under the BITs, most have resorted to hortatory and soft obligations on the investors with questionable enforcement possibilities. The 2016 model BIT falls in the latter category.

Article 12 of the model BIT contains a provision on 'corporate social responsibility' which states:

> Investors and their enterprises operating within the territory the *host state* shall endeavour to voluntarily incorporate internationally recognized standards of corporate social responsibility in their practices and internal policies, such as statements of principles that have been endorsed or are supported by the Parties. These principles may address issues such as labour, the environment, human rights, community relations and anti-corruptions.

This may be noted that although the provision is in the form of a best endeavour clause, without any implementation mechanism. Similar provisions exist in India-Belarus BIT,[125] India-Taiwan BIT,[126] and India-Kyrgyzstan BIT.[127] The CSR provision in India-Brazil BIT states that investors and the investments shall 'endeavour to contribute to economic, social, and environmental progress aiming at achieving sustainable development'[128] and 'refrain from seeking or accepting exemptions that are not established on the legal or regulatory framework relating to. . .environment.'[129]

5.2 EPs in the ISDS Clause

The model BIT has also given some space to the environment in the ISDS provision. Under article 25 of the model BIT, the arbitral tribunal has been empowered, although subject to the approval of the parties, '*to appoint experts to report to it in writing on any factual issue concerning environment. . . .*' The tribunal in an ISDS case related to the environment may require expert analysis to analyze the extent of damage caused to the environment by the activities of the foreign investor, and to

[125] Article 12, India-Belarus BIT.
[126] Article 12, India-Taiwan BIT.
[127] Article 12, India-Kyrgyzstan BIT.
[128] Article 12.2(a), India-Brazil BIT.
[129] Article 12.2(e), India-Brazil BIT.

establish a causal link between the environmental damage and the activities of the investor. This is important to note that although the disputing parties have the right to disapprove the appointment of an expert by the tribunal, the exercise of such right must be subjected to pressing reasons. India-Kyrgyzstan BIT,[130] India – Taiwan BIT,[131] and India-Belarus BIT,[132] all based on the 2016 model BIT, have identical clauses.

Lastly, in footnote 4 to article 26.3 of the model BIT under the ISDS chapter, *'any unremedied harm or damage that the investor has caused to the environment or local community'* has been included as a mitigating factor, which may be considered by the arbitral tribunal while calculating the monetary damages to be awarded to the investor. This provision indirectly will enable the host state to bring a counter-claim against the foreign investor for the damages to the environment, and the breach of domestic environmental norms.[133]

6 Conclusion and Future Pathways

The study of the investment treaties of the states in South Asia presents a grim picture of the EPs. India has the maximum number of investment treaties which contain some form of EPs, while for other states in the region, the number is meagre. The existing EPs take various forms – general exceptions; exceptions to specific provisions such as expropriation, performance requirement, and national treatment; non-lowering of standards clause; and preambles. However, the significantly low number of EPs is worrying causing a major loss of space for environmental regulation.

The South Asian states continue to attract significant foreign investments in various sectors, and they do not seem to be disengaging completely from the IIL regime. Therefore, it is imperative that states in South Asia should actively engage in reviewing their investment treaties to bring them in line with sustainable development goals and climate change objectives. Importantly, these states should actively engage at the ISDS Working Group – III to voice their views and position, as done by various other countries which continue to challenge the piecemeal approach toward reform of IIL in favour of a more radical reform of the IIL regime. This is important as cases such as *Eco Oro v. Colombia* expose the limitations of exceptions and carve-outs as tools to further environmental concerns within IIL, thanks to the arbitral (in)discretion.

The negotiations of new investment treaties must prioritize sustainable development, climate change, environmental protection, labour, and human rights, as the

[130] Article 25, India-Kyrgyzstan BIT.
[131] Article 23, India-Taiwan BIT.
[132] Article 25, India-Belarus BIT.
[133] Ranjan (2022).

core around which the investment protection rules should be framed. Standalone provisions on environmental and climate change flexibilities should be negotiated in addition to provision-specific exceptions. The states must also attempt at restricting the benefit of investment treaties to fossil fuel investors in their investment treaties. While this may appear politically infeasible, at least tabling these issues on the negotiating table will go a long way in consolidating the state practice. Further, mandatory international obligations for foreign investors and procedural rules clearly empowering the host states to bring counterclaims will not only ensure effective regulatory autonomy, but also an avenue for access to environmental justice for these states, and local communities therein. These attempts must be made in conjunction with the creation of a robust and effective domestic environmental governance framework.

References

Alshner W, Hui K (2018) Missing in action: general public policy exceptions in investment treaties. In: Sach L et al (eds) Yearbook on international investment law and policy. Oxford University Press

Chaisse J, Jusoh S (2016) The ASEAN Comprehensive Investment Agreement: the regionalization of laws and policy on foreign investments. Edward Elgar

Chi M (2015) The 'Greenization' of Chinese BITs: an empirical study of the environmental provisions in Chinese BITs and its implications for Chinese future BIT-making. J Int Econ Law 18(3):511–542

Cho S, Kurtz J (2016) The limits of isomorphism: global investment law and the ASEAN investment regime. Chic J Int Law 17:341

D'Aspremont J, Köppen A (2017) Global reform vs regional emancipation: the principles on international investment for sustainable development in Africa. Eur J Int Law 6(2)

Ghouri AA, Mahmood N (2012) Deciphering Pakistan's foreign investment policy: a review of Pakistani BITs. J World Invest Trade 13:812–873

Kathuria V (2018) Does environmental governance matter for foreign direct investment? Testing the pollution haven hypothesis for Indian states. Asian Dev Rev 35(1):222

Kurtz J (2010) Adjudging the exceptional at international investment law: security, public order and financial crisis. Int Comp Law Q 59(2):325–371

Kurtz J (2014) Building legitimacy through interpretation. In: Douglas Z et al (eds) The foundations of international investment law: bringing theory into practice. Oxford University Press

Moehlecke C (2020) The chilling effect of international investment disputes: limited challenges to state sovereignty. Int Stud Q 64:1–12

Musah M et al (2022) Reinvestigating the pollution haven hypothesis: the nexus between foreign direct investments and environmental quality in G-20 countries. Environ Sci Pollut Res 29: 31330–31347

Pathirana D (2016) An overview of Sri Lanka's bilateral investment treaties: status quo and some insights into future modifications. Asian J Int Law 7(2):287–318

Perrone NM (2021) Investment treaties and the legal imagination: how foreign investors play by their own rules. Oxford University Press

Ranjan P (2020) 'Necessary' in non-precluded measures provisions in bilateral investment treaties: the Indian contribution. Neth Int Law Rev 67(3):473–521

Ranjan P (2022) Bilateral investment treaties and environment (on file with author)

Ranjan P, Anand P (2017) The 2016 Model Indian Bilateral Investment – a critical deconstruction. Northwest J Int Law Bus 38(1):1–55
Ranjan P, Anand P (2018) How 'Healthy' are the Investment Treaties of South Asian Countries: an empirical study of public health provisions in South Asian Countries' BITs and FTA investment chapters. ICSID Rev - Foreign Invest Law J 33(2):406–432
Sabir S et al (2020) FDI and environmental degradation: the role of political institutions in South Asian countries'. Environ Sci Pollut Res 27:32544–32553
Sahoo P et al (2014) Foreign direct investment in South Asia policy, impact, determinants and challenges. Springer
Sinha AK (2017) Non-precluded measures provisions in bilateral investment treaties of South Asian countries. Asian J Int Law 7(2):227–263
Tienhaara K, Cotula L (2020) Raising the cost of climate action? Investor-state dispute settlement and compensation for stranded fossil fuel assets. IIED, London
Tienharra K (2018) Regulatory chill in a warming world: the threat to climate policy posed by investor-state dispute settlement. Transnatl Environ Law 7(2):229–250
Titi C (2018) Police powers doctrine and international investment law. In: Fontanelli F, Andrea Gattini A, Tanzi A (eds) General principles of law and international investment arbitration. Brill, pp 323–343
Viñuales JE (2012) Foreign investment and the environment in international law. Cambridge University Press
Xing Y, Kolstad CD (2002) Do Lax environmental regulations attract foreign investment? Environ Resour Econ 21:1–22

Pushkar Anand is Doctoral Research Candidate at the Macquarie Law School, Macquarie University, Sydney, and Assistant Professor (currently on leave) at the Faculty of Law, University of Delhi, India. He received his LL.M. in international legal studies from the South Asian University, New Delhi. His research is focused in the field of public international law, international investment law, and business and human rights. He has also been empaneled as an external consultant for matters relating to international investment law by the Centre for Trade and Investment Law, Ministry of Commerce and Industry, Government of India.

Part II
Regional Trade Agreements

The Interplay of IPEF Between RCEP and CPTPP: An ASEAN Viewpoint

Intan Murnira Ramli, Tomy Waskitho, and Michelle Chandra Kasih

Contents

Abstract ASEAN has emerged as a significant player in the Indo-Pacific region, as evidenced by its active engagement in major multilateral arrangements such as the Regional Comprehensive Economic Partnership (RCEP), Comprehensive and Progressive Agreement for Trans-Pacific Partnership (CPTPP), and the latest addition, the Indo-Pacific Economic Framework (IPEF). IPEF has involved 7 out of 10 ASEAN Member States (AMS) as the initial members, making it apparent that ASEAN's significance and role cannot be overlooked in the economic and security architecture of the region. This paper aims to investigate the interplay of IPEF between RCEP and CPTPP while at the same time examining the current debates and criticisms toward it. We also analysed IPEF's potential to foster a positive and prosperous economic environment that brings practical benefits to ASEAN. Despite IPEF being one of the interests among ASEAN policymakers, there has been insufficient discussion that systematically investigates the interplay of IPEF, RCEP, and CPTPP within ASEAN's perspective, and the understanding of it seems to be limited. Thus, this paper is intended to contribute to the knowledge and nascent debate on the current geo-economic literature in the Indo-Pacific.

I. M. Ramli (✉), T. Waskitho, and M. C. Kasih
Economic Research Institute for ASEAN and East Asia (ERIA), Jakarta, Indonesia
e-mail: intan@eria.org

M. Bungenberg et al. (eds.), *Asian Yearbook of International Economic Law 2023*,
Asian Yearbook of International Economic Law (2023) 2023: 135–152,
https://doi.org/10.1007/16517_2023_23, Published online: 22 June 2023

1 Introduction: The Overview of IPEF, RCEP, and CPTPP

ASEAN has become a hotspot and attractive for multilateral arrangements, and its members have increasingly recognized the importance of promoting regional cooperation. Currently, there are three biggest regional arrangements, the Comprehensive and Progressive Agreement for Trans-Pacific Partnership (CPTPP), the Regional Comprehensive Economic Partnership (RCEP), and the latest addition, the Indo-Pacific Economic Framework for Prosperity (IPEF) where most of the ASEAN Member States are participating. In the first few years of the 2020s, in the middle of supply chain disruption triggered by the COVID-19 pandemic, contrasting economic arrangements have taken shape. On the trade front, Regional Comprehensive Economic Partnership (RCEP) came into effect with ten ASEAN members and five regional partners (Australia, China, Japan, New Zealand, and South Korea), while the Comprehensive and Progressive Agreement for the Trans-Pacific Partnership (CPTPP) was in effect since 2018 and received several new accession applicants including China and Taiwan. The United States, having opted out of the two agreements, then proposed the Indo-Pacific Economic Framework (IPEF) with the other 13 members of the Indo-Pacific in late May 2022 during President Biden's visit to Tokyo for the Quad Summit. The IPEF pursues coalition building in the region with a modular approach for the participants to choose from the four areas of economic cooperation. The IPEF also aims to design the "rules of the road" in the Indo-pacific.[1] The Indo-Pacific region is home to 60% of the world's population[2] and will contribute most significantly to global growth over the next three decades.

In contrast to RCEP and CPTPP, which are primarily based on economic considerations and are a form of Free Trade Agreement (FTA), IPEF, as the White House stated, is not an FTA or merely economic-based either.[3] It was explained that IPEF aims to address the gaps flowing from both CPTPP and RCEP, i.e., seeking cooperation on the digital economy, supply chain resilience, decarbonization, infrastructure, and labour measures, and promoting the highest possible standards in these areas.[4] Additionally, it also aims to fill the void that was created when the U.S. left the Trans-Pacific Partnership (TPP).

Below is the detailed table of the participating members of the three multilateral arrangements (see Fig. 1 and Table 1), with some ASEAN Member States (AMS) participating in all three arrangements, such as Brunei, Malaysia, Singapore, and Vietnam. On the other hand, Cambodia, Lao PDR, and Myanmar only participated

[1] The White House (2022a).

[2] Comprising the tropical waters of the Indian Ocean, the western and central Pacific Ocean, and the seas connecting the two in the general area of Indonesia.

[3] The White House (2022a).

[4] Iwamoto (2022).

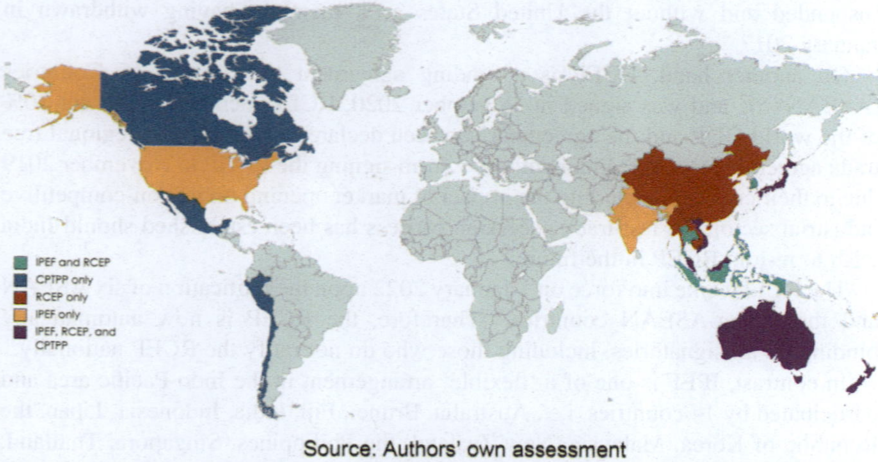

Fig. 1 World Map of IPEF, RCEP, and CPTPP Memberships (Source: Authors' own assessment)

Table 1 Detailed countries participating in the three mega-multilateral agreements

IPEF only	RCEP only	CPTPP only	IPEF, RCEP	IPEF, RCEP, & CPTPP
The United States	China[a]	Canada[b]	Indonesia	Australia
	Cambodia	Chile	Philippines	Brunei Darussalam
		Mexico		Japan
Fiji	Lao PDR	Peru	South Korea	Malaysia
		UK[a] (to join)		New Zealand
India[c]	Myanmar	Taiwan[a] (applied)	Thailand	Singapore
				Vietnam

Source: Authors' own compilation

[a]China formally applied for membership in the CPTPP on September 16, 2021 (Wong 2022); Taiwan submitted its application to join the agreement as a separate customs territory a week later September 22, 2021 (Reuters 2021); The United Kingdom (UK) reached an agreement with Indo-Pacific partners to join CPTPP on March 31, 2023, and currently awaiting formal approval from parliament (CSIS 2023)

[b]Canada has announced that it will seek membership in the IPEF (Reuters 2022)

[c]India opted out of RCEP negotiations during the third RCEP Summit in Bangkok in November 2019 (Gupta and Ganguly 2020)

in RCEP. Meanwhile, Indonesia, the Philippines, and Thailand are members of both IPEF and RCEP.

The CPTPP is a binding agreement that covers 11 countries such as Australia, Brunei, Canada, Chile, Japan, Malaysia, Mexico, New Zealand, Peru, Singapore, and Vietnam, signed in November 2017, which represents 13.5% of the world's GDP. The CPTPP came into force in November 2018, upon the ratification of six Member Countries. The CPTPP is a separate treaty that incorporates the provisions of the original Trans-Pacific Partnership Agreement (TPPA), with some provisions suspended and without the United States as a member, having withdrawn in January 2017.

On another hand, RCEP is a binding agreement that covers 15 Countries (ASEAN+5)[5] and was signed in November 2020. RCEP members represent 30% of the world GDP and the agreement has been declared as the biggest regional free trade agreement to date.[6] India withdrew from signing the RCEP in November 2019 due to their concerns including the impact of market opening on its non-competitive industrial sector.[7] A fast-track accession process has been established should India wish to re-join RCEP in the future.[8]

The RCEP came into force on 1 January 2022 upon the ratification of six ASEAN and three Non-ASEAN countries.[9] Therefore, the RCEP is now automatically binding on all signatories, including those who do not ratify the RCEP nationally.

In contrast, IPEF is one of a 'flexible' arrangement in the Indo-Pacific area and participated by 14 countries, i.e., Australia, Brunei, Fiji, India, Indonesia, Japan, the Republic of Korea, Malaysia, New Zealand, the Philippines, Singapore, Thailand, United States, and Vietnam on 23 May 2022. The IPEF is one of the initiatives in the Indo-Pacific initiated by the US after her withdrawal from TPP (now CPTPP). The IPEF enforces four pillars of commitment in Trade, Supply Chain, Clean Trade, and Fair Trade. This time, India joins but opted out from Pillar I: Trade.[10] Additional Indo-Pacific partners were also invited to join after the signing, with some specific requirements. The IPEF aims to create standardised, inclusive, free, and fair-trade commitments, especially in the digital economy. Other commitments include improving transparency, diversity, security, and sustainability of supply chains, promoting clean energy and environmentally friendly infrastructure projects, and adopting tougher measures against money laundering and bribery.[11] The U.S secretary of Commerce, Gina Raimondo, said that IPEF is "intentionally designed to not be 'same-old, same-old traditional agreement'". Instead, "it is designed as a more innovative and flexible approach, designed to reflect the fact that our economies have changed".[12]

In comparison, once fully implemented, IPEF will be the world's largest mega-multilateral agreement by the coverage of global GDP (see Fig. 2). India's participation in the framework contributes significantly to this scale. Meanwhile, RCEP, which came into force on January 2022, is still currently the biggest multilateral free trade agreement (FTA) in the world, with a total share of GDP reaching 30%, even

[5]Brunei, Cambodia, Indonesia, Laos, Malaysia, Myanmar, the Philippines, Singapore, Thailand, and Vietnam, including Australia, China, Japan, the Republic of Korea, and New Zealand.

[6]Drysdale and Armstrong (2021).

[7]Ward (2022).

[8]ASEAN Secretariat (2020).

[9]ASEAN Secretariat (2020).

[10]Jha (2022).

[11]Johnston (2022).

[12]The White House (2022c).

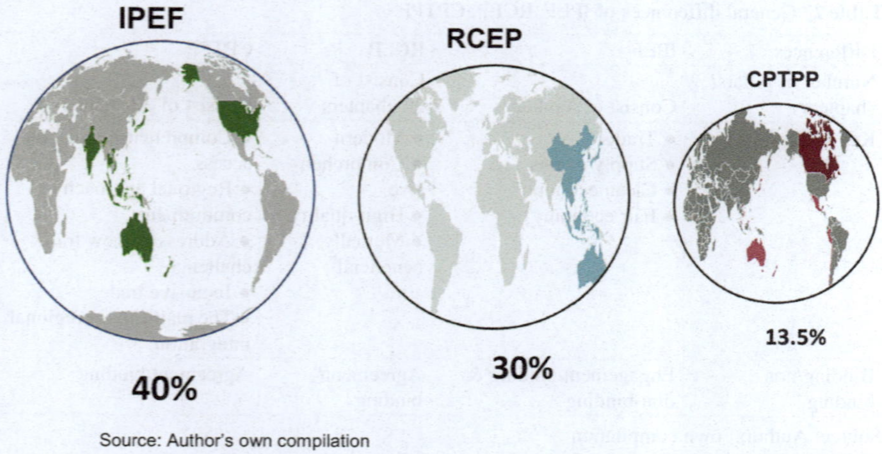

Fig. 2 The share of global GDP % of IPEF, compared to RCEP and CPTPP (Source: Author's own compilation)

after India opted out from the negotiation in 2019. On the other hand, 11 members of CPTPP represent a smaller 13.5% of the world's GDP. Nonetheless, if China's application to CPTPP is approved by member states (and/or Taiwan as a separate customs territory), and once the U.K is formally admitted, the share could go far higher and CPTPP could play a much bigger role in the global economic architecture.

Despite IPEF being one of the interests among our policymakers in the region, there has been not much literature systematically investigating the interplay of IPEF, RCEP, and CPTPP, and potential to be derived from the participation in IPEF and real benefits to the participating ASEAN Member States. Thus, this paper aims to contribute to the knowledge and nascent debate on geo-economic architecture in the Indo-Pacific and multilateral arrangements in the era of heightened global political polarization.

2 The Interplay of IPEF Between RCEP and CPTPP

Negotiating free trade agreements is never easy and the dynamics can be due to many factors such as the membership of the agreement, and the consideration of each member, or even collectively. In the case of IPEF, unlike the CPTPP and RCEP, it will not lower tariffs, but rather, seeks cooperation on strategic pillars, such as supply chain resilience and the digital economy, which are aligned with most member states' priorities (compare Table 2). Moreover, IPEF coverage of GDP is bigger than RCEP and CPTPP. The 14 IPEF members represent 40% of the global GDP with 28% of global goods and services trade. India's membership of IPEF

Table 2 General differences of IPEF, RCEP, CPTPP

Differences	IPEF	RCEP	CPTPP
Number of pillars/ chapters	Consist of 4 pillars	Consist of 20 chapters	Consist of 30 chapters
Key features	• Trade • Supply chains • Clean economy • Fair economy[a]	• Modern • Comprehensive • High-quality • Mutually beneficial[b]	• Comprehensive market access • Regional approach to commitments • Addressing new trade challenges • Inclusive trade • The platform for regional integration[c]
Binding/non-binding	Engagement/binding & non-binding[d]	Agreement/ binding	Agreement/binding

Source: Authors' own compilation
[a]Arasasingham (2022)
[b]ASEAN Secretariat (2020)
[c]USTR (2015)
[d]A mix of both binding and non-binding commitments is likely to be characteristic of IPEF

becomes one of the winning points that IPEF has, reflecting the difficulties of RCEP to invite India back—despite only signing three pillars. Specifically, looking at each IPEF pillar, special attention is given to the ILO Declaration of Fundamental Principles and Rights at Work and the engagement of local communities, indigenous people, and women. However, despite the aim to level the playing field, there is no special treatment or exclusion of obligation towards LDCs. Both RCEP and CPTPP have addressed the need for cooperation and capacity building. Not to mention, the language in the RCEP and CPTPP documents is binding, as opposed to the IPEF.

In signing the framework, the IPEF members agreed to collaborate on at least one of four "pillars". Since its launch, IPEF countries have engaged in intensive discussions to scope out each pillar of the Framework. After the senior officials and ministerial meetings, the members reached a consensus on ministerial statements for each of the four pillars: Trade, Supply Chains, Clean Economy, and Fair Economy.

Pillar I: Trade

In this pillar, IPEF pursue provisions and initiatives related to: (1) benefitting workers and ensuring free and fair trade that contributes to promoting sustainable and inclusive growth; (2) meaningfully contributing to environmental protection and to responses to our common sustainability challenges, including climate change; (3) advance inclusive, trusted digital trade, and resilient, secure digital infrastructure by promoting (a) trusted and secure cross-border data flows; (b) inclusive, sustainable growth of the digital economy; and (c) the responsible development and use of emerging technologies; (4) food security, and sustainable agricultural practice; (5) fair competition policy including in digital trade; (6) transparency and good

Table 3 Similar content and provision of IPEF in RCEP and CPTPP (on Trade Pillar)

Provisions in the IPEF Pillar 1	RCEP	CPTPP
Labour	No chapter on labour	Chapter 19
Environment	No chapter on the environment	Chapter 20
Digital economy	Chapter 12	Chapter 14
Agriculture	No chapter on agriculture	No chapter on agriculture
Transparency and Good Regulatory Practice (GRP)	RCEP Committee on Goods is responsible to enhance cooperation in GRP[a]	Chapters 25 and 26
Competition	Chapter 13	Chapter 16
Trade facilitation	Chapter 4	Chapter 5

Source: Authors' own compilation
[a]RCEP Annex 18 A on functions of the subsidiary bodies of the RCEP Joint Committee

regulatory practices, (7) effective implementation of the WTO's Agreement on Trade Facilitation, (8) inclusivity to benefit indigenous peoples, minorities, women, people with disabilities, rural populations, and local communities, and (9) supporting technical assistance and economic cooperation. The pillar also takes into consideration both trade in goods and services. Concerning services, IPEF will seek to build on the outcome reached in the WTO Joint Initiative on Services Domestic Regulation, as appropriate. IPEF does not provide any market access commitment or tariff reduction in this pillar (see Table 3).

IPEF is intended to address the void in labour and environment measures under the RCEP and enhance the other existing RCEP chapters. Looking at IPEF initiatives in the digital economy, IPEF devotes more attention to cross-border digital trade and digital connectivity than the RCEP. The competition measures under RCEP also have not addressed digital trade. The IPEF initiatives could be an addition to strengthening the supply chain of agriculture products, as RCEP does not regulate much on agriculture except for the elimination of agricultural export subsidies.[13]

Most of IPEF's main initiatives in Trade Pillars are included as chapters in the CPTPP, particularly, in labour and environment. Looking at the e-commerce provisions, CPTPP mandated each member to allow the cross-border transfer of information by electronic means, including personal information, when this activity is for the conduct of the business of a covered person.[14] CPTPP also recognizes the importance of cooperation between their respective national consumer protection agencies or other relevant bodies on activities related to cross-border electronic commerce to enhance consumer welfare.[15] However, the competition chapter in CPTPP has not addressed digital markets, and IPEF may leverage this sector.

[13]RCEP Article 2.13: Agricultural Export Subsidies.
[14]CPTPP Chapter 14.11 on Cross-Border Transfer of Information by Electronic Means.
[15]CPTPP Chapter 14.7 on Online Consumer Protection.

Table 4 Similar content and provision of IPEF in RCEP and CPTPP (on Supply Chain Pillar)

Provisions in the IPEF Pillar 2	RCEP	CPTPP
Anticipate and prevent disruptions in supply chains	Chapter 2 (Trade in goods)	Chapter 22 (competitiveness and business facilitation): – Article 22.3 (supply chain)

Source: Authors' own compilation

Pillar II: Supply Chain

Learning from the COVID-19 shocks, the second pillar of the IPEF sought to support a resilient supply chain by minimising market distortion, protecting confidential business information, promoting regulatory compliance, and respecting market principles and WTO obligations. To achieve the goal, several initiatives have been brought up, such as: (1) jointly establish criteria to identify critical sectors and goods; (2) increase supply chain resiliency and investment in critical sectors and goods; (3) establish a timely information sharing between government and private sector and crisis response mechanisms; (4) strengthen logistics in supply chains; (5) enhance the role of workers and compliance of labour rights; (6) improve the transparency of supply chain.

Along with RCEP and CPTPP, supply chain resilient efforts might be easier to achieve in the regions, due to stronger trade integration. Both RCEP and CPTPP are pursuing more efficient procedures of customs, effective trade facilitation, ensuring more access to services and movement of natural persons (or businessperson in CPTPP), minimising the negative effect of Sanitary and Phytosanitary Measures and Technical Barriers to Trade (for RCEP), participation of SMEs in trade, and others. Looking at IPEF, efforts to establish criteria for critical sectors and goods to national security, health and safety, and economic resiliency; identification of sources of limitations and barriers; crisis response mechanisms; and ensuring sufficient skilled workers in critical sectors might be complementary (see Table 4).

Pillar III: Clean Economy

Under this pillar, the IPEF is expected to focus on building environmental standards that would be common for the members in areas such as energy efficiency and cross-border movement of green technologies.[16] As RCEP does not address the environment, IPEF can help to leverage this sector to pursue a net-zero economy in the ASEAN. The clean economy pillar in the IPEF focuses on a clean energy transition that will require the active participation of all sectors, including private sectors, workers, universities, and research institutions.

There are five main key points, first, energy security and transition; second, greenhouse gas emissions reductions in priority sectors; third, sustainable land, water, and ocean solutions; fourth, innovative technologies for greenhouse gas removal; fifth, incentives to enable the clean economy transition. The negotiation objective of this pillar is to advance efforts to tackle the climate crisis,

[16] Palit (2022).

Table 5 Similar content and provision of IPEF in RCEP and CPTPP (on Clean Economy Pillar)

The provision in the Pillar III	RCEP	CPTPP
Commitments to clean energy and climate-friendly technologies	No chapter on environmental protection	Chapter 20 (Environment)

Source: Authors' own compilation

decarbonisation, and infrastructure that encourage high-paying job creation.[17] The CPTPP had earlier included a chapter on the Environment (Chapter 20), which is emulated by the IPEF under this pillar. IPEF and CPTPP initiatives on the environment will strengthen the prevention and mitigation of pollution, resource depletion, and climate change in the region (see Table 5).

Pillar IV: Fair Economy

RCEP can be leveraged with the existence of IPEF Pillar IV. The Fair Economy pillar focuses on accelerating progress on anti-corruption and curbing tax evasion by—among others, strengthening transparency and promoting integrity within the government and private sector, strengthening measures to counter criminal activities, enhancing transparency in real estate transactions and beneficial ownership of a legal person, prevent corruption that undermines labour rights, countering the financing of terrorism, exchanging information on taxation; improve tax administration, and aligning anti-corruption and tax initiatives within domestic legal frameworks with existing international efforts such as UNCAC,[18] FATF,[19] OECD Anti-Bribery Convention, and OECD/G20 Inclusive Framework on Base Erosion and Profit Shifting's Two Pillar Solution to Address the Tax Challenges Arising from the Digitalization of the Economy—if applicable. Pillar IV also strives to improve domestic resource mobilization through capacity building and cooperation such as technical assistance, development, and application of technology innovation, sharing of expertise, and best practices, including the progress of IPEF goals that engage all stakeholders.

RCEP also mandates each member to prevent and combat corruption in line with its domestic laws. But the initiatives listed under IPEF Pillar IV are far more detailed compared to the RCEP. In terms of government procurement, RCEP has a related chapter (Chapter 16), regulating transparency through the publication of laws and procedures especially in tender, and promoting cooperation to achieve a better understanding of each member's respective government procurement systems. However, LDCs are excluded from undertaking any obligation regarding transparency and cooperation.[20] The RCEP Committee of Business Environment that covers work on government procurement can be guided by the IPEF initiatives to enhance

[17] Jiang (2023).

[18] United Nations Convention against Corruption.

[19] Financial Action Task Force.

[20] RCEP 16.2 on Scope.

Table 6 Similar content and provision of IPEF in RCEP and CPTPP (on Fair Economy Pillar)

Provisions in the IPEF Pillar 4	RCEP	CPTPP
Measures against corruption	RCEP Article 17.9 on measures against corruption Chapter 16—Government Procurement (on transparency information)	Chapter 26 on Transparency and Anti-Corruption: – Article 26.7 (measures to combat corruption)
Measures against tax evasion	No article on tax evasion	No article on tax evasion

Source: Authors' own compilation

the integrity of government officials and private sectors, for example.[21] Meanwhile, CPTPP also detailed the eradication of bribery and corruption,[22] not only in maintaining legislative measures to combat corruption and its forms[23] but also promoting integrity among public officials and participation of private sectors and society.[24] CPTPP also obliges the members to ratify or accede to UNCAC. The measures to ensure integrity against corruption in government procurement and transparency through the publication of laws and procedures especially in tender, are also regulated in CPTPP.[25]

For taxation in CPTPP, applied rates of duties, and taxes of any kind imposed on or in connection with importation or exportation, shall be published as a part of transparency measures.[26] But none of the RCEP and CPTPP regulates measures to improve tax administration and align anti-corruption and tax initiatives. This can be another area that IPEF can address (see Table 6).

3 Criticisms on IPEF

The IPEF was initiated by the US to engage with Asia after the failure of the TPP negotiation.[27] IPEF is often accused as one of the US measures to reduce China's influence in Asia, which could trigger further decoupling.[28] In addition to that, scholars and analysts argue that IPEF benefits are not obvious as compared to

[21] IPEF on Anti-Corruption: "promote transparency and integrity in government procurement practices".

[22] CPTPP 26.6 on Scope.

[23] CPTPP 26.7 on Measures to Combat Corruption.

[24] CPTPP 26.8, 26.9, and 26.10 on Promoting Integrity among Public Officials, Application and Enforcement of Anti-Corruption Laws, and Participation of Private Sector and Society.

[25] CPTPP 15.4 on General Principles and CPTPP 15.6 on Ensuring Integrity in Procurement Practices.

[26] CPTPP Article 2.16 on Publication.

[27] The White House (2022d).

[28] Nikkei Asia (2022).

RCEP and CPTPP. Despite aiming for free, open, and fair trade, IPEF does not offer liberalisation measures, such as the elimination of tariffs, or market access to the U.S. In terms of the supply chain, reflecting the shortage of global chips, Taiwan's exclusion from the IPEF against Taipei's wishes made the agreement's supply chain remains vulnerable, given the importance of its advanced semiconductor industry which now accounts for 92% of the world's manufacturing capacity.[29] Furthermore, the choice of weaker language in the IPEF could only signal an engagement, not a forceful, binding commitment.[30] Also, achieving progress on this could be difficult, given unclear negotiating timelines or measurable outcomes.[31]

Another criticism towards IPEF's push to increase supply chain resilience is that "it tries to push China out of supply chains, which would disrupt the regional network that ASEAN is part of".[32] China continues to be unrivalled as a manufacturing powerhouse given its abundance of skilled workers, extensive supplier networks, and the government's support for enterprises and provision of dependable infrastructure. The economies of China and ASEAN have been entwined in a web of regional production networks, thus increasing their mutual dependence.[33] ASEAN has a significant trade partnership with China on certain products such as electronics, construction materials, chemicals, and agricultural products.[34]

China's criticism towards IPEF could exacerbate the skepticism of the member states, China says that the Asia-Pacific region is "not a chessboard for a geopolitical contest", and Beijing rejects "small circles that smack of the Cold War mentality".[35] ASEAN also has indicated a strong preference for the U.S. to invite all ASEAN Member States (AMS) to join the IPEF. However, the three countries i.e., Cambodia, Lao PDR, and Myanmar. Laos, and are not invited with no clear rationale,[36] making the assumptions of IPEF being a coalition of anti-China grow even stronger. Jiang (2023) concluded in his research that "the economic prospects of IPEF are uncertain, but its political and strategic intentions are evident".[37]

Additionally, there is a question of whether the IPEF will survive beyond the Biden administration, this concern refers to a case where the TPP which was signed by the Obama administration, was later withdrawn by the Trump administration. In addition to that, another concern involves the approach to separate the four pillars. For instance, if the pillars are not linked, perhaps no countries would join the first pillar eventually. India, for example, has made it clear that it will only participate in

[29] Al Jazeera (2022).
[30] Arasasingham (2022).
[31] EIU (2022).
[32] Iwamoto (2022).
[33] Sanchita Basu Das (2017).
[34] Trading Economics, China Exports to ASEAN, https://tradingeconomics.com/china/exports-to-asean.
[35] Iwamoto (2022).
[36] Goodman and Arasasingham (2022).
[37] Jiang (2023).

the other three pillars, citing concerns that the first pillar's environmental provisions may discriminate against developing countries that have the imperative to provide low-cost and affordable energy to support their growing economy.[38]

For IPEF to succeed and be a meaningful multilateral arrangement, IPEF needs to, first, offer more meaningful incentives for countries to be on board and make a stronger commitment. Second, aim for inclusivity beyond close allies to attract more participation in the Indo-Pacific. Third, demonstrate the durability of the framework beyond Biden's administration.[39] Not to mention, some regional governments perceive the IPEF as a framework that contains many demands from the U.S. with few offerings for the other countries, while there exist a variety of credible regional alternatives to the framework e.g., RCEP and CPTPP that could provide more concrete advantages.[40] All IPEF members have to make it clear what they expect from this initiative, including the U.S. itself. Indeed, the anti-China coalition should not be encouraged as it possibly affects the national interest of other participating members. As a final point, the argument that ASEAN is the "centre" of the Indo-Pacific should be deeply considered, as ASEAN tends to prefer its own process and mechanism in the negotiation of multilateral arrangements.[41] It has been argued that the US and ASEAN have very different understandings of the central position of ASEAN in the Indo-Pacific.[42]

4 IPEF: What Could Be the Benefits for ASEAN?

Southeast Asia lies at the heart of the Indo-Pacific and thus, it is in ASEAN's best interest to take the lead in shaping the region's economic and security architecture and to ensure that multilateral arrangements bring about peace, security, stability, and prosperity for the people in the area.[43] IPEF outlined that there have to be resiliency, clean, fair, and connected economies. The "next generation" concerns in IPEF are competitiveness in the digital economy, supply chain resiliency, and climate change. IPEF itself is promoted as a platform where countries can engage in inclusive, cooperative dialogue and not only take-it-or-leave-it kind of multilateral agreements.[44]

There are some benefits of IPEF in ASEAN context. According to the ODI research, IPEF may help bolster the growth of ASEAN. Most of the ASEAN countries' signatories are lower-middle-income countries and are placed at the centre

[38] PBNS (2022).

[39] Goodman and Arasasingham (2022).

[40] Goodman and Arasasingham (2022).

[41] Ram (2023).

[42] Cheng-Chwee (2018).

[43] ASEAN (2019).

[44] Bown and Weisel (2022).

of Indo-Pacific strategies and agreements. This strategically positions ASEAN members in the IPEF to become channels supporting positive spill-over effects to other non-IPEF ASEAN members like Cambodia, Lao PDR, and Myanmar.[45]

Along with the robustness of FDI inflow to ASEAN, IPEF could also maximise cooperation with the U.S. and its partners through investment. The possible reshoring from China and the increasing importance of GVC diversification becomes an opportunity for ASEAN. Currently, China has retained its position as ASEAN's largest trading partner since the 2008 financial crisis, overtaking both the U.S. and European Union. However, ASEAN's trade deficit with China increased drastically with an annual rate of 10.4% from 2010–2019 (pre-pandemic), it increased from US $10.4 billion in 2010 to US $102.9 billion in 2019.[46] ASEAN has also seen robust investment from China in the last decade through both equity and non-equity modes, and ASEAN is the largest target destination for Chinese international infrastructure contracts.[47] Reliance on China on trade and FDI has grown exponentially in the last decade. On the contrary, the US FDI in ASEAN is concentrated only in Singapore, comprising 83% of the US FDI in the region, as of 2020.[48] IPEF could facilitate and promote stronger economic ties between the U.S. and other AMS, in terms of reducing the over-reliance on China, especially on trade, supply chain, and FDI. On the trade front, around a third of the US's imported goods from this region are electronics and machinery according to 2020 WITS data. This can reinforce the trade of value-adding products that are conducive to the transformation of the ASEAN economy.[49] Diversification of FDI and supply chain is crucial to mitigate risk and to ensure resiliency in the era of rising geopolitical risk and fragile global supply chain. That, however, does not imply that ASEAN must "decouple" from China, but rather maintain a balanced relationship.

Inclusive digital economy initiatives can also be beneficial for ASEAN countries that need assistance in digital infrastructures from digitally developed IPEF members. ASEAN can also receive guidance on how to effectively govern their network economies. This can be extended to digitising government transactions, which can be leveraged to increase tax compliance, improve the transparency of procurement and audit agencies, and reduce red tape which is consistent with the IPEF's pillar on tax effectiveness and anti-corruption.[50] In addition to that, due to their nature of being 'flexible' and 'inclusive', IPEF could offer a collaborative process where it looks for input from all of the countries, not only the government but also the private

---

[45] Raga (2022).

[46] ASEAN, ASEAN-China Economic Relations, https://asean.org/our-communities/economic-community/integration-with-global-economy/asean-china-economic-relation/.

[47] ASEAN & UNCTAD (2022).

[48] Raga (2022).

[49] Raga (2022).

[50] Jiang (2023).

sector, who also play key roles in the whole process of the digital economy and supply chain.

The IPEF's clean economy pillar could accelerate efforts to tackle the climate crisis. Several important initiatives such as sharing best practices, cooperation in R&D, and promoting low and zero-emission goods were already discussed. The US committed a US $40 million investment aimed at mobilising roughly $2 billion of blended finance for clean energy and infrastructure in ASEAN.[51] Yet, ADB estimates that ASEAN members need $210 billion annually up to 2030 to adequately finance investment in climate-compatible infrastructure.[52] This is an opportunity for non-CPTPP members of the IPEF to gain cooperation and assistance needed to pursue clean economy goals.

The Fair Economy pillar, too, could provide benefits for ASEAN Member States. IPEF member states could innovate and strengthen shared approaches to implementing anti-corruption and tax measures. It is acknowledged that corruption is a big issue for ASEAN Member States, and it happened mostly in the form of public procurement. By having a strong approach and sharing best practices, AMS could potentially tackle this issue collectively, and further enhance confidence in government. Not to mention, the COVID-19 pandemic has highlighted the critical importance of supply chain resilience in mitigating the amplification of shocks.[53,54] The rise of intricate supply chains has greatly boosted efficiency in the global economy and by understanding the resilience and strengths of these complex supply chains, policymakers in ASEAN could leverage the efficiency benefits of supply chains and mitigation the propagation of future shocks. To this end, diversifying the supply chains is imperative for ASEAN. IPEF has the potential to provide tangible growth and developmental impacts, if the framework extends technical and financial assistance for digital inclusion, facilitates diversified investment, and mobilises climate financing for lower-income IPEF partners in ASEAN.

5 Conclusions: Challenges and Opportunities

This paper examined the interplay of IPEF between the other two mega trade agreements, RCEP and CPTPP. IPEF is a promising initiative that aims to transform the clean energy, digital economy, and technology sectors. This framework, too, seeks to fortify member states' economies against a variety of threats, ranging from fragile supply chains, and corruption, to tax havens. The proponents of IPEF believe that the past economic model and engagement have not effectively these challenges.

[51] The White House (2022b).

[52] ADB (2021).

[53] Khanna et al. (2022).

[54] Fujiy et al. (2022).

The framework thus, focuses on four key pillars to establish high-standard commitments that will deepen the economic engagement among member states.

Projected to be the largest multilateral agreement, covering over 40% of global GDP and still counting (with a potential new member such as Canada), the IPEF is facing several criticisms and setbacks that need to be addressed by both the U.S. and the negotiating parties to unlock its full potential. These issues include the allegations that the IPEF is an anti-China coalition and exclusive to US close allies, that the U.S. is making more 'demand' than 'offer', and the overlapping initiatives that are already covered by RCEP and CPTPP. In addition, if the U.S. attempts to enforce its own rules without considering the perspectives of developing countries, especially ASEAN, IPEF could be viewed as a new form of colonization. Consequently, the notion that IPEF could serve as an alternative to the RCEP and CPTPP would be considered a hollow aspiration by the economic actors in the developing member states.

ASEAN has embraced the "leaving no one behind" principle, yet IPEF is currently open only for upper-middle-income countries and with seemingly political and strategic consideration, thus excluding Cambodia, Lao PDR, and Myanmar, the only less-developed countries in Southeast Asia and often seen as "closer" to China. This could potentially contradict the principle upheld by AMS of "leaving no one behind" and undermine ASEAN's centrality. It should be emphasised that ASEAN requests all major powers to engage in the region, more constructively and comprehensively, but based on its merit, not through the prism of US-China competition or relationships. It is worth mentioning that ASEAN does not view US-China as a dichotomy between "democratic" and "authoritarian" states—rather, it is a crucial matter of its survival,[55] and it is apparent that AMS resist any further "decoupling" because no one in the region could afford the cost of moving away from the Chinese economy. In the case of deteriorating US-China relationships, ASEAN will continue to "hedge" and make foreign policy based on its calculation of material benefits and national interests. Furthermore, a clearer definition of "like-minded" states in the IPEF document could certainly help to clarify the framework's priorities and objectives. Moreover, if that definition aligns with member states' values and principles, IPEF will likely receive an even greater member's support and commitment.

Nonetheless, the authors believe that there are positive impacts that the IPEF could bring on the global economy, and to ASEAN. This paper highlighted several benefits of IPEF for ASEAN, such as its potential to reinforce the trade of value-adding products and diversify global supply chains. Furthermore, ASEAN can receive best practices and knowledge sharing from IPEF on how to manage supply chain resilience. Another way IPEF might be beneficial is the initiative to digitize government transactions to boost tax compliance, promote the openness of procurement and audit agencies, and reduce bureaucratic inertia. Given its flexible and inclusive nature, IPEF could strengthen a collaborative process involving input from all participating countries, from both public and the private sectors. Finally, IPEF

[55] Kamaruddin (2021).

provides non-CPTPP members with the opportunity to advance the transition to clean energy to achieve sustainable development goals. Given that the official negotiating documents have not yet been made public, the outcome of IPEF remains uncertain, leaving room for further research and analysis.

References

ADB (2021) Accelerating sustainable development after COVID-19: the role of SDG bonds, Manila. https://www.adb.org/sites/default/files/publication/712591/sustainable-development-after-covid-19-sdg-bonds.pdf

Al Jazeera (2022) Why China is not sanctioning Taiwan's key chip industry, 4 August 2022. https://www.aljazeera.com/economy/2022/8/4/why-china-is-not-sanctioning-taiwans-crucial-tech-industry

Arasasingham A (2022) Unpacking the Indo-Pacific Economic Framework launch. https://www.csis.org/analysis/unpacking-indo-pacific-economic-framework-launch

ASEAN (2019) ASEAN outlook on the Indo-Pacific. https://asean.org/speechandstatement/asean-outlook-on-the-indo-pacific/

ASEAN & UNCTAD (2022) ASEAN Investment Report 2020–2021: investing in industry 4.0. The ASEAN Secretariat, Jakarta

ASEAN Secretariat (2020) Summary of the RCEP. https://rcepsec.org/wp-content/uploads/2020/11/Summary-of-the-RCEP-Agreement.pdf

Bown CP, Weisel, B (2022) What is the Indo-Pacific Economic Framework and will it work? 12 December 2022. https://www.piie.com/blogs/realtime-economics/what-indo-pacific-economic-framework-and-will-it-work

Cheng-Chwee K (2018) Opening a strategic Pandora's Jar? US-China uncertainties and the three wandering genies in Southeast Asia. https://theasanforum.org/opening-a-strategic-pandoras-jar-us-china-uncertainties-and-the-three-wandering-genies-in-southeast-asia/

CSIS (2023) The United Kingdom is joining the CPTPP. What comes next?, 31 March 2023. https://www.csis.org/analysis/united-kingdom-joining-cptpp-what-comes-next#:~:text=The%20United%20Kingdom%20reached%20an,meeting%20late%20March%2031%2C%202023

Drysdale P, Armstrong S (2021) RCEP: a strategic opportunity for multilateralism. China Econ J 14(2):128–143

EIU (2022) Indo-Pacific Economic Framework falls short, 25 May 2022. https://www.eiu.com/n/indo-pacific-economic-framework-falls-short/

Fujiy BC, Ghose D, Khanna G (2022) Production networks and firm-level elasticities of substitution. Technical report, Working paper

Goodman MP, Arasasingham A (2022) Regional perspective on the Indo-Pacific Economic Framework, 11 April 2022. https://www.csis.org/analysis/regional-perspectives-indo-pacific-economic-framework

Gupta S, Ganguly S (2020) Why India refused to join the world's biggest trading bloc, 23 November 2020. https://foreignpolicy.com/2020/11/23/why-india-refused-to-join-rcep-worlds-biggest-trading-bloc/

Iwamoto K (2022) Indo-Pacific Economic Framework is not an FTA: 5 things to know, 19 May 2022. https://asia.nikkei.com/Politics/International-relations/Biden-s-Asia-policy/Indo-Pacific-Economic-Framework-is-not-an-FTA-5-things-to-know

Jha P (2022) India to join three of four IPEF 'pillars'. India News, 9 September 2022. https://www.hindustantimes.com/india-news/india-to-join-three-of-four-ipef-pillars-101662663955445.html

Jiang F (2023) An analysis of the Indo-Pacific Economic Framework (IPEF): essence, impacts, and prospects. East Asian Aff 2(2)

Johnston E (2022) The IPEF, already a tough sell for Biden at home, seen as limited in scope. Japan Times, 24 May 2022. https://www.japantimes.co.jp/news/2022/05/24/business/ipef-reaction-criticism/
Kamaruddin N (2021) US-China rivalries: what matters for ASEAN. https://www.lowyinstitute.org/the-interpreter/us-china-rivalries-what-matters-asean
Khanna G, Morales N, Pandalai-Nayar N (2022) Supply chain resilience: evidence from Indian Firms (No. w30689). National Bureau of Economic Research
Nikkei Asia (2022) Indo-Pacific Economic Framework needs to bolster free trade, 14 September 2022. https://asia.nikkei.com/Opinion/The-Nikkei-View/Indo-Pacific-Economic-Framework-needs-to-bolster-free-trade
Palit A (2022) IPEF and RCEP not necessarily rivals. China Daily Global, 6 September 2022. https://www.chinadaily.com.cn/a/202209/06/WS63168d25a310fd2b29e7615d.html
PBNS (2022) India agrees to 3 'trade pillars' at Indo-Pacific Meet 2022, 12 September 2022. https://newsonair.com/2022/09/12/india-agrees-to-3-trade-pillars-at-indo-pacific-meet-2022/
Raga S (2022) How will Southeast Asia benefit from the Indo-Pacific Economic Framework? | ODI: Think change, 18 July 2022. https://odi.org/en/insights/how-southeast-asia-will-benefit-from-the-indo-pacific-economic-framework/
Ram V (2023) ASEAN Centrality in the Indo-Pacific Security Architecture. In: Multilateralism in the Indo-Pacific. Routledge, pp 60–72
Reuters (2021) Taiwan applies to join Pacific trade pact week after China, 22 September 2021. https://www.reuters.com/world/asia-pacific/taiwan-applies-join-pacific-trade-pact-cptpp-official-news-agency-2021-09-22/
Reuters (2022) Canada to seek membership to Indo-Pacific Economic Framework, 28 October 2022. https://www.reuters.com/world/canada-will-seek-membership-indo-pacific-economic-framework-2022-10-27/
Sanchita Basu Das (2017) Southeast Asia worries over growing economic dependence on China. Perspective: ISEAS Yusof Ishak Institute. 81
The White House (2022a) FACT SHEET: in Asia, President Biden and a dozen Indo-Pacific partners launch the Indo-Pacific Economic Framework for prosperity. https://www.whitehouse.gov/briefing-room/statements-releases/2022/05/23/fact-sheet-in-asia-president-biden-and-a-dozen-indo-pacific-partners-launch-the-indo-pacific-economic-framework-for-prosperity/
The White House (2022b) FACT SHEET: U.S.-ASEAN special summit in Washington, DC. https://www.whitehouse.gov/briefing-room/statements-releases/2022/05/12/fact-sheet-u-s-asean-special-summit-in-washington-dc/#:~:text=At%20the%20annual%20U.S.%2DASEAN, facilitation%2C%20education%2C%20and%20more
The White House (2022c) On-the-record press call on the launch of the Indo-Pacific Economic Framework. https://www.whitehouse.gov/briefing-room/press-briefings/2022/05/23/on-the-record-press-call-on-the-launch-of-the-indo-pacific-economic-framework/
The White House (2022d) Statement on Indo-Pacific Economic Framework for prosperity. https://mailchi.mp/0298caef72f4/forwarding-from-the-white-housestatement-on-indo-pacific-economic-framework-for-prosperity?e=d2830d7b95
USTR (2015) Summary of the Trans-Pacific Partnership Agreement. https://ustr.gov/about-us/policy-offices/press-office/press-releases/2015/october/summary-trans-pacific-partnership
Ward R (2022) The political significance of the new Indo-Pacific Economic Framework for prosperity. IISS Analysis, 31 May 2022. https://www.iiss.org/online-analysis/online-analysis//2022/05/the-political-significance-of-the-new-indo-pacific-economic-framework-for-prosperity
Wong K (2022) What is the CPTPP and why is China eager to join? 5 May 2022. https://www.scmp.com/economy/china-economy/article/3176487/what-cptpp-and-why-china-eager-join

Inclusive and Responsible Business Conduct in ASEAN: Belt and Road Projects as a Model

Andika Ab Wahab

Abstract China and ASEAN have a long history of economic relations since record began. China and ASEAN have entered into the ASEAN-China Free Trade Agreement, with agreement on trade in goods concluded in 2004, agreement on trade in services concluded in 2007 and agreement on investment in 2009. All ASEAN Member States and China are parties to the Regional Cooperation Economic Partnership Agreement (RCEP). In trade, China is ASEAN's the largest trading partner, whilst ASEAN has been China's third largest trading partner after the European Union and the United States. Foreign direct investment between China and ASEAN has also increased between the two economic partners. Beyond the financial sectors, China's investments in ASEAN are mainly in the natural resource sector, real estates and infrastructure. As a result of the Covid-19 pandemic, many Chinese investors are also relocating their investments into the ASEAN region, mainly to be nearer to the ASEAN Value Chain and Supply Chain. The BRI projects have further increased the prospects of China's FDI in the region. The increase in China's investment, including those under the BRI provides an opportunity for China to promote Responsible Business and Conduct (RBC) among China's investors in the ASEAN Member States, including their contribution towards the Sustainable Development Goals. China is promoting RBC in overseas operations of Chinese enterprises. The question is whether Chinese companies should adopt the "one size fits all" approach in adopting the RBC in ASEAN. ASEAN Member States are of varying economic development and facing varying challenges in ensuring sustainable development. Chinese investors should adopt a high standard RBC in carrying out BRI projects irrespective of the economic standing of the partner economy in ASEAN. This will lead to a win-win outcome for both ASEAN and China. This will also assist China to enhance trust among ASEAN citizens over Chinese investment, which will then further enhance the political-economy relation between the two important partners.

A. A. Wahab (✉)
Institute of Malaysian and International Studies (IKMAS), Universiti Kebangsaan Malaysia (UKM), Selangor, Malaysia
e-mail: andikawahab@ukm.edu.my

M. Bungenberg et al. (eds.), *Asian Yearbook of International Economic Law 2023*,
Asian Yearbook of International Economic Law (2023) 2023: 153–170,
https://doi.org/10.1007/16517_2023_25, Published online: 22 August 2023

1 Introduction

This paper discusses the question whether projects implemented under the China's Belt and Road Initiatives (BRI) promotes sustainable business and responsible investment (SBRI) or commonly known as the Responsible Business Conduct (RBC). China, as one of the largest investors in many ASEAN Member States have been encouraging its businesses and investors to adhere to the RBC. However, there are noises in the ASEAN Member States that some Chinese investors lag behind in complying with the RBC.

There are perceptions in ASEAN that Chinese businesses undertaking BRI projects are not keen to work with local businesses, by ensuring workers, machineries, sub-contractors, professional service providers and capital are all recruited or supplied from China hence limiting opportunities for local workers and businesses in the region. There are also perceptions that Chinese businesses involved in the BRI projects have issues with the environmental protection, workers' rights and rights of the local community.

The paper argues that in carrying BRI projects in ASEAN, Chinese businesses have been mindful of the different development stage of the ASEAN Member States, hence, they should not adopt the "one size fits all" approach in adopting the RBC in ASEAN. ASEAN Member States are of varying economic development and facing varying challenges in ensuring sustainable development. Chinese investors should adopt a high standard RBC in carrying out BRI projects irrespective of the economic standing of the partner economy in ASEAN. This will lead to a win-win outcome for both ASEAN and China. This will also assist China to enhance trust among ASEAN citizens over Chinese investment, which will then further enhance the political-economy relation between the two important partners.

The paper will first discuss the ASEAN-China economic relations, where both sides agree that BRI should play a central role in enhancing the economic relations between them. ASEAN as a grouping needs the BRI to enhance the infrastructure and connectivity between the Member States and other regional partners. The paper will explain the nature of BRI project in ASEAN, followed by the issues arising from the BRI projects in several ASEAN Member States. The paper argues that some of the issues like human rights and environmental concerns are not caused by BRI projects. Rather the BRI projects are used by some local ASEAN parties to encroach the human rights and environmental boundaries. The paper argues that China has taken steps to ensure that Chinese entities involved in the BRI projects in ASEAN adhere to the RBC.

2 ASEAN-China Economic and BRI Work Programs

China is an important Dialogue Partner to ASEAN. In 1991, China expresses its interest to cooperate with ASEAN on areas of mutual benefits, and 5 years later in 1996, China was accorded full Dialogue Partner status.[1] China and ASEAN are also main trading partners, where China is the largest trading partner for ASEAN and a main source of foreign direct investments (FDI), where China is the third largest source of FDI to ASEAN among the ASEAN Dialogue Partners.

To enhance trade and investment between the two partners, ASEAN and China signed the Framework Agreement on Comprehensive Economic Cooperation in 2002. The two parties signed the ASEAN-China Free Trade Agreement (ACFTA) on 1 January 2010 and came into full effect in all ASEAN Member States on 1 January 2015. The ACFTA was upgraded in 2015 through the "Protocol to Amend the Framework Agreement on Comprehensive Economic Co-operation and Certain Agreements thereunder between ASEAN and the People's Republic of China." In addition, ASEAN and China are main parties to the Regional Comprehensive Economic Partnership Agreement (RCEP), concluded in 2021 and came into force on 1 January 2022. It has been suggested that RCEP may affect China's domestic investment regimes and at the same time may affect investment rules relating to BRI projects in ASEAN Member States.[2]

Under the Belt and Road Initiatives (BRI) China sees ASEAN as part of the land bridge connecting China—Southeast Asia—South Asia—Indian Ocean and the China-Indochina Peninsula Corridor sea route (China—South China Sea—Indian Ocean—Europe).[3] On the other hand, ASEAN Member States regard the BRI as an avenue to improve connectivity through infrastructure development which will increase trade and investment in the region through improved logistics. Hence, ASEAN Member States, in collaboration with Chinese entities (construction companies and funding agencies) are developing infrastructure projects as part of government procurement, mainly through joint ventures. The infrastructure development relationship between China and ASEAN is not new and not just because of BRI.

For example, prior to the launching of the BRI, ASEAN and China entered into a Memorandum of Understanding on Transport Cooperation in 2004 (Transport MOU)[4] followed by the Strategic Plan for ASEAN-China Transport Cooperation 2016. Under the Transport MOU, China and ASEAN Member States agree to explore medium and long-term cooperation on transport related initiatives. Such

---

[1] See ASEAN Secretariat (2020).

[2] See Wang (2019), p. 243.

[3] China, 'Vision and actions on jointly building the Silk Road Economic Belt and 21st Century Maritime Silk Road' document (March 28, 2015).

[4] Memorandum of Understanding Between the Governments of the Member Countries of the Association of Southeast Asian Nations and the Government of the People's Republic of China on Transport Cooperation, 2004.

initiatives include transport infrastructure and construction, transport facilitation, maritime safety and security, air transport such as airline cooperation and air services agreements, and human resources management. ASEAN and China agreed to promote cross-border projects like the Singapore Kunming Rail Link, of which the Vientiane-Kunming portion has already been completed; the East Coast Rail Link (ECRL) linking the Port of Kuantan in the East Coast of Peninsular Malaysia and Port Klang in the West Coast of Peninsular Malaysia, where ships and cargo are able to bypass the buys Singapore Port through an alternative rail link; navigation in Lancang-Mekong River; the Port Cities Cooperation Network and Logistics Information Cooperation. China's source of funding into ASEAN are mainly from the China-ASEAN Fund for Investment Cooperation, investing in ASEAN since 2010 and the Asian Infrastructure Investment Bank (AIIB).

In 2018, ASEAN and China agreed to adopt in principle the 2018–2020 Action Programme of the Revised Strategic Plan for ASEAN-China Transport Cooperation.[5] The 2018 Action Program is aligned with ASEAN's goals and actions in the Kuala Lumpur Transport Strategic Plan 2016–2025 and China's BRI. The Action Programme would serve to provide guidance in implementing the Revised Strategic Plan for ASEAN-China Transport Cooperation.

3 China's BRI Projects in ASEAN

ASEAN requires an improved infrastructure to drive economic growth through increased trade, investment, competitiveness and connectivity in the region and with the rest of the world. The ASEAN Development Bank (ADB) estimates that the total infrastructure investment needs in ASEAN from 2016 to 2030, will be US $2.8 trillion (baseline estimate) and US $3.1 trillion (climate-adjusted estimate).[6] These infrastructure needs are important to support the increasing amount of ASEAN trade, which total ASEAN imports and exports of trade in goods totalled to US $2.816 trillion in 2018.[7]

The total merchandise trade is expected to increase as ASEAN grows from the seventh largest economy on the world to the fourth largest economy in the world by the year 2050, with an annual expected gross domestic product (GDP) growth 5.25% between 2016 and 2020, not taking into account the challenge post Covid-19.[8] The IMF predicts that ASEAN-5 will suffer from a negative real GDP growth of −0.6%

[5] Joint Ministerial Statement, The Seventeenth ASEAN and China Transport Ministers Meeting (17th. ATM+CHINA) 8 November 2018, Bangkok, Thailand.

[6] See Asian Development Bank, Meeting Asia's Infrastructure Needs (Manila, February 2017).

[7] ASEAN Secretariat (2019).

[8] IIE, Outlook 2017: ASEAN still beckons, IE Singapore, 2017.

in 2020, followed by a potential growth of 7.8% in 2021.[9] ASEAN needs to work as a group to enhance ASEAN's economic growth as a result of Covid-19. To encourage collective economic growth Post-Covid, ASEAN needs to further develop the infrastructure to further the efficiency in the regional supply-chains.

According to the *Center for Strategic and International Studies and Nikkei*[10] there have been at least 20 BRI related projects in six ASEAN Member States i.e. Brunei (1); Cambodia (5); Indonesia (5); Lao PDR (3); Malaysia (3); and Thailand (1). A few of BRI related projects are under review, either to be cancelled or re-negotiated including the Jakarta Monorail Project[11] valued at US $1.5 billion. The ECRL Project in Malaysia has been delayed due to re-negotiations between successive Malaysian Government and China. The Jakarta-Bandung Railway project which was under threat, mainly due to the delay in the release of loan from the China Development Bank[12] and delayed due to the Covid-19 pandemic has now been completed[13] and would be launched soon.[14] The Melaka Gateway Project in Melaka, which is a mixed property development project is now considered as white-elephant, especially after the change of the Government in Malaysia.[15]

Most of the BRI projects are developed through joint-ventures (JV) between ASEAN host country entity and China's entity with financing from China's linked financial organisations.[16] These JVs carry out their projects under concessions or direct government procurement. Such concession projects include Muara Container Terminal and Oil Refinery Project in Brunei; the Melaka Gateway Project in Melaka, Malaysia; the Jakarta-Bandung Railway and the Morowali Industrial Park in Indonesia. Examples of government procurement projects include the ECRL and Gemas-Johor Bharu railways in Malaysia and the Lao PDR's Vientiane-Boten Railway.

Upon the completion of the BRIs, export of goods from continental ASEAN into China and Europe will be facilitated by the land bridges being built in Laos and Malaysia such as the Vientiane-Boten Railway, ECRL and Gemas-Johor Bharu, Phongsaly-Yunnan projects. The completion of the "last mile", Vientiane to Kunming will connect ASEAN to its main global partners, alleviating the needs to rely on the sea route to certain parts of China, Central Asia, Russia and Eastern Europe. The ECRL project, although mainly conceived as part of the domestic connectivity,

---

[9] International Monetary Fund, (2020), World Economic Outlook, April 2020: The Great Lockdown, https://www.imf.org/en/Publications/WEO/Issues/2020/04/14/weo-april-2020.

[10] Center for Strategic and International Studies and Nikkei, Is China's Belt and Road working? A progress report from eight countries Beijing's infrastructure push clouded by project delays and mounting debt, 28 March 2018.

[11] Center for Strategic and International Studies.

[12] Negara and Suryadinata (2018).

[13] Rahman (2020).

[14] Soeriaatmadja (2023).

[15] Shepard (2020).

[16] This type of activity clearly falls within the definition of investment which involves commitment of capital, the expectation of gain or profit or the assumption of risk. For an example of definition of investment, see the ASEAN Comprehensive Investment Agreement (ACIA), Article 4.

could act as the land bridge between South China Sea Port of Kuantan to the Port Klang in the Straits of Malacca, thus reducing the needs for vessels to travel through the busy Straits of Singapore.

Completion of BRI projects will also mean ASEAN will be able to increase investment in the logistic sector. This could contribute towards spill-over effects in the economy through other investments, such as manufacturing, oil and gas, mining and quarrying and agriculture. The completion of the BRI will plug the investment gaps in infrastructure, which if not addressed, will have a negative impact on the overall economic growth in ASEAN.[17]

BRI projects not only involved investments or flow of capital but also importation of goods from China to ASEAN. These goods may directly and indirectly be used in the BRI projects. Selected goods possibly linked to the BRI projects imported from China to ASEAN. Since 2010, importation of construction related products from China into ASEAN such as chemical products, ceramic products, glassware, iron and steel and its related articles, copper and articles, tools, metal products and boilers have been on an increasing trend.

On the other hand, it is possible that importation of some of the products will reduce once the BRI are fully completed. Rather, there could be an increase in the imports and exports of the intermediate goods, both from ASEAN into China and to the world and from China into ASEAN. This would be able to assist ASEAN to address the trade in goods imbalance between ASEAN and China. Between 2014 and 2016, ASEAN trade in services with the world has shown an increase in import of services in the sub-sectors related to the BRI projects. ASEAN has been importing construction services, ranging from US $6.2 billion in 2014 to US $ 5.4 billion in 2016. China's exports of services into ASEAN increased from US $161 billion to US $657 billion, whereas, for ASEAN, it rose from US $252 billion to US $643 billion.[18] China has mainly been exporting engineering and labour services to ASEAN and imports transport, financial and construction services from ASEAN countries.

The BRI may change the balance in favour of China with more export of construction services and related financial services into ASEAN. It can be assumed that ASEAN Member States will import more financial services to help finance the infrastructure projects, based on the projects in Table 1. Upon completion of the BRI projects, it is expected that some ASEAN Member States may see an increase in the export of transportation and travel services, especially in tourism, through the BRI completed infrastructure projects. The BRI projects will enhance connectivity within ASEAN Member States, which contributes to both trade and investment facilitations.

[17] See Asian Development Bank, Meeting Asia's Infrastructure Needs (Manila, February 2017).

[18] See Basu Das (2018). See also Yoon (2017).

Table 1 Related-sustainable and responsible business initiatives

Year	Sustainable & responsible business initiatives
1976	• OECD Guidelines for Multinational Enterprises
1997	• Global Reporting Initiative (GRI)—sustainability reporting
2000	• Establishment of the United Nations Global Compact (UNGC)—on sustainable and responsible business
2005	• Principles for Responsible Investment (PRI)
2008	• 10 Principles of the UNGP
2009	• Sustainable Stock Exchange Initiative (SSE)—as a UN partnership program with the United Nations Conference on Trade and Development, the UN Global Compact and the United Nations Environment Program Finance Initiative
2011	• United Nations Guiding Principles on Business & Human Rights (UNGP-BHR) (2011)
	• OECD Guidelines for Multinational Enterprises—fourth vision with the enhanced standards (2011)
2015–2018	• Sustainable Development Goals (SDGs) (2015)
	• Paris Agreement—United Nations Framework Convention on Climate Change (UNFCC) (2016)
	• Implementation of the UNGP-BHR & National Action Plan (NAP) in 21 countries (Chile, Korea and U.S.A have developed a NAP)
	• Establishment of the OECD's National Focal Points for responsible business [a]
	• Creation of G20 Inclusive Business Framework (2015)
	• The proliferation of market-based initiatives (e.g., human rights benchmark; enhanced principles and criteria for Roundtable Sustainable Palm Oil)
2019	• Legally Binding Instrument on Human Rights for Multinational Enterprises—in progress (*draft*)

Source: Author's analysis based on efforts by various international organisations
[a] Australia, Canada, Chile, Japan, Korea, Mexico, New Zealand, Peru and U.S.A are among the APEC Economies who have established National Focal Points for responsible business

4 China's SBRI and Enhancing Trust in ASEAN

China introduced the Go Global Policy in 1999, which leads to the accession of the country into the World Trade Organisation (WTO) in 2001, which has further increased its incorporation in the global economy.[19] To further enhance its position on the global economy, China undertakes the expansionary policy in the global trade and investment. These approaches brings about, among others the Belt and Road Initiatives (BRI). China's BRI is not just about President Xi Jinping's approach to foreign policy, but also remain true to the late Deng Xiaoping's maxim on China's foreign policy that is "to create a stable external environment for China's domestic economic growth."[20] This is a truly important policy, as the BRI is not just about supporting progress in the target countries but also ensuring the progress in the target

[19] Chaisse (2019).

[20] See for example the discussion in Hass and Rubenstein (2017).

countries such as the ASEAN Member States will support China's economic growth. BRI project is well planned with good execution strategy, where target countries are needed to deal with China's contractors, buy China's products, utilise China's services and most importantly utilise China's financing scheme to fund these projects.

Yu Jie correctly states that the BRI brings opportunities in trade, engineering and in finance, particularly in supporting the internationalisation of the Renminbi.[21] Yu Jie also supports the author's assertion that China, in building the BRI must maintain a close understanding of how countries across Southeast Asia are reacting to the BRI, and respond to their concerns. The main challenge for China in pursuing the BRI in ASEAN is not just about the completion of the projects or the benefits to China's domestic economy, but also about building the long term political-economic relation with the countries and also the people. As Yu Jie states, the challenge for China going forward is as much about winning hearts and minds as it is showering dollars and pounds.[22]

One of the biggest challenges facing the BRI is to ensure those projects in ASEAN fit within the sustainable development goals (SDG). Sustainable development is often referred to as development that meets the needs of the present without compromising the ability of future generations to meet their own needs. Based on this broad-based expression of sustainable development, in 2015, the global development framework—the Sustainable Development Goals (SDGs) was formed. It integrates three aspects of sustainable development, namely, economic, social and environmental protection. The three aspects are crucial for the well-being of individuals and societies at large. Each of the aspects is interlinked to one another, and that the failure to achieve one will trigger failure in others. For example, the failure to act on climate change will have severe implications to basic elements of human life such as access to clean water, food, health and land use. As such, climate change initiatives are often seen as a prerequisite for sustainable economic growth and development.

Inequality emerges uniquely in many developing countries, and that poses another challenge for sustainable development. Inequality cannot be removed without addressing other challenges such as the lack of access to quality healthcare and education; poor governance and inefficient public spending; wide-spread discrimination and social exclusion; lack of human rights protection and fundamental freedoms. In practical term, development policy in many developing countries should address the inequality of opportunities and the inequality of outcomes—responding to the specific needs and circumstances of each country.[23] As such, the successful implementation of the global development vision (SDGs) by 2030 requires strong national actions as well as global collective efforts that generate public goods for all.

---

[21] Jie (2019).

[22] Jie (2019).

[23] United Nations Development Programme (UNDP) (2013).

In parallel to this development, China has risen as the second-largest economy and an engine of global growth and trade.[24] Indeed, it plays a substantial role in contributing to or advancing sustainable development. Particularly, the China's BRI—an economic framework that covers more than 70 countries across the globe will have a significant role to accelerate the fulfilment of sustainable development. In other words, the BRI may serve as an important accelerator for the successful implementation of the SDGs by 2030. However, this prospect relies heavily on how the BRI is designed, implemented and contributed to fulfilling development gaps—in China and elsewhere.

As it stands, the BRI's broad vision to create shared growth around the globe, and its priorities to strengthen connectivity and people-to-people linkages—are strongly aligned with the SDGs' targets and goals. Their relationship (BRI and SDGs) may be seen as complementary—through which can generate synergies and opportunities to address many current developmental issues, including inequality and social exclusion. At the same time aligning the two will pave the way for more dialogues and partnership between counties and many segments of non-state actors, including multinational enterprises.

The BRI implementation has been progressing relatively well, with a high prospect to be the world's largest economic corridor covering a population of more than four billion and economic output of US $21 trillion.[25] As this reflects the potential of China's BRI to shape the landscape of international cooperation, risks and challenges exist in many forms, including political instability and regulatory risks; social and environmental threats; as well as negative reputation associated with BRI's projects. In facing the domestic political risk, BRI investors and business face the reality of domestic politics. For example, in the Malaysia and Thailand, BRI projects have been subject to changes due to the changes in the governments, which lead to the delay and cancellation of some projects. Kuik Cheng-Chwee contributes this to the political power struggle based on elite legitimation and a process shaped by inter-elite and societal contestation that explains individual countries' distinctive patterns of rail engagement with China.[26]

While managing these risks require a whole-of-government approach on the side of the Government, industry players associated with the BRI's projects play an equally important role in ensuring such risks are foreseen and prevented from occurring, or mitigated when they happen.

In recent time, large and multinational corporations have been criticized for contributing, directly or indirectly, to various forms of environmental calamities and damages, including climate change.[27] This is becoming even more explicit when multinational corporations invest and operate in developing countries, including

---

[24] Horvath (2016).

[25] *Xinhua*. (2015, April 24th). China Focus: Belt and Road Initiative a boost to China, regional economy. Xinhua. Available at http://news.xinhuanet.com/english/2015-04/26/c_134186100.htm.

[26] Cheng-Chwee (2020).

[27] Islam and McPhail (2011). Also see Varkkey (2015) and Wahab (2019).

BRI's recipient countries—where there is a lack of a regulatory framework.[28] This demands businesses to have integrity and standards to guide the way they operate.

Generally, there is no mutually agreed definition of what constitutes responsible business. The Organisation for Economic Co-Operation and Development (OECD), however, defines responsible business as the baseline standards for how businesses should understand and address their risk, and how governments should support and promote such responsible business practices. Despite the lack of consensus on the definition of responsible business, there is a plethora of global initiatives and actions attempting to influence the way businesses are conducted.

In 1997, for instance, a Global Reporting Initiative (GRI) was established in view of encouraging corporate's transparency and accountability through sustainability reporting and disclosure. Three years later, in 2000, the United Nations Global Compact (UNGC) was established to promoting sustainable and responsible business. From the years 2000–2010, several related initiatives were established in areas related to sustainable and responsible financing and investment. Among the most significant initiatives were the creation of the United Nations' Principles for Responsible Investment (PRI) in 2005 and the Sustainable Stock Exchange Initiative (SSE) in 2009.

In 2011, the Office of the United Nations High Commissioner for Human Rights (OHCHR) produced the United Nations Guiding Principles on Business and Human Rights (UNGP-BHR) as the first authoritative global framework that aims to address the business impact on human rights.[29] This is the first document of its kind that applies to both states and businesses in addressing governance gaps and ensure corporate accountability.[30] The adoption of the UNGP-BHR had also prompted the OECD to revise its Guidelines for Multinational Enterprises in 2011 (which was first adopted in 1976)—by incorporating several new chapters pertaining corporate respect to human rights. One of the crucial chapters in the revised OECD Guidelines is the enhanced labour chapter (employment and industrial relations).

Since 2011 to recent years, several new initiatives were established, including the SDGs in 2015; the creation of the G20 Inclusive Business Framework in 2015; the United Nations Framework Convention on Climate Change (UNFCC) in 2016; and the Corporate Human Rights Benchmark (CHRB) in 2017. Table 1 depicts the key initiatives related to sustainable and responsible business until recent time.

---

[28] Preuss and Brown (2012).

[29] United Nations Human Rights Council (UNHRC). (2011). United Nations Guiding Principles on Business and Human Rights: Implementing the United Nations Protect, Respect and Remedy Framework. [Online]. Available: https://www.ohchr.org/documents/publications/GuidingprinciplesBusinesshr_eN.pdf.

[30] Ramasastry (2015).

5 China's Efforts to Address RBC

Given its position as the world's leading country in electricity production from renewable energy, China, in many ways, is also seen as an environmental leader.[31] Mckinsey reported that China had invested more than US $100 billion in domestic renewables every year. Renewable energy has become an in important energy mix in China. It has been reported that China's coal intensity declines sharply, with its overall coal consumption falling, more than offset by a large rise in renewable energy mainly from hydro, account for over 80% of the increase in China's energy demand out to 2040.[32] This shows domestically China is encouraging a higher level of sustainable use of energy and this approach should be built and applied in China's economic diplomacy through BRI abroad.

To further claim its position as an environmental sustainability leader, the Chinese Government released two governance directives in 2018 known as the Belt and Road Ecological and Environmental Cooperation Plan (BREECP) and Guidance on Promoting Green Belt and Road. The overall objective of these directives is to strengthen cooperation and ensure that BRI's projects are moving towards environmental-friendly and sustainability routes. The BREECP, in particular, consists of 25 green BRI projects—of which six of them are projects that aim to strengthen policy coordination to support eco-friendly projects; four projects for facilities connectivity; three for unimpeded trade; two projects for financial integration; four projects related to people-to-people bonds; and six other projects for capacity building.[33] At least two of the green BRI projects are implemented at the ASEAN (region) level, namely, the China-ASEAN Partnership on Eco-Friendly Cities, and China-ASEAN Environmental Technology and Industrial Cooperation Demonstration Bases.

The Guidance document promoting Green Belt and Road, on the other hand, prioritizes infrastructure and capacity building projects for energy conservation, emission reduction and eco-environment protection, as well as business guidance for corporate behaviour. Despite critics that these directives lack accountability mechanism, the issuance of these governance directives has further positioned China at the forefront of the global environmental sustainability initiatives. Importantly, these initiatives were created and implemented as part of the BRI's projects, including those operated in many ASEAN member states.

Back in 2014, the Chinese Government announced a state-owned investment fund amounting to US $55 billion, focuses specifically to fund BRI projects. Besides, China's National Development Bank (CNDB) had signed more than 100 agreements related to BRI projects since 2013 with another pool of investment

[31]Escobar (2019).

[32]BP Plc, BP Energy Outlook 2018 Edition, (London, BP, 2018), pp. 100 and 101. See also Sufian (2021).

[33]Further see The Belt and Road Ecological and Environmental Cooperation Plan, available at https://eng.yidaiyilu.gov.cn/zchj/qwfb/13392.htm.

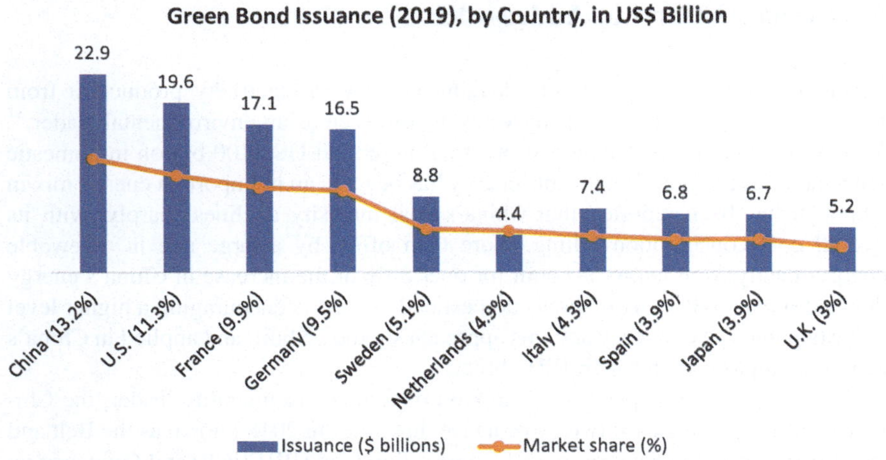

Fig. 1 Green Bond by Country 2019. Note: in bracket [country(%)] above refers to market share (Source: Green Belt and Road Initiative Center, 2019. Available at https://green-bri.org/green-finance)

amounting nearly US $100 billion. With this financial strength, China wants environmental protection to become one of its pillar industries.[34] This depicts China's position as an investment and infrastructure powerhouse with an immense opportunity to play a leading role in green finance development. In other words, the BRI projects provide an opportunity to scale China's green finance market through green bonds (also known as climate bonds). In 2019, China was reported to have the highest amount of green bond amounting to US $22.9 billion, with a total of 13.2% market share (see Fig. 1). This achievement and its subsequent progress may be attributed to the issuance of the Chinese' governance directives (discussed above), the BREECP and the Guidance on Promoting Green Belt and Road.

At individual country level among the ASEAN Member States, the impacts of BRI projects can be evaluated on several fronts. On the people-to-people bond, Cambodia reported that about 3000 scholarships had been provided to Cambodian students to undertake bachelor's up to doctoral degrees in various Chinese universities in fields such as civil engineering, business administration, health, international trade, finance, economics and international relations.[35] On top of that, Cambodia had received some two million Chinese tourists in the year 2018, boosting the total number of foreign tourists to Cambodia to 6.2 million. This has contributed immensely to many tourism-related activities and informal economic sector in the Kingdom.

In Thailand, the Thai-Chinese high-speed rail project—a flagship BRI project in the country offers a host of opportunities for connectivity, not only among

---

[34] Escobar (2019), p. 4.

[35] Runsinarith (2019).

businesses but rural and ordinary citizens. This project once completed—is expected to boost the Thai's economy, raising land values among the agricultural community and reducing trade cost.[36] This public infrastructure project and the opening of special economic zones at the border areas will address urban-rural gaps and subsequently alleviate inequality among vulnerable and poor segments of society in Thailand. Similarly, in Myanmar, the BRI projects such as the Kyaukphyu Deep Sea Port, the Muse-Mandalay Railway Project, the New Yangon Development Project, as well as various border economic zones—are expected to boost public infrastructures, connectivity and financial cooperation, as well as reducing barriers for trades. This, in turn, will benefit many different segments of the society, including rural entrepreneurs and rural citizens.[37]

5.1 *Impacts on the Environment and the Environmental Governance*

China's leadership and influence on environmental sustainability offer a great opportunity—both financial and institutional strengthening in many BRI's recipient countries. The governance directives, particularly the BREECP and Guidance on Promoting Green Belt and Road issued in 2018 have led to the creation of various operational guidance for many Chinese companies operating in BRI's recipient countries—with a view to avoiding adverse environmental impacts of the BRI projects and at the same time promoting sustainable and environmentally-friendly development projects. At the same time, the link between BRI projects and investment related to fossil fuel infrastructure development around the world[38]—points out that China is seen as both promoting green projects but also putting more pressure on earth through coal investment and exploration.

In several ASEAN Member States, BRI projects have been linked to a range of violations of domestic laws concerning environment and health. In Indonesia, for instance, local civil society claimed that the implementation of the landmark BRI-project, the Jakarta-Bandung high speed rail had breached many of Indonesia's domestic environmental laws. The BRI-sponsored project with an investment value of US $5.5 billion was accused of rushing the environmental impact assessment process, subsequently disregarding the voices of the local community and public grievance mechanism.[39] These processes are part of Indonesia's domestic

[36] Chaisrisawatsuk (2019).

[37] Soe (2019).

[38] International Institute for Sustainable Development. 2019, May 2nd. SDG Knowledge Weekly: Update and Perspectives on Belt and Road Initiative. Available at https://sdg.iisd.org/commentary/policy-briefs/sdg-knowledge-weekly-update-and-perspectives-on-belt-and-road-initiative/.

[39] Ward (2020).

environmental laws, and any efforts to pass or not to follow the standards are considered breaching these legal instruments.

The expansion of BRI infrastructure projects especially along the Mekong River, which spans Cambodia, Lao PDR, Myanmar, Thailand and Viet Nam have raised biodiversity and ecosystem issues in the region. A study conducted by the World Wildlife Fund (WWF) has listed over 1700 critical biodiversity spots and 265 threatened species that will be adversely affected by the BRI.[40] In the meantime, the Fisheries Action Coalition Team (FACT) claimed that fish stocks have declined due to hydropower dams built along the Mekong River region, leading to a loss of livelihood for many local communities.[41]

5.2 *Limited Employment Creation*

One of the immediate outcomes of the BRI projects is employment creation, especially for the host population that can ultimately lift them out of poverty and raise the standards of living. The Chinese' government official claimed that the BRI projects across the world have created more than 300,000 jobs for local citizens of the BRI-recipient countries.[42] While this is uncontested, countries such as Lao PDR, Myanmar and Cambodia claimed that the employment opportunity created through the BRI projects might not necessarily be filled by the local. In Lao PDR, for instance, only about 4763 local hired in BRI projects as compared to nearly 23,500 posts being filled by foreign workers—the majority of which are the Chinese nationals.[43] The Chinese's migration to Lao PDR is characterized as both skilled and unskilled workers, typically employed by the state-owned Chinese companies managing the BRI projects in the country. The case in Lao PDR is not an isolated one. The Chinese's migration to Africa and Middle East where the BRI projects are implemented has also been on the rise. In these two regions alone, the Chinese

[40] World Wildlife Fund (WWF). 2017, November 2nd. WWF and Greening the Belt and Road Initiative. Available at https://www.wwf.org.hk/en/?19680/Feature-Story-WWF-and-Greening-the-Belt-and-Road-Initiative.

[41] ASEAN Post. 2019, December 24th. China's BRI negatively impacting the environment. Available at https://theaseanpost.com/article/chinas-bri-negatively-impacting-environment.

[42] Xinhua. 2019, April 7th. BRI-related economic, trade cooperation zones create 300,000 local jobs. Available at http://www.chinadaily.com.cn/a/201904/07/WS5ca9349aa3104842260b4ad1.html.

[43] Vanxay, Sayavong. 2019. BRI and SDGs progress in Lao PDR. Paper presented at UNESCAP's Jointly Building Belt and Road towards SDGs, Bangkok, on 25 and 26 September 2019. Resources available at https://www.unescap.org/sites/default/files/4_Lao%20PDR%20BRI%20and%20SDGs.pdf.

migrant population is estimated between one to two million—the majority of which concentrated in South Africa and Jordan.[44]

5.3 Legal Risk and Lack of Transparency

A study conducted by the CIMB-ASEAN Research Institute (CARI) has alerted several legal issues arising from the BRI projects in ASEAN, highlighting that risk allocation between the Chinese Government and BRI-recipient countries in the region must be negotiated and dealt carefully. Based on BRI projects currently implemented in Lao PDR, Indonesia and Malaysia, the study found that conflicting priorities may occur in concession agreement since national governments of Lao PDR, Indonesia and Malaysia are playing a dual role as a commercial actor and the regulator as the same time.[45] Conflicting priorities may also exist between governing the country's resources and safeguarding the interest of its citizens and the environment. The Chinese Government's strategy in dealing with legal and regulatory issues, including conflicting priorities in ASEAN member states should not be a one-size-fits-all approach. This is because each of the ASEAN Member State has a different and unique regulatory and legal system (i.e., Malaysia and Singapore employ common law), and that conflicts and disputes are inevitable.

As much as the legal risk is a concern, there is no lack of transparency and accountability issues being raised around BRI projects in ASEAN. The lack of information on BRI projects and non-transparent procurement system may not only hinder public participation but jeopardize national efforts among the ASEAN Member States to address issues around corporate and Government transparency and accountability. Some companies are allegedly hand-picked by the Chinese Government and/or the hosting governments to participate in BRI projects. This has limited the opportunity for local firms to enter into a fair competition, and being evaluated based on their merit and expertise. Issue of transparency has a tremendous implication for the continuity and completion of BRI projects. The lack of transparency, proper due diligence and allegation of funds misappropriation associated with three landmark BRI projects in Malaysia had led to the cancellation of the East Coast Rail Link (ECRL), the Multi-Product Pipeline (MPP) and Trans-Sabah Gas Pipeline (TSGP) in 2018. The projects later being reconsidered and finally resumed following the signing of a revised agreement in April 2019.

---

[44] Wang, Hui. 2017, July 14th. The opportunities and challenges of migration in the Belt and Road region. Available at https://doc-research.org/2017/07/opportunities-challenges-migration-belt-road/.

[45] Hamzah (2018).

6 Conclusions

The above discussions show that in conducting the BRI projects in the ASEAN Member States, China will have to deal with myriad of issues. For example, as second largest economy in the world, China has to avoid criticisms of the projects and to build trusts not just among the ASEAN Member States but also other economic players in the region. The BRI projects have faced many levels of criticisms, such as the lowering of environmental and labour standards and non-compliance with transparency rules. However, these issues are not unique and not new ASEAN Member States. Some ASEAN Member States have been facing these issues domestically even prior to the BRI being launched. Some of the ASEAN Member States should have undertaken reforms in their domestic political economic and legal systems to ensure transparent and trust in the implementation of the infrastructure projects. Hence, these criticisms are considered BRI-pushed rather than BRI-caused and will have to be tackled jointly between the ASEAN Member States and China together.

The BRI projects landed into these myriads of issues, and have been subject to criticisms by ASEAN domestic economics and political oppositions. These oppositions have exploited to certain extent the way China conducts its business when compared to the other investors in the region. This also means that when investing in ASEAN Member States, China's investors and businesses will have to study the economic, political and social nature of each member state. China's investors and businesses cannot assume that ASEAN Member States are all the same as they are different. Each member state has different uniqueness, identities and peculiarities. The ability of China's BRI investors and businesses to address the issues in each ASEAN Member State will enable them to initiate targeted business initiatives, which in return will enhance the trust building in the China's backed BRI in the region.

References

ASEAN Secretariat (2019) ASEAN Key Figures 2019

ASEAN Secretariat (2020) Overview of ASEAN-China dialogue relations, ASEAN Secretariat Information Paper, April 2020

Basu Das S (2018) Do the economic ties between ASEAN and China affect their strategic partnership? ISSUE: 2018, No. 32, ISEAS – YUSOF ISHAK perspective, Singapore, 21 June 2018

Chaisrisawatsuk S (2019) Regional workshop on assessing the potential impact of the Belt and Road Initiative on sustainable development goals in Asian economies. Paper presented at UNESCAP's jointly building Belt and Road towards SDGs, Bangkok, 25 and 26 September 2019

Chaisse J (2019) China's international investment law and policy regime – identifying the three tracks. In: Chaisse J (ed) China's international investment strategy, bilateral, regional and global law and policy. Oxford

Cheng-Chwee K (2020) The politics of Thailand-China Railway Cooperation: domestic determinants of smaller state BRI engagement, file with authors
Escobar M (2019) The importance of sustainability in China's Belt and Road Initiative. Yale Review of International Studies. http://yris.yira.org/essays/3436
Hamzah H (2018) Legal issues and implications of the BRI. https://www.cariasean.org/publications/chinas-belt-and-road-initiative-bri-and-southeast-asia-publication/legal-issues-and-implications-of-the-bri/#.Xra21i-w2-V
Hass R, Rubenstein DM (2017) The trajectory of Chinese foreign policy: from reactive assertiveness to opportunistic activism. Center for East Asia Policy Studies, Brookings Institution
Horvath B (2016) Identifying development dividends along the Belt and Road Initiative: complementarities and synergies between the Belt and Road Initiative and the sustainable development goals. https://www.undp.org/content/dam/china/docs/Publications/UNDP-CH-BRI%202017%20Scoping%20Paper1%20(Final).pdf
Islam A, McPhail K (2011) Regulating for corporate human rights abuses: the emergence of corporate reporting on the ILO's human rights standards within the global garment manufacturing and retail industry. Crit Perspect Account 22(8):790–810
Jie Y (2019) China and Southeast Asia: many belts and roads to turn. In: The impact of the BRI on trade and investment in ASEAN. London, 2018
Negara SD, Suryadinata L (2018) Jakarta-Bandung High Speed Rail Project: little progress, many challenges, ISEAS perspective, ISSUE: 2018 No. 2 ISSN 2335-667
Preuss L, Brown D (2012) Business policies on human rights: an analysis of their content and prevalence among FTSE 100 firms. J Bus Ethics 109(3):289–299
Rahman DF (2020) Jakarta-Bandung high speed railway project delayed amid pandemic. The Jakarta Post, 15 April 2020
Ramasastry A (2015) Corporate social responsibility versus business and human rights: bridging the gap between responsibility and accountability. J Hum Rights 14(2):237–259
Runsinarith P (2019) Belt and Road Initiatives and Southeast Asia: the case of Cambodia. Paper presented at UNESCAP's jointly building Belt and Road towards SDGs, Bangkok, 25 and 26 September 2019
Shepard W (2020) Inside the Belt and Road's Premier White Elephant: Melaka Gateway. Forbes, 31 January 2020
Soe AK (2019) Trade promotion and SDGs implementation in Myanmar. Paper presented at the national workshop on the opportunities for Myanmar on trade promotion under the Belt and Road Initiative, Yangon, December 2019
Soeriaatmadja W (2023) Jakarta Bandung in one hour, Indonesia's new high speed train completes first trial run. Straits Times, 31 May 2023
Sufian J (2021) Energy cooperation in Asia. In: Faure M (ed) Elgar encyclopaedia of environmental law. Elgar, London, pp 145–155
United Nations Development Programme (UNDP) (2013) Humanity divided: confronting inequality in developing countries. United Nations Development Programme, New York
Varkkey H (2015) The human rights dimension in the revised RSPO principles and criteria. Malaysian J Int Relat 3(1):153–158
Wahab A (2019) Human rights anchored in business: practice and challenges in the palm oil sector in Malaysia. Asian Int Stud Rev 20(1):1–20
Wang H (2019) The RCEP investment rules and China, learning from the malleability of Chinese FTAs. In: Chaisse J (ed) China's international investment strategy, bilateral, regional and global law and policy. Oxford, pp 243–247
Ward O (2020) Is China meeting its international environmental and human rights obligations on BRI? ASEAN Today. https://www.aseantoday.com/2019/04/is-china-meeting-its-international-environmental-and-human-rights-obligations-on-bri/
Yoon O (2017) China's economic ties with Southeast Asia. World Economic Brief, 4 September 2017, Vol. 7 No. 18 ISSN 2233-9140

The Comprehensive and Progressive Agreement for Trans-Pacific Partnership: Intellectual Property Chapter and Research in Biotechnology

Sufian Jusoh

Contents

Abstract Four of ASEAN Member States are parties to the two largest free trade agreements, i.e. the Comprehensive and Progressive Agreement for Trans-Pacific Partnership (CPTPP) and the Regional Comprehensive Economic Partnership Agreement (RCEP). Of the four countries, Malaysian and Singapore have established biotechnology industry and research and development activities. Biotechnology is important for these two countries economic growth; and to address pressing domestic issues such as disease eradication, addressing environmental concerns and increasing food production. However, much of the biotechnology related activities in these two countries are dominated by foreign investors, with foreign registered patents. These patent-owned patents may hinder the development of indigenous research and development activities involving local research institutions are their research activities may be subject to complying with foreign owned patents. The paper examines how the CPTPP Intellectual Property Chapter could affect the research and development activities in the biotechnology sector in these two countries, and how these two countries can employ research exemption flexibility as provided in the WTO TRIPS Agreement and also the CPTPP Intellectual Property Chapter.

S. Jusoh (✉)
Universiti Kebangsaan Malaysia, Institute of Malaysian and International Studies, Bangi, Malaysia
e-mail: sufianjusoh@ukm.edu.my

M. Bungenberg et al. (eds.), *Asian Yearbook of International Economic Law 2023*,
Asian Yearbook of International Economic Law (2023) 2023: 171–188,
https://doi.org/10.1007/16517_2023_24, Published online: 24 June 2023

1 Introduction

Last decades brought a large progress in improving and using both science and technology, putting forward a lot of possibilities for emerging economies like Malaysia and Singapore to become a player in several biotechnology-based sectors such as health especially in facing challenges in health issues like Covid-19 and any future challenge, food security especially in ensuring consistent food production in the face of food security and food price crisis, environment and human development generally. Between 2006 and 2016, there were 131,349 patents applied for biotechnology fields worldwide with an average annual increase of 5.2%; and 249,744 applications for pharmaceutical patents, with an annual increase of 4.1%. Most of the applications are dominated by developed countries, with the exception of China.[1]

Among the major concerns of many countries, including parties to the Comprehensive and Progressive Agreement for Trans-Pacific Partnership (CPTPP), in using biotechnology are to enhance their economic growth; and to address pressing domestic issues such as disease eradication, addressing environmental concerns and increasing food production. With the increasing cost of living and challenge in food security, countries need to do more research and development in biotechnology that could accelerate the production of food across the globe. Nevertheless, many countries in the ASEAN region, including Malaysian and Singapore, continue to rely on imported patented and generic medicine, vaccines and food which affect domestic food security and economy including balance of trade and balance of payment.

Malaysia and Singapore are among countries in ASEAN which would like to progress in the science and technology by promoting research and development, either to create new technologies or to work on existing technologies, which include patented ones. Nevertheless, they have to grapple with constraints that affect the advancement of local science and technology. The constraints include lack of domestic direct investment and capital, technology advancement and research and development. These countries have a choice of either developing their own research and development capabilities both in the private and the public sector; or contracting through partners either locally or abroad; or to purchase technologies either by way of outright purchase or by paying licence fees and royalty. Developing one's own research and development capability will require heavy expenses, including setting-up infrastructure and facilities and making sure to have the right number of experts and support staff.

The following pages will elaborate research exemptions in the legal frameworks of in Malaysia and Singapore, being two of the ASEAN Member States which have major biotechnology activities and being part of CPTPP. Malaysia is an upper-middle income country, whereas Singapore is a high-income country. The CPTPP is a trade and investment agreement between 11 countries in the Asia-Pacific region. Those countries are New Zealand, Australia, Brunei Darussalam, Canada, Chile, Japan, Malaysia, Mexico, Peru, Singapore, and Viet Nam. The CPTPP is based on

---

[1] WIPO (2018).

the Trans-Pacific Partnership Agreement (TPP) signed by the same countries, as well as the United States, on 4 February 2016. In January 2017 the US withdrew from the TPP. The resulting CPTPP was signed on 8 March 2018.

In Article 2.29, CPTPP Parties confirm the importance of transparency, cooperation and exchanging information related to the trade of "products of modern biotechnology", as defined in CPTPP. The text specifically acknowledges that it does not require any changes to CPTPP Parties' existing laws, regulations and policies. The paper will outline the scope of research exemptions in several emerging countries including Malaysia and Singapore. The paper will then discuss whether the CPTPP Intellectual Property (IP) Chapter will restrict any research and development activities in the pharmaceutical and biotechnology sectors in Malaysia and Singapore.

2 Research Exemptions Defined

In general, the research exemption allows for the use of a patented invention without the patent holder's authorisation and without financial compensation.[2] However, it only does so in as far as this use is conducted for research or for experimental purposes and this always depends on the exact nature and scope of research and experimental purposes, and to delineate them from commercial activities. Research exemption normally refers to the research or experimental purposes, either academic research or private research which excludes any acts done with a commercial intent. However, it is unclear whether the exemption is limited to acts done on the protected invention or if it also exempts acts done with the patented product or process, using it as a tool.

The main function of research exemption is to allow research on (or with) protected subject matter. Researchers conducting research are still required to abide by the terms of the law of patents, be it the need to obtain the necessary licence to use any patented tools; and not to infringe any third-party patents in conducting the research. Research exemption provision is no longer applicable after a particular product of the research being produced and introduced into the market. Research exemption is only practically relevant where the protected invention that is needed for one's research can be reproduced or purchased by the researcher claiming the exemption. In addition, the research exemption does not imply an obligation of the patent holder to deliver the protected invention for the planned research.[3]

[2]Michelangelo Temmerman, Patent Research Exemption Defined, 2011, unpublished text, file with author.

[3]Michelangelo Temmerman, Patent Research Exemption Defined, 2011, unpublished text, file with author.

The scope of the research exemption is discussed in Article 30, read together with Article 27 of the TRIPs Agreement. Article 27 of TRIPs requires no discrimination as to the field of technology. whereas Article 30 allows exceptions granted to the patent holder's rights in as far as they are to be limited, do not to unreasonably conflict with a normal exploitation of the patent and do not to unreasonably prejudice the legitimate interests of the patent owner, taking account of the legitimate interests of third parties.

Research exemption is also closely linked with the private use exemption or generally known as the Bolar exemption. The Bolar is limited to pharmaceuticals.[4] It allows acts undertaken with a view to obtain regulatory approval for generic drugs and a similar exemption is also established under European Union law, under the Directive 2004/27/EC.

Research exemptions will need to be linked with the issue of competition policy. Intellectual property does not actually consider any impact that an invention may have on competition before granting patent protection[5] Patent law and patent offices do not normally consider competition issue in granting patents or whether such patents will restrict any future research. In examining innovation, IP officials exclusively focus on legal and scientific conditions of patentability and the 'prior art'. On the other hand, there is a widely accepted perception in antitrust policy of the patent right as a form of monopoly.[6] Although a patent holder is conferred rights to exclude others from exploiting the patent, it does not actually generate a monopoly in the antitrust sense as these rights do not in fact offer significant market power on their own.[7]

Competition issue may also play a role in the case of broad patents, which will then restrict the potential further research in the same field of science and technology. For example, after obtaining a broad patent, the owner may decide not to conduct further research; being satisfied with the power of his patent. Excessive protection allows patent holders to be relaxed, slowing down considerably innovation process. After obtaining patent protection, the invention can become an idle innovation, if the patent owner does not have any intention to complete the research

[4]The World Intellectual Property Organisation (WIPO) has issued a draft reference document on the exceptions regarding acts for obtaining regulatory approval from authorities under the Bolar Exception. See WIPO (2017).

[5]Prepared Remarks of James E. Rogan under Secretary of Commerce for Intellectual Property and Director of the United States Patent and Trademark Office at the Hearings on Competition and Intellectual Property Law and Policy in the Knowledge-Based Economy, February 6, 2002, US Federal Trade Commission (USFTC).

[6]Prepared Remarks of James E. Rogan under Secretary of Commerce for Intellectual Property and Director of the United States Patent and Trademark Office at the Hearings on Competition and Intellectual Property Law and Policy in the Knowledge-Based Economy, February 6, 2002, US Federal Trade Commission (USFTC).

[7]Prepared Remarks of James E. Rogan under Secretary of Commerce for Intellectual Property and Director of the United States Patent and Trademark Office at the Hearings on Competition and Intellectual Property Law and Policy in the Knowledge-Based Economy, February 6, 2002, US Federal Trade Commission (USFTC).

process and transform its invention into a product suitable for commercialization. Depending on the significance of the innovation, the patent owner without doubt is in a position to slow down technological progress, given the fact that his patent would not allow others to find a substitutable product either.[8]

Broad patents are not unusual in the biotechnology field. Claims in biotechnology are actually broadly formulated by their very nature.[9] The most obvious example is an invention related to a process of setting a particular gene into a particular organism with a specific method. If the claim would have been limited to a specific gene, organism or process, the invention could be utilized without infringement by simply using another gene, organism or processing method. Expectedly, as a consequence of a narrowly defined claim, the patent potentially is of very limited commercial value.[10] This is the main reason why applications relating to biotechnology area are as broadly formulated as possible, seeking patent protection covering more than the invention to which it actually relates. Given the trend of PTOs awarding broad patents to biotechnology related claims, we have to be aware of the consequence that exclusive rights are not only conferred on the unique invention, but they are extending to a development that is only supposed to have equal effect or a purpose.[11]

These problems are accelerated as patent protection is of great importance to biotechnology. The majority of biotechnology companies are small in size, with rather limited technologies available to dispose with, as opposed to technologies available to large companies.[12] In addition, developing a biotechnology product requires a long period of time, and extensive, time is needed before these companies are able to commercialize their inventions. Thus, conferring a patent to biotech companies in the early stage of ongoing development is essential to secure sufficient investment required to continue research that may lead to the development of either final or an intermediate product.

---

[8] Thomas Cottier and Ana Jevtic, Competition, Patents and Innovation – An interdependent relation, 2011, unpublished text, file with author.

[9] Thomas Cottier and Ana Jevtic, Competition, Patents and Innovation – An interdependent relation, 2011, unpublished text, file with author.

[10] Barton (1995), pp. 605–618. For example, the biological effectiveness of a transformation technique on strains other than those used in inventor's disclosure may not be known at the time of patenting. A later researcher who finds it impossible to make the technique work for a new strain is ipso facto demonstrating that the technique was not enabled for that strain. (The case, however, give only limited comfort to those considering action that might infringe a broad claim that they suspect is invalid).

[11] West (2005).

[12] West (2005).

3 The Scope of Research Exemptions in Selected Countries

Research exemption provisions exists in patent laws in most countries around the world. The United States appear to provide research exemptions in biotechnology, in particular in drug discovery through written law i.e. Hatch-Waxman Act 1983,[13] which sets up a system to "balance the need to stimulate innovation against the goal of furthering the public interest." and judge-made laws (case laws). However, there are arguments that recent court decisions such as in *Helsinn Healthcare S.A.* v. *Teva Pharmaceuticals USA, Inc.*[14] in the United States under the America Invents Act[15] has further narrowed the scope of the experimental research exemption in the country.[16]

The European Union (EU) members also provide for research exemption in the national patent laws. For example, the German Patent Act (GPA), §11 No. 2 states that the effects of a patent shall not extend to "acts done for experimental purposes relating to the subject matter of the patented invention."

Biotechnology appears to be the area where many countries could benefit the most from implementing research exemptions in their legal framework, considering the potential that certain end result may have within health-related issues or agriculture. Taking the example of agricultural biotechnology and its implication in improving agricultural capacity of emerging countries, research exemptions can be considered in these countries as a tool to reduce poverty and provide more food security on sustainable level.

Given the increasing pace of a tendency to straightening and enforce IP rights, in particular favouring adherence to a stringent IPRs beyond the TRIPs minimum standards, as contained in many preferential trade agreements (PTA) such as the CPTPP, countries undertaking domestic technological development will have to design the national law and PTA template to suit their national research and development and technology advancement agenda. For example, research in pharmaceutical sector is important as a mean to creating a sustainable public health policy. The World Health Organisation (WHO) sees the necessity to build research ability of developing countries and calling for "work with developing countries to build systems of science, technology and innovation for economic and social development, and to promote the education and training of their future leaders particularly in science, engineering, technology and medicine."

Research exemption provision is an indispensable tool for facilitating access to existing knowledge. When more country promotes and foster innovations the more

[13]The Drug Price Competition and Patent Term Restoration Act (Hatch–Waxman Act), Pub. Law No. 98-417, 98 Stat. 1585 (1984) (codified in relevant part at 35 U.S.C. §271(e)). See discussion in Russo and Johnson (2015).

[14]Helsinn Healthcare S.A. v. Teva Pharmaceuticals USA, Inc., 855 F.3d 1356 (Fed. Cir. 2017).

[15]Pub. L. No. 112-29, 125 Stat. 284 (codified at 35 USC §§ 100 et seq.).

[16]For discussion see Kostolanksy and Salgado (2018).

space should be available for research exemptions. This would leave enough liberty for local inventors to use disclosed information and contribute with incremental developments, mostly for the purpose of adopting the innovation for a better use locally.

Many countries have introduced research exemption provisions in their national patent laws, although the scope of exemptions differs among them to the great extent.[17] Many emerging and developing countries turned to the WIPO Model Patent Law for Developing Countries in order to address the issue of research exemptions. Article 23 of the Model Patent Law indicated that the "use of the patented invention for strictly private or experimental purposes is not to be deemed to be use for industrial or commercial purposes." On this basis, implemented provisions are however not uniform and are based on different criteria.[18] Characterising developing countries research exemptions is very hard given the lack of jurisprudential guidance. This on the other hand makes it difficult to assess the concrete scope of research exemptions in each country; and on the other points at a seldom use of the concept.

The diversity in the way emerging and developing countries have stipulated experimentation or research exceptions can be roughly summarized in three groups. Many countries provide for exceptions of 'experimentation' or 'experimental purposes' where in some cases the law requires that the act is done only and exclusively for experimental purposes.[19] Other countries limit patent exception for research conducted for scientific purposes exclusively or extend exceptions in a way to include both experimental and scientific purposes.[20] In these countries, if not explicitly defined, either formulation implies non-commercial nature of the exception. Some countries like Albania,[21] Antigua and Barbuda,[22] Kyrgyzstan,[23]

[17] For example, countries without explicit research exemption provision are: Guyana, Haiti, Kuwait, Libya, Madagascar, Nigeria, Sudan, Yemen, Vietnam and Zimbabwe. See Correa M. C., The International Dimension of the Research Exceptions, January 2005, AAAS/SIPPI Paper.

[18] Garrison (2006).

[19] For example Belize, Bhutan, Botswana, Cambodia, Chile, Mongolia, Guatemala, Pakistan, Philippines, Singapore, South Korea, Turkey.

[20] Reference to scientific research is provided in Algeria, Barbados, Cuba, Egypt, Malaysia and so on, while the reference to both scientific research and experimental purposes may be found in countries like Panama, the Republic of Chine, Costa Rica, Guatemala, Mongolia, Nicaragua and Paraguay.

[21] See Albanian Law No 9947 on Industrial Property, including as the limitation of the patent rights, among others, "acts performed merely for experimental purposes relating to the subject matter of the invention".

[22] Patent Act No 23, stating that the rights under the patents shall not extend to acts done only for experimental purposes relating to patent invention.

[23] Patent Law of the Kyrgyz Republic No 8, 14 January 1998, as amended by the Laws of Kyrgyz Republic No 130 as of 25 July 2002, and No 46 as of 27 February 2003, in its Article 13 states that the following is not recognized as an infringement of the exclusive rights of the patent owner: (2) conducting scientific research or an experiment with an article containing an object of industrial property.

Lithuania[24] and Moldova[25] opted for a modern language of exemptions, in the same way as accepted in the European Union. These countries limit exception only to the acts related to subject matter of the patent.

4 Emerging Biotechnology Sectors in Malaysia and Singapore

4.1 Malaysia

This part analyses the impact of research exemption provision in the Malaysian patent law on biotechnology research and development and commercialisation activities in Malaysia. Malaysia is ambitious in developing its biotechnology sector to build up its economy into a knowledge economy in order to compete with its neighbours as well as with China and India in the Asia Pacific region. The Malaysian Patents Act 1983 as amended provides in Section 37 that "...The rights under the patent shall extend only to acts done for industrial or commercial purposes and in particular not to acts done only for scientific research." Hence, under the Malaysian Patents Act 1983, the rights of the patent shall not be applicable to scientific research, including research relating to biotechnology.

This is very critical for Malaysia as most of patents filed for applications and granted by the Malaysian Patents Office belonged to foreign applicants. Based on the Malaysian Patent Statistics, between 1986 to March 2023, there were 197,885 applications for patents with 96,313 granted by the Malaysian Patent Office. Out of total applications, only 11% (23,343) were filed by Malaysians, and out of the total patents approved granted, only 9.4% were Malaysians.[26]

Malaysia's National Biotechnology Policy[27] aims to give impetus to developing the biotechnology sector into a new economic engine enhancing prosperity and wellness of the nation. Under this policy, Malaysia intends to concentrate on all

[24] Patent Law No I-372 of January 18, 1994, as amended by the Law No IX-118 of December 21, 2000 in its Article 21 provides that the patent owner shall have no rights to prevent third parties from performing acts referred to in the paragraph 1 and 2 provided that (2) the act is done for purely experimental purposes or for scientific research.

[25] The Law of Patents for Inventions No 461-XIII of 18 May 1995, as amended by the Law No 1079-XIV as of 23 June 2000. Article 24 goes: The use of an invention protected by the patent shall not constitute an infringement of the patent owner's exclusive right: (b) for the performance of research work or scientific experimentation for assessing the application of the subject matter of the invention or for non commercial purposes.

[26] Intellectual Property Corporation of Malaysia, Patent—Statistic—Application and Registration, https://www.myipo.gov.my/en/statistic-application-registration/#toggle-id-1.

[27] This Policy was launched on 28th April 2005. It encompasses three phases, namely capacity building (2005–2010), creating business out of science (2011–2015) and turning Malaysia into global player (2016–2020). The 9th Malaysia Plan says that 'biotechnology is poised to be the next wave of knowledge based industries that will contribute to growth and wealth creation, new

aspects of biotechnology such as agriculture biotechnology, healthcare biotechnology development and industrial biotechnology. At the same time Malaysia plans to conduct research and academic development activities into seven areas: molecular biology, plant biotechnology, animal biotechnology, medical biotechnology, environmental and industrial biotechnology, and bio-pharmacy and food biotechnology.

Malaysia also intends to increase its research and development capacity by establishing Centres of Excellence, such as the National Pharmaceutical Institute, the Agriculture Biotechnology Institute and the Malaysia Genome Institute. By establishing these Centres of Excellence, Malaysia hopes to bring together multidisciplinary research teams to co-ordinated research and commercialisation initiatives. These Centres of Excellence are being set up in addition to the existing universities and research institutions such as Malaysian Agriculture Research and Development Institute (MARDI), Malaysian Palm Oil Board, Malaysian Rubber Board, Institute of Medical Research and Forest Research Institute of Malaysia (FRIM).

Many of the Malaysian biotechnology companies concentrate on agriculture biotechnology such as tissue culture and cross breeding but none is involved in the commercialisation of genetic modification, which does not receive favourable response in Malaysia. Several companies are involved in healthcare biotechnology such as creating stem cell banks, production of nutraceuticals and health and functional food especially from local biodiversity and herbs and at the early stage of biopharmaceuticals. None of the biopharmaceutical companies area capable of producing patented drugs and many are still at stage 1 of clinical trials, meaning that Malaysia still has a long way make any significant marks in the field of pharmaceutical production. Some companies are involved in the industrial biotechnology such as production of health enzymes from tobacco, industrial enzyme, ethanol and biofuel from oil palm.

The issue now is whether the progress in the indigenous biotechnology activities may also result in the increase in the domestic technology and innovation and whether Malaysia requires stronger patent regime or whether Malaysia requires a more flexible approach in allowing research and development hence a higher degree of flexibility in the patent research exemption. The answer lies with the number of patented indigenous innovation and patent applications. It is submitted that a higher number of locally owned patents will mean Malaysia will tilt towards a higher degree of patent protections in order to encourage more local patents and at the same time to have a less flexible research exemption due to protect local innovation and a higher degree of enforcement of patent rights by the patent owners.

The dominance of foreign patents could hinder the development of indigenous technology if such development in local technology falls foul of foreign patents. In the author's interviews with local researchers from 10 biotechnology companies and research institutes, the researchers and biotechnology companies are aware of the

investment and employment opportunities as well as deliver social and environmental benefits. See Government of Malaysia, the 9th Malaysia Plan 2006–2010, 2006, Ch. 6.

need to conduct research within the parameter of the patent, not to infringe any patents in conducting research using patented research tools and, although many are not aware of the exact existence of the research exemption provision, many are aware of the implications of research exemption provision in Malaysian patent law.

For example, a senior researcher at the Malaysian Agriculture Research and Development Institute (MARDI), admits that researchers at MARDI are aware of the possible infringement of patented markers, such as in the development of new specifies of high nutrient rice, which were used as research tools. MARDI would invest in buying markers or arranging for a royalty-based payment to the patent owner in conducting such research. However, MARDI is worried about the implication of royalty on the final price of commercialised products, as they need to factor in the royalty payable to third party technology provider.

In the healthcare sector, Malaysia does not have the capability of producing patented and novel drugs yet. Pharmaniaga and CCM Duopharma, are the largest local pharmaceutical manufacturers produce generic drugs and conduct contract manufacturing for international pharmaceutical companies. The research and development activities of these companies do not have the capability of producing new patented drugs or novel drugs in Malaysia hence there is little need for research exemption to be applicable to this company.

To generate products, Malaysia's biotechnology companies mainly rely on technology transfer and technology collaboration with foreign technology partners. The move from relying on the foreign technologies to the development of indigenous and locally research products may mean that Malaysia will require a flexible approach towards research exemption whilst trying to achieve a balance in the high degree of protection of patented biotechnology products.

In conclusion, a clear research exemption policy is important if Malaysia wants to encourage for more indigenous research in the field as at the moment Malaysia has little research and development including in biotechnology.

4.2 Singapore

Singapore has the most developed biotechnology industry in ASEAN. One of the efforts is building a physical infrastructure, such as '*Biopolis*', an 18 million square foot biomedical sciences hub, housing public research institutes, corporate research and development centres and start-ups, where Singapore sets up priority in developing pharmaceutics and diagnosis that were expected to yield high value. Singapore has also established the Biomedical Research Council and a Biomedical Grid, a high-security network enabling the biomedical research information to be shared and distributed between interested parties.

Singapore's effort to become the manufacturing and research hub for major multinational biotechnology companies has shown some success where more than thirty leading biomedical sciences companies, such as Takeda and Quintiles have set up regional and international headquarters in the country. Multinational biotechnology companies in Singapore do not serve Singapore's market alone as it is very small, but their main market is the whole of Southeast Asia which has around 650 million populations. These operations have also set up their research and development activities either on their own or in collaboration with Singapore's research institutes, for example the Institute of Chemical Engineering and Sciences and Bioprocessing Technology Institute.[28] The main purpose of the research and development collaboration is mainly to optimise manufacturing processes and the formulation of new products.

In relation to research and development, it could be assumed that Singapore will impose a high level of IP protection which means a narrow approach towards research exemption. This is because biotechnology is fast gaining foothold in the country. Under the Singapore Patent Act 1994, Section 66 (2), an act is not an infringement of a patent if (a) it is done privately and for purposes which are not commercial; or (b) it is done for experimental purposes relating to the subject matter of the invention. Note the difference here, where Malaysia's Patent Act provides for "scientific research" whereas the Singapore Patent Act provides for "experimental purposes relating to the subject matter of the invention."

Research exemption is important for Singapore homegrown technology, where most patents filed and approved in Singapore are dominated by foreign own inventions and patents. For example, according to the Intellectual Property of Singapore patent statistics, local patent applications represent 13.6% (3802) of all patent applications (27,855) in in 2020 and 2021. Further, local approved patents only represent 6.3% (763) of all approved applications (11,874).[29] This shows that Singapore's technology, in the same way as Malaysia, is still dominated by foreign patent holders.

For the lack of latest data, it is reported that patenting data shows Singapore innovators having a higher interest in the field of Biotechnology, with a total of 350 inventions and a further 180 inventions in pharmaceuticals in 2016.[30] Singapore's policy is to offer a high level of IP protection as a strategy to attract investment in the biotechnology fields. In addition of using IP protection to attract foreign multinational companies to invest in Singapore the country also has a policy of attracting global talents in biomedical and biotechnology. Complementing Singapore's strengths in early innovation and translational research, the city-state has also established a core base of 20 leading contract research organisations (CROs) and pharmaceutical companies that manage regional clinical trials from Singapore.

The issue whether there should be broad or narrow application of research exemption should be looked at from two different angles, one from the perspective

[28] Singapore Economic Development Board (2010–2011), pp. 13–20.

[29] Intellectual Property Office of Singapore, Statistics 2020–2021, https://www.ipos.gov.sg/docs/default-source/about-ipos-doc/statistics/statistics-2020-2021.pdf.

[30] Intellectual Property Office of Singapore (2016).

of attracting foreign researchers and multinational companies; and another from the perspective of local or rather indigenous Singaporean researchers and investors. Multinational companies form part of an important component for Singapore's goal to grow the biomedical sciences sector which comprises pharmaceuticals, medical technology, biotechnology and healthcare services to become the fourth pillar of its manufacturing sector, offering world-class capabilities across the whole value chain of activities.

It could be argued that foreign researchers attached to multinational companies and multinational companies with special funding for research and development and that own high degree of patents would prefer narrow interpretation of research exemption and Singapore would likely entertain this view in order to continuously import foreign capital and foreign researchers. On the other hand, Singapore's indigenous researchers and companies may prefer a broader interpretation of research exemption as this group of people would need to work within the constraint of budgets and the patent rights in order to develop their innovations.

In an attempt to comply with Singapore's obligations under the US-Singapore Free Trade Agreement, the Patents Act was amended on July 1 2004 to introduce a Bolar-type exemption to patent infringement. Under this provision, any acts to support an application for marketing approval for a pharmaceutical product in Singapore will be exempt from infringing a Singapore patent if such acts are in support of an application for marketing approval. Before the Bolar-type exemption provision came into force, the Patents Act provided statutory exemptions from infringement for acts done "privately and for purposes which are not commercial" and "for experimental purposes relating to the subject matter of the invention."

It was uncertain then if clinical trials of patented drugs would fall within these exemptions since there was no case law in Singapore that has dealt with this aspect of patent infringement. However, Singapore Courts will often decisions made in other Commonwealth Courts as persuasive on judges. In the UK case of *Monsanto Co v Stauffer Chemical Co*[31] and *Auchincloss v Agricultural and Veterinary Supplies*,[32] it was found that acts done to support an application for marketing approval would fall outside of the experimental use provisions. This is because such acts are considered to ultimately be for commercial purposes.

The inclusion of the Bolar-type exemption provision in the Patents Act, which explicitly excludes from patent infringement clinical trials of patented drugs for the purpose of seeking regulatory approval, clarifies Singapore's position on this aspect of infringement. Accordingly, drug companies are now able to engage in activities seeking to obtain marketing approval for a pharmaceutical product without infringing any Singapore patent rights. Thus, Bolar type exemption is an important provision in the patent law which allows pharmaceutical companies seeking marketing approvals prior to expiry of patents and this would encourage more

[31] [1984], FSR 669.

[32] [1997] RPC 662.

investment and commercial activities especially from companies producing generic or competing drugs.

Singapore's position can also be compared to the position of Korea, when Korea advances in biotechnology, there have been concerns about access to technology and negative impact of patents on innovation in Korea's small and medium enterprises. It was found SMEs in Korea faced restricted access when dealing with patented research tools where about 30% of respondents actually made their own tools, and another 30% acknowledged that they used research tools without licence.[33] It was found that most of the respondents believed that the research exemption under the Korean Patent Law should be applied more broadly.[34] Thus, Singapore's indigenous small and medium enterprises may face similar problems as in Korea where they may face difficulties in accessing research tools especially in biomedical field, as those tools may have been patented and owned by foreign multinationals.

5 CPTPP IP Chapter and Research Exemptions

Article 18 of the CPTPP addresses the protection of intellectual property in the Parties to the agreement, which adopts many TRIPs Plus measures including patent extension term and marketing arrangement for generic pharmaceuticals. In analysing the agreement, Article 18 of the CPTPP does not seem to prohibits or restricts patent research exemptions as provided for in the existing patent laws of the Parties. This position is clear when of the objectives of the CPTPP is only to protect and enforce intellectual property rights, but also to "...contribute to the promotion of technological innovation and to the transfer and dissemination of technology, to the mutual advantage of producers and users of technological knowledge and in a manner conducive to social and economic welfare, and to a balance of rights and obligations."[35]

It could be implied that the above provision allows the Parties to adopt provisions in the national IP that promotes research and development through research exemption provision. This argument is further supported by the fact that Parties to the CPTPP are given the flexibility to adopt measures necessary to protect public health and nutrition and to promote the public interest in sectors of vital importance to their socio-economic and technological development.[36] The Parties also recognise the need to promote innovation and creativity; facilitate the diffusion of information, knowledge, technology, culture and the arts; and foster competition and open and efficient markets, through their respective intellectual property systems.[37]

[33] Kang et al. (2009).
[34] Kang et al. (2009).
[35] CPTPP, Art. 18.2.
[36] CPTPP, Art. 18.3.
[37] CPTPP, Art. 18.4.

The argument that CPTPP allows Parties to retain the flexibility for research or research exemption lies in the provision of Article 18.40, that "*A Party may provide limited exceptions to the exclusive rights conferred by a patent, provided that such exceptions do not unreasonably conflict with a normal exploitation of the patent and do not unreasonably prejudice the legitimate interests of the patent owner, taking account of the legitimate interests of third parties*." This provision is consistent with Article 30 of the TRIPS Agreement, which introduces the three steps test, namely that the activities (1) *do not unreasonably conflict with a normal exploitation of the patent; (2) do not unreasonably prejudice the legitimate interests of the patent owner; and (3) taking into account of the legitimate interests of third parties.*

Nevertheless, it is argued that Parties to the CPTPP would adopt a narrower approach towards research exemption. This is because Parties only agree to provide limited exceptions to the exclusive rights conferred by a patent, "provided that such exceptions do not unreasonably conflict with a normal exploitation of the patent and do not unreasonably prejudice the legitimate interests of the patent owner, taking account of the legitimate interests of third parties."[38]

The narrow scope of patent research exemption is further exacerbated by the provision to allow to allow protection of new usage of existing pharmaceuticals (generally known as "ever--greening") as long as they meet the requirement of patentability outlined by the national laws of the Parties. Article 18.37 allows for patents to be available for "inventions new uses of a known product, new methods of using a known product, or new processes of using a known product." This allows certain pharmaceutical products to obtain new patents if it could be shown that they have new uses. The ever-greening provision allows patent holders to extend the use and terms of the patent for further protection, to the exclusion of third parties who could have conducted research and development in the same field.

The term ever-greening has been defined as "in the absence of any apparent additional therapeutic benefits, patent-holders use various strategies to extend the length of their exclusivity beyond the 20-year patent term".[39] There are concerns that product ever-greening could lead to the higher pharmaceutical price and lead to the constraint on the public health spending as they could lead to continues purchase of follow-on or improved products by hospitals or doctors and/or the blocking of the generic products of the original patented and approved pharmaceuticals. The Trilateral Study by the WHO, WTO and WIPO raises concern that ever-greening could be used to prolong patents protection in an appropriate manner, thus creating negative impact on access to medicine.

With due respect, the term "ever-greening" as defined by the CIPIH Report, which refers to "strategies" may not meet the term of "new use" in the CPTPP. It is submitted that new use refers to the scientifically proven use and meet the requirement of patentability of the relevant Patents law in the CPTPP member countries. Patentability criteria are still important and being applied by the national patent

[38] CPTPP, Art. 18.42.

[39] World Health Organisation (2006). See also discussion on the issue in Patel (2015).

offices. In applying the requirement of industrial application, one of the important criteria for patentability, some national patent offices may prevent the patenting of pharmaceutical compounds in a situation in which the inventor synthesizes compounds "without knowing how they can be applied to reach a result."[40] Thus, it is very important for a national patent office to develop a set of criteria to examine any application for new patent relating to ever-greening.

Commercialisation of new products resulting from the research and development activities, especially in the new of usage of pharmaceuticals with expiring patents also faces obstacles caused by the provision on the Undisclosed Test or Other Data for marketing approvals for new chemical entities and biologics.[41] Under Article 18.49, undisclosed data for new chemical entities are protected for a minimum period of 5 years from the date of the marketing approval of the new pharmaceutical product. The period of protection for biologics is divided into two options, namely for 8 years for from the date of first marketing approval or 5 years for a new pharmaceutical product that is or contains a biologic, that is a product that is a protein or contains a protein produced using biotechnology processes, for use in human beings for the prevention, treatment, or cure of a disease or condition.

However, the data protection for new chemical entities and biologics are only applicable to a situation where the regulators require the submission of undisclosed test or other data concerning: (a) only the safety of the product, (b) only the efficacy of the product or (c) both that has not been previously disclosed. Recognising that international and domestic regulation of biologics is in a formative stage, Parties agree to hold consultation after 10 years from the date of entry into force of the CPTPP.

Under Annex 18-C, in order to obtain protection for Undisclosed Test and Other Data for new chemical entity and biologics in Malaysia, an applicant is required to commence the process of obtaining marketing approval for pharmaceutical products within 18 months from the date that the product is first granted marketing approval in any country. The periods of protections for both new chemical entities and biologics begin on the date of marketing approval of the pharmaceutical product in Malaysia.

Malaysia needs to introduce new measures, possibly both in the Patents Act 1983 and the regulations or administrative measures by the National Pharmaceutical Control Bureau relating to the linkages between the owners of the marketing approval and their registered patents for products linked to the marketing approval, specifically where third persons are seeking marketing approvals for such patented products with marketing approvals.

Article 18.53 provides that, in the event of a third person seeking a marketing approval for a pharmaceutical product using information on safety and efficacy from

[40] WIPO, According to the WIPO's "*Study on the Role of Patent Systems in Promoting Innovative Medicines, and in Fostering the Technology Transfer Necessary to Make Generic and Patented Medicines Available In Developing Countries And Least Developed Countries*", Standing Committee on the Law of Patents Twenty-First Session Geneva, November 3 to 7, 2014, SCP/21/8, October 10, 2014. See also t'Hoen (2016).

[41] CPTPP, Art. 18.49.

a previously approved product, the Government is required to provide a system to provide a notice to a patent holder linked to the previously approved product about the new marketing approval application during the term of the patent; and adequate time and opportunity for such a patent holder to seek, prior to the marketing of an allegedly infringing product, available remedies through "certain procedures, such as judicial or administrative proceedings, and expeditious remedies, such as preliminary injunctions or equivalent effective provisional measures, for the timely resolution of disputes concerning the validity or infringement of an applicable patent claiming an approved pharmaceutical product or its approved method of use." In the alternative, Malaysian may have to adopt a system to preclude the issuance of marketing approval to any third person seeking to market a pharmaceutical product subject to a patent claiming that product, without the consent or acquiescence of the patent holder.

6 Conclusions

The above discussion shows that research exemption in the CPTPP preserves the same flexibility as contained in the TRIPS Agreement. The implementation of the flexibility in research exemption depends on the policy needs of the CPTPP member. Analysing the position of Malaysia and Singapore, it is safe to state that Malaysia and Singapore may take different approaches in utilising the provision of research exemption in biotechnology. Singapore's biotechnology development is due to investment made by foreign multinationals. Thus, Singapore will have to work on a policy that meets the need and the expectations of foreign multinationals and this will normally involve a narrow interpretation of research exemption in the patent law in order to protect the interest and investment made by the multinational companies.

On the other hand, Malaysia could adopt a broader approach towards research exemption.as the country does not have a strong pharmaceutical and healthcare biotechnology sector. Malaysia's focus is to gather its own strength, like biodiversity-based biotechnology such as production of biopharmaceuticals and nutraceuticals, fermented products, agriculture biotechnology and environmental biotechnology. This requires local technology development, either through locally based research and development or through joint research and development with foreign based commercial and foreign organisations.

References

Barton HJ (1995) Patent scope in biotechnology. Int Rev Intellect Prop Competition Law 26(5): 605–618

Garrison C (2006) Exceptions to patent rights in developing countries. UNCTAD-ICTSD Project on IPRs and Sustainable Development, August 2006

Intellectual Property Office of Singapore (2016) Singapore Patents Landscape 2016
Kang K, Ryu TK, Lee YS (2009) Effects of research tools patents on biotechnology patents in a developing country; a case study of South Korea. BMC Biotechnol 9:25
Kostolanksy K, Salgado D (2018) Does the experimental use exception in patent law have a future? The Colorado Lawyer, January 2018, pp 32–40
Patel R (2015) A public health imperative: the need for meaningful change in the trans-pacific partnership's intellectual property chapter. Minnesota J Law Sci Technol 16(1):Article 10
Rogan JE (2002) Hearings on competition and intellectual property law and policy in the knowledge-based economy. US Federal Trade Commission (USFTC), 6 February 2002
Russo AA, Johnson J (2015) Research use exemptions to patent infringement for drug discovery and development in the United States. Cold Spring Harb Perspect Med 5(2):a020933
Singapore Economic Development Board (2010–2011) Overview of Singapore's pharmaceutical and biotechnology industry. Singapore Biotech Guide 2010/2011, Singapore, pp 3–20
t'Hoen E (2016) Private patents and public health, changing intellectual property rules for access to medicines. Health Action International
West JK (2005) Intellectual property rights and competition policy with a focus on biotechnology. In OECD paper, best practice roundtables in competition policy working paper no. 50, 21 January 2005
World Health Organisation (2006) Public health, innovation and intellectual property rights: report of the Commission on Intellectual Property Rights, Innovation and Public Health 131
World Intellectual Property Organisation (WIPO) (2014) Study on the role of patent systems in promoting innovative medicines, and in fostering the technology transfer necessary to make generic and patented medicines available in developing countries and least developed countries. Standing Committee on the Law of Patents Twenty-First Session Geneva, 3–7 November 2014, SCP/21/8, 10 October 2014
World Intellectual Property Organisation (WIPO) (2017) Draft reference document on exception regarding acts for obtaining regulatory approval from authorities. Standing Committee on the Law of Patents, Twenty Seventh Session, SCP/27/3, 20 November 2017
World Intellectual Property Organisation (WIPO) (2018) World Intellectual Property Indicators 2018. WIPO, Geneva

Part III
International Dispute Resolution

Balancing Substantive Fairness and Procedural Efficiency: An Analysis of the ISDS Appeal Mechanism Under the Rules of Beijing International Arbitration Center

Yeqiong Wang and Fuyong Chen

Contents

Abstract Investor-state dispute settlement (ISDS) faces a profound legitimacy crisis. Establishment of an ISDS appeal mechanism is an important reform option for confronting such a crisis. The key issue in weighing this option lies in properly balancing substantive fairness and procedural efficiency. The Rules for International Investment Arbitration of Beijing International Arbitration Center (BAC Rules) of 2019 are the first set of investment arbitration rules at the global level to introduce a specialized ISDS appeal mechanism. The BAC Rules makes rational arrangements with regard to the initiation of appeal proceedings, grounds of appeal, independence and impartiality of the members of appellate tribunal, procedural transparency, time limit and other aspects. Such arrangements are expected to help strike a proper balance between substantive fairness and procedural efficiency. While its practical

Y. Wang (✉) and F. Chen
Beijing Arbitration Commission/Beijing International Arbitration Center (BAC/BIAC), Beijing, China
e-mail: wangyeqiong@bjac.org.cn; chenfuyong@bjac.org.cn

M. Bungenberg et al. (eds.), *Asian Yearbook of International Economic Law 2023*, Asian Yearbook of International Economic Law (2023) 2023: 191–206,
https://doi.org/10.1007/16517_2023_19, Published online: 11 April 2023

impacts remain to be observed, the BAC Rules could be a valuable reference for the international community in exploring an ISDS appeal mechanism in confronting the legitimacy crisis of ISDS.

1 Introduction

International investment arbitration, also known as investor-state arbitration (ISA) is the prominent form of investor-state disputes settlement (ISDS), and is often deemed as a largely depoliticized form of ISDS.[1] Over the past several decades, ISA has been frequently resorted to by investors in defending investment interests against sovereign states. As shown by the statistics of the United Nations Conference on Trade and Development (UNCTAD), over 1200 ISA cases have been initiated up to the present.[2]

ISDS is facing a legitimacy crisis in recent years. Both developing and developed countries have shown concerns over the existing ISA mechanism. While ISA remains a popular form of ISDS, some countries have taken measures to limit the use of ISA. For instance, Bolivia, Venezuela, and Ecuador have announced their withdrawal from the Convention on Settlement of International Investment Disputes between States and Nationals of Other States (ICSID Convention).[3] In the U.S.-Mexico-Canada Agreement (USMCA), the U.S. and Canada "abandoned" the ICSID arbitration arrangement and returned to domestic judicial recourses to settle international investment disputes, and ICSID arbitration is only available for international investment disputes between the U.S. and Mexico in certain industrial areas. Several European countries, such as the Netherlands, Spain and France, have announced that they will withdraw from the Energy Charter Treaty (ECT),[4] which provides energy companies the right to sue host governments and claim damages for policies that jeopardize their investments.

The causes of legitimacy crisis of ISDS are complex, mainly including inconsistency and unpredictability of international investment arbitration awards, imbalance in protection of interests of investors and host states, lack of independence and impartiality of arbitrators. The existing ISDS error-correcting mechanisms for ensuring the correctness and consistency of ISA awards have many deficiencies.[5] In more detail, grounds for annulling or setting aside awards in existing ISDS system are

---

[1] Shihata (1986), pp. 1–25.

[2] UNCTAD, Investment Policy Hub, available at https://investmentpolicy.unctad.org/investment-dispute-settlement.

[3] St John (2018), p. 239.

[4] Paul Messad, France must withdraw from Energy Charter Treaty, https://www.euractiv.com/section/energy/news/france-must-withdraw-from-energy-charter-treaty-climate-advisors-say/.

[5] See ICSID (2016), pp. 9–31.

restricted to procedural matters. Substantive issues are not involved. Moreover, a uniform standard of annulling or setting aside awards is missing. So does the award enforcement mechanism. Moreover, the effect of the award setting aside or annulling mechanism on enforcement of the award is uncertain.

To resolve legitimacy crisis of ISDS, fresh and continued efforts should be made in seeking an efficient ISDS error-correcting mechanism. Establishment of an ISDS appeal mechanism is one of the important ISDS reform options. It is well-accepted that establishment of an ISDS appeal mechanism could help ensure the correctness and consistency of awards to some extent. Opponents argue that such a mechanism will further burden the disputing parties with time and pecuniary costs, which is contrary to the principle of efficiency of arbitration. Whether an ISDS appeal mechanism is feasible or not depends largely on how the mechanism is shaped and enforced. A delicate set of rules for ISDS appeal proceeding can promote the unity of fairness and efficiency in ISDS.

In 2019, BAC formally issued its Rules for International Investment Arbitration (BAC Rules), which is the first set of arbitration rules in the world to include rules for an ISDS appeal mechanism. The BAC Rules has made rational arrangements on ISDS appeal proceedings. It is not only an innovative aspect of the BAC Rules, but more importantly, it also provides the international community an opportunity for a potential "test run" of an novel ISDS appeal mechanism.

This article provides a comprehensive overview of the appeal mechanism in the BAC Rules, clarifies the features and advantages of this appeal mechanism and rules and analyzes how it could help balance fairness and efficiency for ISDS. It is expected that stakeholders of ISDS may better evaluate the potential efficacy and deficiency of an ISDS appeal mechanism as a reform alternative of ISDS. Section 2 raises the question, that is, whether an ISDS appellate mechanism is needed and Sect. 3 attempts to figure out what possible obstacles establishing an ISDS appellate mechanism might face. Sections 4 and 5 take BAC Rules as a sample, analyzing how the Rules deals with those potential problems and balances fairness and efficiency respectively.

2 Necessity and Feasibility of an ISDS Appellate Mechanism

International investment arbitration is an important mechanism for resolving investment disputes between investors and host states, which has largely depoliticized international investment dispute settlement. However, the ISDS regime faces a legitimacy crisis in recent years.

The causes of the ISDS legitimacy crisis are complex. The first reason is the inconsistency and unpredictability of international investment arbitral awards. Some arbitral tribunals have made inconsistent or even conflicting awards in cases involving same or similar treaties, facts, and parties. Some arbitral tribunals have even made different awards on the same standard of treatment in the same investment treaty.[6] The inconsistency and unpredictability of arbitral awards has led to the loss of trust in the ISDS regime by disputing parties.

The second reason is the imbalance in protection of the interests of investors and host states. Guided by the purpose of protecting investment, some arbitral tribunals overly favor the protection of investors' interests and pay insufficient attention to the public interests of host states. Compounded by the defective design of investment treaty provisions, such imbalance has been gradually expanded with the rapid growth of the number of treaties and ISDS cases, thus triggering a crisis of legitimacy.[7]

The third reason is the lack of independence and impartiality of arbitrators. Arbitrators in the field of international investment arbitration are relatively a "small club." Some arbitrators act as lawyers in some cases and as arbitrators in others, resulting in a potential conflict of interests due to their "double hats." Moreover, ISDS cases are usually initiated by investors who claim that regulatory measures taken by host states have harmed their interests. If the disputants are given the right to choose arbitrators, it is likely that arbitrators will tend to favor investor's interests to increase the chance to be reappointed in subsequent cases.[8] Thus, the fairness of investment arbitration cannot be guaranteed.

While the existing ISDS regime has several defects has discussed above, it also has an error-correcting mechanism to remedy "incorrect arbitral awards," which mainly includes the award annulment mechanism and the award setting aside mechanism during the enforcement stage. The existing error-correcting mechanism can, to a certain extent, ensure the correctness and consistency of awards and balance the interests of investors and host states. Yet, this mechanism has deficiencies in its institutional design and practical effects, with a limited role to play in correcting awards.[9]

Notably, the existing ISDS regime emphasizes the finality and enforceability of awards. The grounds for annulling or setting aside of awards are usually limited to procedural matters, and do not involve substantive issues, such as errors in application and interpretation of law or errors in appreciation of facts. Besides, the criteria for setting aside awards is not uniform at the global level, depending largely on the attitude of state courts. Therefore, the existing award-correcting mechanism cannot adequately ensure the correctness and consistency of awards, nor can it maximize the balance between the interests of investors and host states, and is not sufficient to resolve the ISDS legitimacy crisis.

---

[6] See Myers, Inc. v. Canada, UNCITRAL, First Partial Award of 13 December 2000; Metalclad Corporation v. Mexico, ICSID Case No. ARB(AF)19711, Award of 30 August 2000 (ICSID); Pope & Talbot Inc. v. Canada, UNCITRAL, Award of 10 April 2001.

[7] See Schill (2017).

[8] Gaukrodger (2017), pp. 28–30.

[9] See ICSID (2016), pp. 9–31.

To address the crisis, sovereign states, international organizations, investment dispute settlement institutions and other stakeholders have begun to pursue ISDS reform. Establishing an ISDS appellate mechanism is an important reform option, which is well acknowledged to have certain advantages.

An ISDS appellate mechanism is conducive to ensure the correctness of awards. Under the objective of protecting and promoting investment, arbitral tribunals are likely to make mistakes in law application or interpretation, which will lead to the incorrectness of awards and do harm to the public interest of host states. For example, in CMS v. Argentina,[10] the arbitral tribunal misapplied and misinterpreted the law by equating the requisites of the security exception clause in the Argentina-US BIT with the requisites of necessity under customary international law and by giving precedence to rules of customary international law.[11] The establishment of an ISDS appellate mechanism, if realized, would mark the change from the era of efficiency or finality to the era of fairness. Grounds of appeal should include errors in the interpretation and application of the law generally. In addition to errors in the application and interpretation of the law, other grounds for appeal should include manifest error in the appreciation of the facts, including the appreciation of relevant domestic law. The identification and correct interpretation of the content of the host state's domestic law is directly related to the outcome of the award. To conclude, entrusting disputants with rights to appeal based on "errors in the interpretation and application of law" and "manifest errors in the appreciation of facts" is beneficial in ensuring the correctness of awards.

An ISDS appellate mechanism is also helpful in ensuring the consistency and predictability of arbitral awards. In general, the establishment of such a mechanism makes it easier to create a de facto system of stare decisis. Currently, international investment arbitration is characterized by a decentralized decision-making model with ad hoc arbitral tribunals.[12] There is no hierarchy among arbitral tribunals. In an ISDS appellate mechanism, lower-tier bodies are more likely to recognize the binding nature of decisions rendered by higher-tier bodies, and to achieve the same conclusion with the higher-tier body in the same or similar circumstances. The concept of consistency goes far beyond the request that arbitral tribunals constituted under different investment treaties reach same conclusions when dealing with the same set of facts; it also covers uniformity and coherence in the interpretation of basic principles.[13] To avoid the legal findings or conclusions in a provisional award being modified or reversed by an appellate tribunal, the tribunal will apply and interpret the law more judiciously and be more likely to follow the basic

[10] CMS Gas Transmission Company v. The Argentine Republic, ICSID Case No. ARB/01/8.

[11] CMS Gas Transmission Company v The Argentine Republic, ICSID Case No. ARB/01/08 (Annulment proceeding). Decision of the Ad Hoc Committee on the Application for Annulment of the Argentine Republic, 25 September 2007, para. 128–136.

[12] Kriebaum (2014), p. 48.

[13] K. Yannaca-Small, Improving the System of Investor-State Dispute Settlement: An Overview, www.oecd.org/dataoecd/3/59/36052284.pdf.

rules set out in the Vienna Convention on the Law of Treaties (VCLT). Consistency and correctness of the award are mutually complementary, meaning that the appellate mechanism can not only guarantee the correctness of the award, but also enhance the consistency of the award through uniformly following the fundamental standards of interpretation and application of law.

3 Potential Obstacles for Establishing an ISDS Appellate Mechanism

In the 1990s, during the negotiation of the Multilateral Agreement on Investment (MAI) led by the Organization of Economic Cooperation and Development (OECD), the representative of France proposed the establishment of an appellate mechanism in the MAI to be applied to disputes between the home state of investors and the host state, as well as to disputes between the host state and the investor.[14] This proposal was supported by many delegations during the informal consultation procedure. However, as the inclusion of an appellate mechanism could lead to delays and additional costs, which is contrary to the principle of efficiency, low-cost and finality of arbitration, the final draft of the MAI did not formally include an appellate mechanism, but left it as an option to be considered for the next 5 years.[15] With the failure of the MAI, the proposed appellate mechanism has never been put to practice.

In 2004, ICSID Secretariat proposed the inclusion of a uniform, optional Appeals Facility Rule to replace the bilateral appellate mechanism under BITs and FTAs for enhancing the consistency and coherence of the awards.[16] However, most member states considered it premature to establish an ICSID Appeals Facility at that stage, especially because of the technical and policy obstacles.[17] Finally, ICSID Secretariat withdrew its proposal to establish an appellate mechanism.

The reasons for opposing the establishment of an appellate mechanism for ISDS can be divided into two main types. First, finality is the basic feature of arbitration, and establishment of an appellate mechanism would hurt the finality. Second, an obvious advantage of arbitration as a form of dispute settlement is its high efficiency

[14] See Organization for Economic Co-operation and Development, Selected Issues on Dispute Settlement (Note by the Chairman), DAFFE/MAI (98) 12, 13 March 1998, p. 5, https://www.oecd.org/daf/mai/pdf/ng/ng9812e.pdf.

[15] See Organization for Economic Co-operation and Development, Selected Issues on Dispute Settlement (Note by the Chairman), DAFFE/MAI (98) 12, 13 March 1998, p. 5, https://www.oecd.org/daf/mai/pdf/ng/ng9812e.pdf.

[16] See International Centre for Settlement of Investment Disputes, Possible Improvements of the Framework for ICSID Arbitration, available at https://icsid.worldbank.org/sites/default/files/Possible%20Improvements%20of%20the%20Framework%20of%20ICSID%20Arbitration.pdf.

[17] See International Center for Settlement of Investment Disputes, Suggested Changes to the ICSID Rules and Regulations, available at https://icsid.worldbank.org/sites/default/files/Suggested%20Changes%20to%20the%20ICSID%20Rules%20and%20Regulations.pdf.

and low cost, whereas an appellate mechanism for arbitration is likely to create delays in dispute settlement and increase in costs.

The above arguments could be rebutted. For the first objection, it has been argued that the fundamental characteristic of arbitration is that its jurisdiction is based on the voluntary consent of the parties, which distinguishes arbitration from domestic courts. There have been practices for appellate mechanism of arbitration. For instance, Arbitration Act 1996 of the United Kingdom expressly allows the parties to an arbitration the right to appeal to the court on questions of law in the course of the arbitration upon satisfaction of certain conditions. Upon review, the court may issue a decision upholding the arbitral award, modifying the award, remanding for reaffirmation or setting aside the award.[18] As can be seen, the binding and enforceable nature of an arbitral award does not prevent the parties from exercising the right to apply to the court for review or appeal of the arbitral award.[19] Besides, Court of Arbitration for Sports has also established an appellate mechanism.[20]

For the second objection, there has been discussions on whether establishment of an appellate mechanism for investment arbitration can ensure the correctness and consistency of awards while preserving the efficiency and low cost depends on the specific arrangements on the rules of appeal procedure, including grounds of appeal, time limits, allocation of costs and other critical elements. In essence, whether an appeal mechanism should be allowed is a question of balancing between correctness and efficiency of awards. Admittedly, there is no fixed answer to this question. As the first set of rules for international investment arbitration in the world to introduce appeal proceedings, BAC Rules tries to explore this balancing question through its specialized appeal rules. The following two parts deals respectively with how the BAC rules tries to improve the correctness of arbitral awards and in the same time ensuring the efficiency of arbitration.

4 The BAC Rules and the Substantive Fairness of Arbitral Awards

While there is no uniform definition of the term "fairness" or "correctness" of arbitral awards, it seems reasonable to argue that for an arbitral award to be persuasive, it has to be perceived fair and correct in substance especially by the disputants.[21] In a sense, such substantive fairness of awards forms a pillar of the legitimacy of the

[18] See Arbitration Act 1996 of the United Kingdom, section 69.

[19] See Arbitration Act 1996 of the United Kingdom, section 58(2).

[20] See Statutes of the Bodies Working for the Settlement of Sports-Related Disputes, S3 and S12.

[21] See, generally, Academic Forum on ISDS Working Group Four, "Incorrectness of ISDS Decisions," available at https://www.cids.ch/images/Documents/Academic-Forum/4_Incorrectness_of_ISDS_Decisions_-_WG4.pdf.

awards and the ISDS mechanism. Establishing an ISDS appeal mechanism is deemed as a method for achieving such substantive fairness.

The BAC Rules provides for an appeal mechanism for international investment arbitration. Article 46 of the BAC Rules provides for the appeal of the award in general, expressly granting the disputing parties the right to appeal based on their consent. The specific appeal procedures are set out in Appendix E of the BAC Rules. The appeal proceedings will be analyzed from the perspectives of improving the correctness of arbitral awards.

4.1 Grounds of Appeal

Under rule 3 of Appendix E of the BAC Rules, an appeal may only be initiated based on three grounds: (a) the arbitral award contains error(s) in the application or interpretation of the applicable law or rules of law; (b) the arbitral award contains manifest and material errors of fact; and (c) the BAC or the Arbitral Tribunal lacked jurisdiction, or the arbitral tribunal exceeded its powers, in so far as they are not covered by the two circumstances above.[22]

In contrast to the existing error-correcting mechanism, the grounds of appeal provided in the BAC Rules are not limited to procedural matters, but also include substantive issues, such as errors in interpretation and application of law and errors in appreciation of facts. As mentioned above, arbitral awards are frequently criticized for lack of substantive correctness. For instance, a series of arbitration cases arising from regulatory measures taken by Argentine during the economic crisis have been criticized for lack of correctness,[23] such as CMS v. v. Argentina,[24] and Enron v. Argentina.[25] International investment arbitration often involves important public interests, making the correctness and fairness of awards important. The BAC Rules specifies that the grounds of appeal include errors in application and interpretation of law and manifest errors in appreciation of facts, providing the losing party an opportunity to get remedy on these grounds and to achieve a fair and equitable award.

The third ground of appeal deals with jurisdictional issue, namely, the BAC or the arbitral tribunal lacked jurisdiction, or the arbitral tribunal exceeded its powers. This ground is quite similar to one for setting aside arbitral awards in the existing ISDS regime. Specifically, the term "the arbitral tribunal exceeded its powers" is a broad one, which includes the situations where there is no arbitration agreement or where the award deals with a difference not contemplated by or not falling within the terms

---

22 Appendix E of the BAC/BIAC Rules for International Investment Arbitration, Rule 3.

23 See Burke-White (2008).

24 CMS Gas Transmission Company v. The Argentine Republic, ICSID Case No ARB/01/8.

25 Enron Creditors Recovery Corporation (formerly Enron Corporation) and Ponderosa Assets, LP v. Argentine Republic, ICSID Case No ARB/ 01/3.

of the submission to arbitration.[26] The fundamental feature of arbitration is that the jurisdiction of arbitration derives from the consent of the disputing parties. Allowing the disputing parties to appeal on such jurisdictional ground reflects the respect for party autonomy and the emphasis on procedural legality.

4.2 *Independence and Impartiality of Arbitrators*

To address the growing concerns over of the independence and impartiality of arbitrators, chapter III of the BAC Rules provides for qualifications, nomination or appointment, disclosure, challenge to and replacement of arbitrators. Appendix E of the BAC Rules further confirms that these relevant rules also apply to the members of appellate tribunal.[27] Meanwhile, BAC also issued the Code of Conduct for Arbitrators in International Investment Disputes (hereinafter referred to as "BAC Code of Conduct"). Article 2 of the BAC Code of Conduct provides that it shall apply to arbitrators in international investment arbitration cases submitted to the BAC and to members of the Appellate Tribunal in international investment arbitration appeals submitted to the BAC. The BAC Code of Conduct provides for performance of duties, independence and impartiality, obligation of disclosure and other requirements separately.

To address the conflict of interests caused by of the "double hats" of arbitrators, the BAC Code of Conduct provides that arbitrators shall refrain from acting as arbitrator, representative, counsel, expert appointed by the arbitral tribunal or court, or expert witness at the same time as they are acting on matters that involve the same parties, the same international investment agreement, or the same facts.[28] Also, arbitrators shall not act as the party's representatives in arbitration cases administered by the BAC.[29] Furthermore, where arbitrators on the BAC Panel of Arbitrators for International Investment Disputes have breached the BAC Code of Conduct, the BAC may, depending on the circumstances, consider not renewing or dismissing the arbitrators.[30] Both the BAC Rules and the BAC Code of Conduct require arbitrators, upon acceptance of nomination or appointment, to ensure that they have recognized competence in law (particularly knowledge of public international law) and high moral character. It is to be noted that the emphasis on knowledge of public international law is a response to the recent criticism over the qualification of arbitrators for lack of public international law knowledge, which could lead to their lack of competence in recognizing the specialness of sovereign states in regulating foreign investment and economic activities.

[26] See Tsolakidis (2014), p. 834.

[27] See Appendix E of the BAC/BIAC Rules for International Investment Arbitration, Rule 2(5).

[28] See BAC/BIAC Code of Conduct for Arbitrators in International Investment Disputes, Art. 3(4).

[29] See BAC/BIAC Code of Conduct for Arbitrators in International Investment Disputes, Art. 4(3).

[30] See BAC/BIAC Code of Conduct for Arbitrators in International Investment Disputes, Art. 10.

Here, the proposal of a two-tiered international investment court by the European Union (EU) worth mentioning. Such a proposal aims mainly at addressing the "double hat" issue of arbitrators.[31] Members of the Appellate Tribunal shall serve on a full-time basis. The president of the Appeal Tribunal shall appoint the Members composing the division of the Appeal Tribunal hearing the appeal on a rotation basis. Disputing parties have no rights to nominate particular adjudicators to hear the specific case. Members of Appeal Tribunal appointed for a long term through a transparent process are not permitted to engage in any occupation, whether gainful or not. Members shall be paid a retainer fee and daily fees which may be permanently transformed into a regular salary.[32] Although the arrangements of international investment court are more likely to guarantee independence and impartiality of arbitrators, it seems that a permanent appellate body can be established only through bilateral or multilateral treaty practice at the state level. as Arbitration institutions, such as the BAC, may not be in a position to establish a permanent appellate body. That been said, the BAC Rules has tried to ensure the independence and impartiality of arbitrators, including members of appellate tribunal, through its arbitration rules, appeal rules and code of conducts, which could be a helpful reference for other international arbitration institutions in further exploring the issue in the future.

4.3 Requirements of Transparency

The issue of transparency in international investment arbitration is related to the limited obligation of the arbitral tribunal to provide information and the inability of third parties to participate in the arbitration to promote the protection of private or public interests.[33] As argued by some scholars, since investment treaty arbitration not only involve the rights and obligations of disputing parties, but also of other specific stakeholders and the public,[34] it is unreasonable to directly apply the principle of confidentiality as in commercial arbitration. In the absence of transparency, other stakeholders and the public cannot participate in the investment treaty arbitration. As a result, the arbitral tribunal cannot consider their opinions and is more likely to make an award in favor of the investor with the purpose of investment protection.

The degree of confidentiality varies among arbitration rules and international investment treaty. Under the BAC Rules, where the disputing parties have agreed in

---

[31] UNCITRAL, Submission from the European Union and its Member States, A/CN.9/WG.III/WP.159/Add.1, https://documents-dds-ny.un.org/doc/UNDOC/LTD/V19/004/19/PDF/V1900419.pdf?OpenElement, para. 47.

[32] For example, Investment Protection Agreement between the European Union and its Members States, of the One Part, and the Republic of Singapore, of the Other Part, Art. 3.10.

[33] Adeleke (2015), p. 7.

[34] St John (2018), pp. 240–248.

writing, Articles 3–7 of the UNCITRAL Rules on Transparency in Treaty-based Investor-State Arbitration 2014 (the "UNCITRAL Transparency Rules") shall apply to the arbitration in whole or in part, and shall prevail over the relevant provisions of the Rules; where the disputing parties have no agreement on the application of the UNCITRAL Transparency Rules, the Notice of Arbitration, Notice of Appeal, orders, decisions and the award of the Arbitral Tribunal and the Appellate Tribunal shall be made public, except for confidential or otherwise protected information therein.[35] As can be seen, the BAC Rules maintains a certain level of compulsory transparency of arbitration. The disclosure of relevant arbitration information enables stakeholders, such as the public, industry associations, other NGOs and non-disputing Parties to the treaty, to participate in the arbitration proceedings to provide opinions and monitor arbitration cases, thus contributing to the fairness of arbitration proceedings and inclusiveness of arbitral awards.

5 The BAC Rules and the Procedural Efficiency of Arbitration

As mentioned, inception of an appeal procedure in ISDS could cause delay in dispute settlement and higher cost. It seems justified that commentators and practitioners may concern over the efficiency of investment arbitration. The BAC Rules also addresses this concern from the following aspects.

5.1 Optional Nature of Appeal Proceeding

The BAC Rules specifies the conditions for appeal. The appeal proceeding can only be initiated based on agreement by both disputing parties in writing.[36] The BAC Rules does not set specific requirements on the form of writing. According to the Interpretation of BAC Rules, the form of written agreement is generally considered to be sufficient in any way that can be left in writing, such as an appeal agreement or an appeal arrangement. The state party may either incorporate an agreement to appeal through a treaty with the investor's home state before the investment dispute arises, or it may consent to appeal after the dispute arises on a case-by-case basis.[37]

The optional appellate mechanism is flexible in that it leaves the trade-off between procedural efficiency and substantive fairness to the parties to an international investment dispute. The parties may choose to apply the appellate mechanism

[35] See BAC/BIAC Rules for International Investment Arbitration, Art. 50.

[36] See BAC/BIAC Rules of International Investment Arbitration, Art. 46.

[37] See BAC/BIAC (ed.), the Interpretation of BAC/BIAC Rules of International Investment Arbitration, Law Press·China, 2021, p. 5.

to review the original award to ensure the fairness of the award, but they will bear the time and monetary costs of the appeal. If the parties prefer to pursue procedural efficiency of ISDS, they may also choose not to appeal. Such an optional appellate mechanism essentially reflects a greater degree of flexibility, which could be attractive to the disputants and the international community at large.

In summary, the optional ISDS appeal mechanism provided in the BAC Rules retains the fundamental attribute of arbitration, that is, respecting party autonomy, without judicializing the appellate mechanism. At the same time, given the difficulties of ISDS reform and of the establishment of a multilateral appellate mechanism, the optional appellate mechanism gives disputing parties the right to decide whether to apply for appeal, and leaves it to the parties to decide the trade-off between procedural efficiency and substantive fairness.

5.2 *Avoidance of Procedure Duplication*

If award setting aside or annulment procedure is retained with the inception of an ISDS appellate mechanism, it may lead to the de facto creation of a three-tier dispute resolution mechanism. As a result, time and pecuniary costs of dispute resolution will increase, which will ultimately hurt the efficiency and finality of arbitration.[38] Therefore, to guarantee the efficiency of ISDS, the relationship between appeal procedure and award setting aside or annulment procedure needs to be properly dealt with.

United Nations Commission for International Trade Law (UNCITRAL) Working Group III, in the Initial Draft on Appeal Mechanism and Enforcement Issues, notes that if the grounds for annulment and setting aside under the ICSID Convention and the UNCITRAL Model Law on International Commercial Arbitration ("Model Law")[39] are made grounds for appeal, it would be necessary to ensure that disputing parties would not be able to commence annulment or setting aside procedures and that states would be required to waive the right of review of decisions made by the appellate mechanism.[40] However, The implementation of such a waiver would depend on how the appellate mechanism is to be set-up. EU, for instance, does so by expressly providing in its BITs that the appellate award is binding as final and that the final award cannot be further appealed, reviewed or set aside. Even if a party waives its right through a treaty, not all domestic laws would necessarily recognize such a waiver as a valid agreement to exclude the right to seek setting aside before

[38] See UNCITRAL Working Group III, Initial Draft on Appellate Mechanism and Enforcement Issues, para. 8.

[39] The Model Law has been referenced in domestic law in many countries, including China.

[40] UNCITRAL Working Group III, Initial Draft on Appellate Mechanism and Enforcement Issues, para. 9.

their courts, states parties to the appellate mechanism might need to consider passing legislation to make the waiver take effect in domestic law.

The Arbitration Law of the People's Republic of China (CAL) provides that the people's courts have the right to review arbitral awards and may decide to set aside arbitral awards under certain circumstances.[41] Judicial review of awards by domestic courts is a statutory power conferred by domestic law. As discussed above, the appeal mechanism is included in BAC Rules. According to the CAL, if disputing parties choose to apply appeal proceeding of BAC Rules, the appeal award is likely to be reviewed judicially by people's court again. To avoid duplication of appeal procedure and award setting aside procedure, there are only two approaches. The first approach is to pass legislation to make a waiver to review the final arbitral awards by the Government of China. However, from a practical point of view, this approach is hard to realize at the present stage. Alternatively, the arbitration institution could make a reasonable arrangement on grounds of appeal to avoid the procedure duplication.

The BAC limits the grounds of appeal. Specifically, not all grounds for annulment under the ICSID Convention and the grounds for setting aside awards under the Model Law qualify as grounds for appeal under the BAC Rules. As discussed, under the BAC Rules, an appeal may only be initiated on three grounds, namely, errors in the application or interpretation of the applicable law or rules of law, manifest and material errors of fact, and excess of powers by the arbitral tribunal. The grounds of setting aside an award provided in the CAL, such as "the formation of the arbitration tribunal or the arbitration procedure was not in conformity with the statutory procedure," "the evidence on which the award is based was forged," "the arbitrators have committed embezzlement, accepted bribes or done malpractices for personal benefits or perverted the law in the arbitration of the case," "the award violates the public interest," are not grounds for appeal under the BAC Rules. By this way, although appeal procedure and award setting aside procedure exist concurrently in form, duplication of procedures has been avoided to the greatest extent in content. Thus, the efficiency can be improved.

5.3 *Strict Time Limit*

The BAC Rules also stresses efficiency and cost control of the appeal process. With respect to the initiation of the appeal, the BAC Rules promotes efficient resolution of disputes by providing the parties with the option to reach a consensus at the latest point in time. Under Article 46(2) of the BAC Rules, the parties shall notify their agreement to appeal to the BAC as early as possible, and in any event no later than the expiration of the time limit fixed by the arbitral tribunal for the filing of comments on the draft of the award. The term "notice" in this Article refers to

[41] See CAL, Art. 58 and Art. 70.

informing the arbitrator of the parties' consent to the application of the appeal procedure, and does not mean that the parties have commenced the appeal procedure or that the appeal procedure is going to be commenced thereafter. If the parties wish to initiate an appeal procedure, they should submit a written notice of appeal to the BAC within 60 days from the date on which the award is made, and the appeal procedure is deemed to be initiated from the date of the parties' successful submission of the notice of appeal. In theory, the investor and the host state can agree to appeal at any point in time, but to ensure reasonable use of the appeal procedure and to avoid abuse of the appeal procedure, the BAC Rules requires the parties to notify the BAC of their agreement to appeal as early as possible.

In terms of time constraints, the BAC Rules limits the time for arbitrator appointment and arbitration proceedings. First, the BAC Rules sets a reasonable time limit for selection and appointment of arbitrators. The appellate tribunal should be constituted no later than 30 days after the appellee receives the notice of the commencement of the appeal proceedings, as provided in Rule 2(2) of the Appendix E.

Second, the BAC Rules provides for a time limit for the disputing parties to submit written statements. Rule 5(2) of Appendix E provides that, unless the appellate parties have agreed otherwise, the appellant shall file an appellant's submission within 15 days of its receipt of the notice of the commencement of the appeal proceedings, and the appellee shall file an appellee's submission within 30 days of its receipt of the appellant's submission. The length of time taken by the parties to submit written statements has been a hurdle for the efficiency of investment arbitration. Setting a reasonable limit on the time for submission of statements encourages the parties to respond promptly to each other's statements; it could also facilitate the appellate tribunal to resolve the disputes promptly.

Third, the time for the appellate tribunal to make an award is also subject to a time limit. Rule 8(1) of Appendix E stipulates that the appellate tribunal shall render an award on the appeal within 90 days from the date of its constitution. This time limit may be extended at the request of the appellate tribunal, but the extension shall not exceed 30 days. The aforementioned time limit shall not apply to any extension(s) on which the appellate parties have agreed. It can be seen from this provision that unless the appellate parties unanimously agree to extend the time limit for appeal, the appellate tribunal will render the final arbitral award within 120 days at the latest from the date of constitution of the appeal tribunal. This provision is in line with some other rules at the international level. For instance, the EU-Singapore IPA stipulates that a final arbitral award shall be rendered within 180 days, and that if the appellate tribunal is unable to render a decision within that period, the period shall be extended to no more than 270 days upon written notice of reasons.[42]

For the costs of appeal, the BAC Rules stipulates for the sanctions for parties that unduly delay the appellate proceeding. Rule 9(7) and (10) of Appendix E provides

[42] See Investment Protection Agreement between the European Union and its Members States, of the One Part, and the Republic of Singapore, of the Other Part, Art. 3.19.4.

that the appellate tribunal may, at the request of a party or on its own initiative, determine in the appeal award the division and apportionment of the costs of the appeal between the parties, and order one party to pay any reasonable costs incurred by the other party in whole or in part, including the costs of legal representation, having regard to the outcome of the appeal, each party's contribution to the efficiency and expeditiousness of the appeal and any other circumstances it considers relevant. These provisions give the appellate tribunal needed discretion to apportion the costs of the appeal and the reasonable expenses incurred by the parties. They could help discourage parties from filing unnecessary or false applications for appeal, and could reduce the financial burden suffered by one party as a result of undue delay caused by the other party.

6 Conclusion

As international investment activities and international investment law keep developing, the number of ISDS cases has increased rapidly in recent years. The legitimacy crisis of ISDS has become increasingly outstanding and challenging. Although the existing ISDS regime include certain error-correcting mechanisms, these mechanisms have defects in both procedural and substantive aspects, and need to be improved.

Against such a background, it is broadly deemed that the establishment of an ISDS appellate mechanism could be conductive to address the legitimacy crisis of the existing ISDS regime. Establishment of an ISDS appellate mechanism has certain advantages, but it also has defects. Plainly put it, while an ISDS appeal mechanism helps to improve the fairness of the award, the appeal is likely to cause delay as it necessitates more time and cost. Thus, the efficacy and success of such a mechanism relies essentially on how it can balance substantive fairness with procedural efficiency.

The BAC Rules, as the first investment arbitration rules with an appeal mechanism in the world, have made fresh efforts in striking such a balance from different aspects, providing helpful reference for other arbitration institutions and the international community in addressing the ISDS legitimate crisis. They could also be a helpful supplement to the international efforts made by other international institutions, such as the EU and UNCITRAL Working Group III.

References

Adeleke F (2015) The role of law in assessing the value of transparency and the disconnect with the lived realities under investor-state dispute settlement. SECO/WTI Academic Cooperation Project Working Paper Series 2015/06

Burke-White WW (2008) The Argentine financial crisis: state liability under BITs and the legitimacy of the ICSID system. Asian J WTO Int Health Law Policy 3(1):199–234

Gaukrodger D (2017) Adjudicator compensation systems and investor-state dispute settlement. https://www.oecd-ilibrary.org/finance-and-investment/adjudicator-compensation-systems-and-investor-state-dispute-settlement_c2890bd5-en

ICSID (2016) Updated background paper on annulment for the Administrative Council of ICSID. https://icsid.worldbank.org/sites/default/files/Background%-20Paper%20on%20Annulment%20April%202016%20ENG.pdf

Kriebaum U (2014) The nature of investment disciplines. In: Douglas Z, Pauwelyn J, Viñuales JE (eds) The foundations of international investment law: bringing theory into practice. Oxford University Press, Oxford, pp 45–72

Schill SW (2017) Reforming investor-state dispute settlement: a (comparative and international) constitutional law framework. JIEL 20(3):649–672

Shihata IFI (1986) Towards a greater depoliticization of investment disputes: the roles of ICSID and MIGA. ICSID Rev 1(1):1–25

St John T (2018) The rise of investor-state arbitration: politic, law, and unintended consequences. Oxford University Press, Oxford

Tsolakidis N (2014) ICSID annulment standards: who has finally won the Reisman v. Broches debate of two decades ago? In: Kalicki JE, Joubin-Bert A (eds) Reshaping the investor-state dispute settlement system. Leiden, Brill Nijhoff, pp 828–853

Yeqiong Wang is the Case Manager of Beijing Arbitration Commission/Beijing International Arbitration Center (BAC/BIAC). She received an LL.B. degree from East China University of Political Science and Law (2016), an LL.M. degree in International Commercial Law from University College London (2017), and a PhD. Degree from Renmin University of China (2022).

Fuyong Chen is the Deputy Secretary General of Beijing Arbitration Commission/Beijing International Arbitration Center (BAC/BIAC) and the Vice-President of Asia Pacific Regional Arbitration Group (APRAG). He received an LL.B. degree from China University of Political Science and Law, an LL.M. degree from Peking University, and a PhD. Degree from Tsinghua University. He was a Visiting Researcher at University of California at Berkeley School of Law (2007–2008).

Tashkent International Arbitration Centre at the Chamber of Commerce and Industry of Uzbekistan: Taking Stock on Its Fourth Anniversary

Diana Bayzakova and Adrian Mak

Contents

Abstract The Tashkent International Arbitration Centre ('TIAC') was founded in 2018 to put Uzbekistan on the global arbitration map. This article first reviews the broad powers and features of the TIAC in the 4 years since its establishment. Second, it examines the increasing diversity and volume of its current caseload. Third, it discusses the 2022 TIAC-HKIAC Cross-institutional Rules of Arbitration. Lastly, it examines the challenge, recognition and enforcement of foreign arbitral awards in Uzbekistan. This article reflects that TIAC's unique features and arbitral rules, along with a pro-arbitration and pro-enforcement stance taken by the Uzbek judiciary, will enable Uzbekistan to position itself as a leading regional dispute resolution centre in the coming years.

D. Bayzakova (✉)
Tashkent International Arbitration Centre, Chamber of Commerce and Industry of Uzbekistan, Tashkent, Uzbekistan
e-mail: dbayzakova@tiac.uz

A. Mak
Singapore International Commercial Court, Singapore, Singapore
e-mail: adrianm@connect.hku.hk

M. Bungenberg et al. (eds.), *Asian Yearbook of International Economic Law 2023*,
Asian Yearbook of International Economic Law (2023) 2023: 207–216,
https://doi.org/10.1007/16517_2023_16, Published online: 12 April 2023

1 Background

Since 2016, Uzbekistan has been implementing significant reforms which aim to enable business development, bolster economic stability, improve trade connectivity and attract foreign investment. According to the World Bank, despite the economic setbacks in the post-pandemic world, Uzbekistan's GDP is projected to grow at 4.9%, making it one of the fastest growing economies in Europe and the Central Asian region's 23 countries, along with Armenia, Croatia, Georgia and Montenegro.[1]

As part of the reforms, the Tashkent International Arbitration Centre ('TIAC') at the Chamber of Commerce and Industry of Uzbekistan was founded in 2018 to put Uzbekistan on the global arbitration map and to promote arbitration as an alternative dispute resolution method in Uzbekistan and beyond. November 5, 2022 marks the fourth anniversary of the establishment of TIAC. It is apposite to take stock of the institution which has received overwhelming support from leading international arbitration practitioners, who have in concerted effort joined to build the necessary infrastructure for the region's leading arbitral institution.[2]

Before TIAC's establishment, there were merely a handful of local institutions offering arbitration services in Uzbekistan. Their services were limited to domestic arbitrations, and were administered in accordance with the 2006 Domestic Arbitration Law that had two major limitations: it restricted the parties to appoint foreign arbitrators and apply foreign law. Considering these limitations, the Decree establishing TIAC ('the Decree') granted TIAC broad powers to make it a competitive arbitral institution in Central Asia as well as internationally:

- Parties have been enabled to choose the substantive laws of non-Uzbekistan jurisdictions as the governing law in disputes.
- Parties have been empowered to appoint foreign arbitrators to resolve their disputes.
- Foreign (but not local) arbitrators appointed under the TIAC Rules have become exempt from income tax for their services.
- No work permits have become required for foreign arbitrators (and experts) to serve in TIAC-administered cases.
- No bar admissions or permits are required for foreign advocates or counsels acting in local Uzbek courts on matters related to TIAC arbitrations, such as in applications for the setting-aside or recognition and enforcement of arbitral awards.
- For cases administered by TIAC, the parties' costs of arbitration (filing fees and arbitrators' fees) are exempt from VAT.[3]

[1] Bjerde (2022).

[2] Ross (2021).

[3] Decree establishing TIAC №4001 of 5 November 2018, https://lex.uz/docs/4039518.

The TIAC organizational structure was formed with the support of the TIAC Supervisory Board (whose members were invited by the Chamber of Commerce and Industry of Uzbekistan in December 2018 following the TIAC establishment), and is currently composed of the following bodies:

1. The TIAC Court of Arbitration ('TIAC Court'), which is a fully autonomous organ within the TIAC and is the only body within the TIAC's structure that administers disputes under the TIAC Rules of Arbitration in complete independence from TIAC, its founders, or any other entities or individuals. The exclusive powers of the TIAC Court include confirmation, appointment or replacement of the arbitrators, fixing the arbitration costs and overseeing the arbitral process and scrutinising the awards to ensure their enforceability.
2. The TIAC Supervisory Board, which is an organ within TIAC, which observes and advises on the operational standards of the TIAC and is in charge of selecting the TIAC Court.
3. The TIAC Secretariat, which assists the TIAC Court in the procedural matters, which is under the competence of the TIAC Court in accordance with the TIAC Arbitration Rules.

As arbitration is becoming increasingly popular globally, it is important for TIAC (being one of the youngest arbitral institutions globally) not only to comply with the best international practices, but also to create and deliver a unique value proposition to its prospective users. Therefore, the following features were introduced.

1.1 Zero Admin Fee Policy

In the landmark empirical survey conducted in 2018 by the School of International Arbitration at Queen Mary University of London, it was found that 'cost' continues to be seen as arbitration's worst feature.[4] Under the TIAC Schedule of Costs (see Fig. 1), users do not pay administrative fees, which provides a significant saving. It is also worth noting in this context that the remuneration of TIAC arbitrators may at times be even higher when compared to the fees they would have received at other arbitral institutions.

1.2 Strictest No-Conflict Rules

TIAC has also implemented a reinforced 'no conflict of rules' policy. Unlike many institutions in the region, the members of the TIAC Court, the TIAC Secretariat and

[4]2018 International Arbitration Survey: The Evolution of International Arbitration, https://arbitration.qmul.ac.uk/research/2018/.

Fig. 1 TIAC Schedule of Costs 2021 (https://www.tiac.uz/tiac-rules-of-arbitration)

Claim amount (USD)	TIAC's admin fee	Arbitrator's fees (USD)	
		Minimum	Maximum
Up to 35,000	0%	2300	4,500
From 35,001 to 75,000	0%	2,300 + 8% of and over 35,000	4,500 + 10% of and over 35,000
From 75.001 to 200,000	0%	7,500 + 4,5% of and over 75,000	9,500 + 5,3% of and over 75,000
From 200,001 to 500,000	0%	9,500 + 2,5% of and over 200,000	26,500 + 4,8% of and over 200,000
From 500,001 to 700,000	0%	22,500 + 1,4% of and over 500,000	28,500 + 3,7% of and over 500,000
From 700,001 to 1.500.000	0%	29,500 + 0,9% of and over 700,000	45,500 + 2.4% of and over 700,000
From 1,500,001 to 3.500.000	0%	30,300 + 0.500% of and over 1,500,000	65,500 + 1.200% of and over 1,500,000
From 3,500,001 to 7,000,000	0%	51,500 + 0.12% of and over 3,500,000	90,000 + 0.700% of and over 3,500,000
From 7,000,000 to 35,000,000	0%	52,500 + 0.11% of and over 7,000,000	115,000 + 0.200% of and over 7,000,000
From 35,000,001 to 55,000,000	0%	62,500 + 0.1% of and over 35,000,000	200,000 + 0.15% of and over 35,000,000
From 55,000,001 to 75,000,000	0%	68,500 + 0.07% of and over 55,000,000	220,000 + 0.07% of and over 55,000,000
From 75,000,001 to 350,000,000	0%	72,500 + 0.06% of and over 75,000,000	210,000 + 0.06% of and over 75,000,000
From 350,000,000	0%	74,500 + 0.040% of and over 350,000,000 up to a maximum of 1,000,00	220,500 + 0.040% of and over 350,000,000 up to a maximum of 1,000,00

other TIAC employees are prohibited from sitting as arbitrators in cases administered by TIAC under the TIAC Rules of Arbitration during their term of service. All decisions of the TIAC Court are made on a collegial basis, where there must be a quorum of at least three Members and for a decision to be made, there must be a simple majority. Under the TIAC's institutional framework, Uzbek representation in the TIAC Court cannot exceed 20%. Notably, in 2021 *Global Arbitration Review* wrote that TIAC's 'strict no conflict of interest' rules go further than IBA guidelines on conflicts.[5]

1.3 State-of-the-Art TIAC Rules of Arbitration and the Statutory Framework

In 2021, in view of the pandemic, the increased use of technology, rising cybersecurity threats (which subjected the Permanent Court of Arbitration to a cyber-attack in 2015[6]) and the vicissitudes of the post-pandemic world, TIAC has decided to form a working group of prominent arbitration practitioners to address the rising use of technology in dispute resolution as well as the growing number of technology-related disputes. As a result, the updated 2021 TIAC Rules of Arbitration were adopted,[7] which now contain opt-in cybersecurity rules and updated provisions related to treatment of documents and data production, and use of experimental evidence, technical primers, reference materials and tutorials in arbitrations involving complex subject-matters.[8]

In addition to establishing TIAC in 2018, another important milestone in strengthening Uzbekistan's resolve to become a preferred seat for the arbitral proceedings in the Commonwealth of Independent States ('CIS') region and beyond has been the adoption of the new Law on International Commercial Arbitration (No. O'RQ-674)[9] and the official recognition of Uzbekistan as a model law jurisdiction by UNCITRAL. Albeit not incorporating the body of the UNCITRAL Model Law on international commercial arbitration as a whole, the new law largely mirrors the provisions thereof, and was recognised by UNCITRAL as Model Law-compliant. There are, however, several important additions, such as, inter alia, the provision on immunity of arbitrators, which stipulates that arbitrators, experts appointed by an arbitral tribunal, and the arbitration institution and its employees shall not be liable to the parties or other persons for any actions or omissions in connection with the arbitration proceedings, unless their action or omission is proved to be intentional. Importantly, they are also exonerated from giving any explanations on any issue related to the arbitral proceedings and may not be called as witnesses in a judicial or any other process that arose as a result of such arbitral proceedings.

[5] Ross (2021).
[6] Lowther (2019).
[7] TIAC Rules of Arbitration, https://www.tiac.uz/tiac-rules-of-arbitration.
[8] Cheung et al. (2021).
[9] Law of the Republic of Uzbekistan on International Commercial Arbitration, No. ZRU-674, dated 16 February 2021, https://lex.uz/docs/5294087 (in Russian and Uzbek).

2 Current Caseload at TIAC

The promise of TIAC to become the region's leading arbitral institution is also reflected in the diversity and increasing number of its cases: from its official launch, TIAC has received over 40 requests for arbitration with disputes in various industry sectors, ranging from construction, real estate, supply and sale of goods, agriculture, oil and gas, even including one for sports arbitration. All commercial cases are international in nature (except for one domestic sports dispute), with at least one party not being from Uzbekistan. There have also been two applications for emergency relief, and one request for expert determination in connection with a project financed by an international financial institution.

It should be also noted that in a recent case administered by TIAC both parties to the dispute were foreign, with the claimant originating from Russia and the respondent from Singapore, which underpins the fact that TIAC is gaining traction not only as a regional, but also as an international arbitral institution. The geographical representation of the parties ranges from the jurisdictions within the CIS region such as Uzbekistan, Kazakhstan, Russia to the jurisdiction from Europe and Asia such as Turkey, Italy, the Netherlands, Moldova to the Far East such as Singapore, the Philippines.

3 TIAC-HKIAC Cross-Institutional Rules of Arbitration

The unprecedented measures that the governments needed to take to fight the pandemic and the post-pandemic crises, which included, among others, the calls for a cooperative and coordinated global response not only among governments and nations, but also among institutions, whose role in contributing to certainty and stability for businesses and individuals, including those, who have been affected by the pandemic, cannot be understated. Faced with unprecedented challenges and to further simplify the procedures for the users of alternative dispute resolution mechanisms in the pandemic and post-pandemic times, TIAC has proposed to HKIAC that arbitral institutions join forces to further contribute to the stability and foreseeability in this volatile economic environment.

The main objective of this initiative was to find a common ground in which the two independent arbitral institutions could consolidate their efforts during the COVID-19 and the post-pandemic era. One particular common ground concerns certain disputes which may be resolved more effectively and efficiently with the assistance of more than one institution due to, among others, the nature of the disputes and the location of the parties. This includes, for instance, disputes related to the Belt and Road Initiative ('BRI') projects. The potential that the BRI projects may have in bolstering the economies along the BRI calls for a more proactive and collaborative approach, emphasising on delivering access to dispute resolution avenues and reducing the costs of arbitration during the post-pandemic times.

This cooperation in delivering arbitration services is essentially focused on the allocation of roles and tasks between the cooperating arbitral institutions. Certain services that are not decision-intensive (such as registering the notices/requests for arbitration, initial liaison with the parties) are to be provided by institutions that are in closer proximity to the parties, while the services that require the institutions to exercise critical decision-making powers (such as appointing arbitrators, deciding on the challenges of arbitrators) are to be provided by other arbitral institutions of choice.

As a result, in September 2022 TIAC entered into the TIAC-HKIAC Cross Institutional Arbitration Rules (TIAC-HKIAC Rules), an exclusive cooperation agreement with the HKIAC. Under the TIAC-HKIAC Rules, TIAC and HKIAC will jointly administer cases and TIAC will refer to HKIAC on certain procedural issues arising in arbitrations filed under the TIAC-HKIAC Rules. HKIAC will make its decisions without charging administrative fees except in limited, pre-defined circumstances.[10]

In sum, these ongoing initiatives of the TIAC, combined with its unique features and arbitral rules, will enable Uzbekistan to position itself as a leading regional dispute resolution centre. Uzbekistan's success would also depend on it becoming a leading regional arbitral seat with a pro-arbitration and pro-enforcement approach, which will be discussed in the next section.

4 Challenge, Recognition and Enforcement of Foreign Arbitral Awards

Uzbekistan is a party to the 1958 New York Convention on the Recognition and Enforcement of Foreign Arbitral Awards (NY Convention), which broadly provides that regardless of the country in which the award was issued, arbitral awards may be recognized and enforced upon written request to a competent court by the claimant. The norms and provisions on the recognition and enforcement of foreign arbitral awards provided for in the NY Convention have been incorporated into the national procedural legislation of Uzbekistan. These include the Code of Economic Procedure (No. ZRU-461)[11] ('CEP'), the new Law on International Commercial Arbitration (No. ZRU-674),[12] and 'On amendments and additions to certain legislative acts of the Republic of Uzbekistan in connection with the adoption of the Law "On International Commercial Arbitration"' (No. ZRU-769).

[10] HKIAC and TIAC sign cooperation agreement to adopt TIAC-HKIAC Cross-Institutional Rules of Arbitration (2022), https://www.hkiac.org/news/hkiac-and-tiac-sign-cooperation-agreement-adopt-tiac-hkiac-cross-institutional-arbitration.

[11] Code of Economic Procedure of the Republic of Uzbekistan, dated 24 January 2018, https://lex.uz/docs/3523895 (in Russian and Uzbek).

[12] Law of the Republic of Uzbekistan on International Commercial Arbitration, No. ZRU-674, dated 16 February 2021, https://lex.uz/docs/5294087 (in Russian and Uzbek).

Particularly, Chapter 33 of the CEP, which broadly mirrors Articles IV &V of the NY Convention, provides that the enforcement of foreign arbitral awards shall be conducted by the Economic Court. This includes those administered by the TIAC.

4.1 Time Limits

Under Article 252 of the CEP, unless otherwise provided for in an international treaty of the Republic of Uzbekistan, a number of documents shall be attached to the application for the recognition and enforcement of an arbitral award. These include the original arbitral award or its certified copy; the original of the arbitration agreement or its certified copy (both translated into Uzbek).

Under Article 254 of the CEP, an application for recognition and enforcement of an arbitral award unless otherwise provided for in the relevant international treaties of the Republic of Uzbekistan, shall be considered at a court session within 6 months from the date of its receipt by the Economic Court.

4.2 Grounds for Refusal

The grounds for refusing to recognise and enforce an arbitral award are listed in Article 256 of the CEP, according to which the Economic Court of the Republic of Uzbekistan may refuse to recognise and enforce a foreign arbitration decision upon the application of the party against whom the decision is directed, if the party furnishes proof:

1. that the parties to the arbitration agreement were incapacitated, or that the arbitration agreement was invalid under the law to which the parties submitted it, or failing any indication thereon, under the law of Uzbekistan;
2. the party against whom the award is directed was not properly informed about the appointment of an arbitrator or about the arbitration proceedings, or was unable to present its case;
3. that the award deals with a dispute not arbitrable or not falling within the terms of the submission to arbitration, or it contains decisions on matters beyond the scope of the arbitration agreement. If the decisions on matters that are arbitrable can be separated from those that are not arbitral, that part of the award which contains decisions on arbitral matters may be recognised and enforced;
4. that the composition of the arbitral tribunal or the arbitral procedure were not in accordance with the agreement of the parties.

Furthermore, recognition and enforcement of a foreign arbitration decision may also be refused in the following cases, if:

1. the subject matter of the dispute is not arbitrable according to the legislation of the Republic of Uzbekistan;

2. the recognition and execution of the award contradicts the public order of the Republic of Uzbekistan;

According to statistical data of cases related to arbitration and foreign arbitration courts, from 2020 to June 2022, the first instance of the Tashkent City Court has reviewed 50 cases on the recognition and enforcement of a foreign court judgment or of a foreign arbitral award, of which 44 were satisfied, 5 were rejected and 1 was terminated. With 17 such cases in 2020, 24 in 2021 and 9 as of June 2022, the number of cases on the recognition and enforcement of a foreign court judgments or arbitral awards is expected to steadily increase.

5 Conclusion

The use of arbitration to resolve international disputes provides overarching economic benefit by facilitating cross-border trade and investment. As the fulcrum of the world economy has tilted towards the higher growth economies in the emerging markets, the disputes brought to international arbitration are increasingly drawn from trade and investment in and between emerging economies, including countries of the Central Asian region. The TIAC's unique features and its state-of-the-art institutional framework have enabled it to provide all the necessary infrastructure to administer high-profile, complex international disputes.

At the same time, arbitral institutions may also amplify the cordial spirit of their relationships through effective cross-institutional collaboration initiatives, such as the TIAC-HKIAC Cross Institutional Rules of Arbitration. The benefits of such collaboration include drawing on the local expertise, language, and the cultural affinity with the parties. Lastly, it also allows exposure of younger institutions to different types of arbitral proceedings.

References

Bjerde A (2022) To withstand global shocks, Uzbekistan needs to continue reforms and build an inclusive market economy. https://www.worldbank.org/en/news/opinion/2022/11/01/to-withstand-global-shocks-uzbekistan-needs-to-continue-reforms-and-build-an-inclusive-market-economy

Cheung K, Kot D, Mirabdullaeva D (2021). Technology and 2021 rules of arbitration of the Tashkent International Arbitration Centre (TIAC) at the Chamber of Commerce and Industry of Uzbekistan, Kluwer Arbitration Blog. https://arbitrationblog.kluwerarbitration.com/2021/12/31/technology-and-2021-rules-of-arbitration-of-the-tashkent-international-arbitration-centre-tiac-at-the-chamber-of-commerce-and-industry-of-uzbekistan/

Lowther J (2019) Report on Arbitration Committee session at the 2019 IBA Annual Conference in Seoul. https://www.ibanet.org/article/eef13a7d-b31f-4362-b868-c7bc7edce52b

Ross A (2021) Uzbekistan's offering on show at first arbitration week. https://globalarbitrationreview.com/article/uzbekistans-offering-show-first-arbitration-week

Diana Bayzakova is Director of the Tashkent International Arbitration Centre (TIAC), Arbitrator and Dispute Resolution Specialist.

Adrian Mak is an Arbitration Associate to Prof. Anselmo Reyes SC of the Singapore International Commercial Court.

Part IV
Book Reviews

Henry Gao and Weihuan Zhou, Between Market Economy and State Capitalism China's State-Owned Enterprises and the World Trading System

Cambridge University Press, 2022, ISBN: 978-1-108-90879-5

Simon Lester

Contents

1 Countering the China Trade Narrative

When narratives take hold, they are hard to cast aside. Policymakers and politicians are prone to groupthink, and suddenly everyone just knows a particular thing is true. A prime example from early this century is the U.S. "War on Terror." After the September 11 terrorist attacks, the U.S. foreign policy establishment just knew that U.S. military intervention in the Middle East was necessary for security and would promote freedom and democracy. It took many years to recognize the absence of evidence for the claims being made in support of this approach, and to pull back from the flawed strategy that developed.

The latest foreign policy narrative that has taken hold is that China is out to spread its socialist ideology to the entire world. As the newly appointed Chair of the U.S. House of Representatives China Select Committee recently put it, China is out to "destroy the capitalist system led by the United States and make way for the

S. Lester (✉)
Falls Church, VA, USA
e-mail: simon.lester@worldtradelaw.net

M. Bungenberg et al. (eds.), *Asian Yearbook of International Economic Law 2023*,
Asian Yearbook of International Economic Law (2023) 2023: 219–226,
https://doi.org/10.1007/16517_2023_21, Published online: 11 April 2023

ultimate triumph of world socialism with, you know, Chinese characteristics."[1] Whether assertions such as this one reflect actual Chinese foreign policy goals is barely scrutinized. Once a general narrative about the threat from China catches on, embellishments proliferate and extreme variations are accepted as truth.

The China narrative also has a trade policy component. In trade, the story goes, China is a cheater that manipulates the system created by the West and flouts the rules with abandon. Letting China into the WTO was a mistake, under this view, because it allowed China to rise economically and take advantage of the West. China uses the trading system as a weapon against the West while simultaneously ignoring its own obligations. And for those critics who support the WTO (some of the China trade critics are critics of the WTO as well), these actions have the side effect of undermining the WTO itself.

The China trade narrative has a tiny grain of truth to it, in the sense that China does engage in some practices that constitute "unfair" trade and it has violated some WTO rules. But for the most part, the narrative is a distortion. An objective analysis of what China agreed to when it acceded to the WTO, and how it has behaved as a WTO Member, demonstrates that the current narrative is disconnected from reality. Whether such an analysis can change the narrative remains to be seen, but it is a worthwhile and necessary task for those seeking better policies. Therefore, it is good news that scholars such as Henry Gao and Weihuan Zhou have taken on this task.

In their work over the past few years, Gao and Zhou have made important contributions to the study of China's participation in the trading system. They have published a series of papers that weigh in on some of the biggest technical China trade policy issues. And in their new book, "Between Market Economy and State Capitalism," they synthesize their past work into an overarching look at the core of the issue: Is China's state-led economic system compatible with a trade regime that is intended for domestic economic systems that are more market-oriented?

To be clear, we are not talking here about a centrally planned economy trying to integrate with purely market-oriented economies. Rather, we have a particular brand of what is often referred to as "state capitalism" trying to fit with the relatively market-driven, but still somewhat interventionist, economies of the West. Thus, the differences in the level of state involvement in each set of economies are matters of degree, not of kind. As Gao and Zhou put it, a "nuanced definition of state capitalism . . . refers to the magnitude of government involvement in business activities depending on 'state ownership stake in or significant influence over' the business sector" (p. 4).

The fundamental question here is whether the major world economies of today—particularly China on the one hand, and the United States, the European Union, Japan, and various others, on the other hand—have levels of economic intervention that are so different that they are incompatible and cannot operate within the same trading system. Can international economic rules be crafted that bring these different

[1] Thiessen (2022).

domestic systems together in a trade regime that everyone considers fair? Or do the differences create a sense of unfairness that no set of technical trade rules can overcome? Gao and Zhou take the optimistic view of the situation, and lay out a strong case for how the existing multilateral trade rules can do a better job than proponents of the current narrative have claimed.

2 Challenging the Narrative

Gao and Zhou are clear in their objective from the outset: They have observed the current narrative and they are trying to challenge it. As they put it in the introduction: "[s]ome observers argue that the triumph of China and the decline of the WTO are not mere coincidence but deeply correlated." According to this view, "China manipulated its trade practices through its state capitalism model to get where it is today, and this is exactly what precipitated the crisis at the WTO, because its rules are ill-equipped to deal with China's practices which violate the spirit but not necessarily the letter of the world trade law, thus leading to the collapse of its dispute settlement and negotiation functions" (p. 1).

Gao and Zhou recognize how this narrative became popular in the West, as it "combines all of the right elements: the economic rise of China, its practice of state capitalism and the decline of the world trading system." However, they say, the narrative is fundamentally flawed because "it mistakes correlation with causation." While it is true that the trading system has suffered some setbacks in recent years, China's economic practices are not the primary cause. The full story of "the interactions between China's state capitalism and the world trading system," Gao and Zhou argue, is "much more nuanced than this simplistic narrative." Indeed, rather than China's GATT/WTO accession being a mistake by past government negotiators who did not anticipate the problems with China's entry, these negotiators "noticed the problems and carefully crafted China-specific rules to tackle them in the final accession package" (p. 2). To this end, these negotiators "meticulously identified specific aspects of the Chinese system that might undermine its WTO commitments and carefully crafted surgical solutions to address these problems in WTO-consistent ways" (p. 10).

The book is thus intended to "challenge[] the conventional wisdom that the existing WTO rules are inadequate to address China's state capitalism, particularly the market-distortive conduct of Chinese SOEs supported by industrial policies and subsidies." Its key argument is that "China's WTO-plus obligations, coupled with the general rules on subsidies, can be applied to tackle these problems." And what follows from this conclusion is "a major policy recommendation ... that WTO Members should continue to resort to the WTO dispute settlement system to challenge China's state capitalism using existing rules" (pp. 3–4).

Having set out this big picture at the start, the bulk of the book provides a detailed analysis of specific sets of industrial policy issues related to China's state capitalism, along with the relevant WTO obligations that might address these practices. SOEs and subsidies are at the core of the concerns here, and make up a good portion of the book's substantive analysis.

3 The Fall and Rise of Chinese SOEs

In Chapter 2 of the book, Gao and Zhou explain that, during the opening up that began in 1978, China recognized the flaws of its central planning system, and sought to transform its SOEs into functioning commercial entities and profitable players in a competitive market. At the same time, the authors point out that even in the reform stage, there were signs that there were limits to the degree of market-orientation that the Chinese government would tolerate, with efforts underway by 2003 to turn SOEs into "national champions" (pp. 19–23). And more recently, the government has enlisted the SOEs in its broader economic and foreign policy goals (pp. 23–39).

As noted above, however, negotiators from other governments were well aware of the potential pitfalls regarding competition with Chinese SOEs. These governments had concerns about SOEs all along, and crafted WTO rules designed to address the issue. The Working Party report from the accession negotiations, some parts of which were incorporated into the Accession Protocol and made binding and enforceable, discussed the issue in some detail, emphasizing that the purchases and sales of SOEs "should be based solely on commercial considerations, without any governmental influence or application of discriminatory measures." In its statements to the Working Party, China went so far as to "ensure that all state-owned and state-invested enterprises would make purchases and sales based solely on commercial considerations, e.g., price, quality, marketability and availability, and that the enterprises of other WTO Members would have an adequate opportunity to compete for sales to and purchases from these enterprises on nondiscriminatory terms and conditions"[2] (pp. 54–55).

Such a promise is a bold one for a government whose SOEs were surely not completely in compliance with this commitment at the time of accession. China might have expected some formal WTO disputes against its SOE behavior at some point, but they never came, and this provision remains untested. How well such an obligation can constrain Chinese economic practices remains to be seen, but given the structure of enforcement under the WTO dispute settlement system, it can only have an impact if other governments bring complaints.

---

[2]Report of the Working Party on the Accession of China, WT/ACC/CHN/49, 1 October 2001, para. 46.

4 The Size and Nature of Chinese Subsidies

With SOEs, while every country has them, China has more of them and their non-market behavior tends to be of greater concern. Similarly, with subsidies, every country offers them, but it is the size and nature of the Chinese subsidies that is the particular problem. There are WTO rules in this area, and they have been somewhat effective in addressing conflicts over subsidies. However, there are limits to the impact of these rules on Chinese practices, due in part to issues such as non-transparency on the Chinese side and the use of trade remedy measures as a response on the other side.

Gao and Zhou note the "growing concerns about the effectiveness of WTO rules in dealing with Chinese subsidies," but argue that these concerns "are flawed in two major aspects": (1) "they do not distinguish between deficiencies specific to China and those generally applicable to all WTO Members"; and (2) "they are not based on a detailed assessment of specific types of Chinese subsidies and the potential issues in applying the existing rules to these subsidies," and "[s]ignificantly, they pay little attention to China's WTO-plus obligations" (p. 102).

A key issue in this regard is that governments often try to address foreign subsidies through domestic countervailing duty actions, under which there will be a domestic investigation of the foreign subsidies, and tariffs imposed in response. The problem with this approach is that WTO panels and the Appellate Body have often been skeptical of the objectivity of these domestic proceedings. Thus, as Gao and Zhou discuss, when the United States or other governments impose countervailing duties on Chinese products, these duties may be found inconsistent with WTO rules. The conclusions that many critics of China and of the WTO draw from these WTO dispute settlement rulings is that China does not belong in the system and that the system itself is flawed. However, a more accurate description of the situation may be that in practice, countervailing duties have inherent limitations as a way to address foreign subsidies, in part because governments may deviate, in various ways, from the WTO rules governing countervailing duties, leading to WTO dispute settlement rulings that the response to foreign subsidies has violated the rules. Thus, while in theory countervailing duties can be used in a targeted and effective way here, as Gao and Zhou advocate, it may also be worth utilizing WTO subsidies rules that provide a multilateral way of addressing subsidies through the provisions on "adverse effects."

In general terms, Gao and Zhou conclude that the WTO's subsidies rules are "broad enough to capture the major subsidies provided under China's ambitious industrial policies, including those granted via SOEs." For those measures of concern that fall outside the existing rules, "new and better rules" may be needed, they say, and should be "created by WTO Members through negotiations" (p. 125).

5 Multilateralism Is the Best Answer

Countering the existing narrative, Gao and Zhou make the case for the WTO to be the focus of efforts to tackle China's state capitalism, with two areas of emphasis: Litigation and negotiations.

On litigation, they argue that "the conventional narrative about the inadequacy or ineffectiveness of the existing WTO rules is untenable and misleading," and that "to unleash the full potential of these rules, WTO Members need to invoke these rules to challenge the relevant Chinese laws and practices via litigation" (p. 8). In Chapter 7, they consider several claims that have been put forward about the "futility of WTO litigation": (1) "existing WTO rules do not cover China's trade practices"; (2) "even if there are such rules, they will not be interpreted with sufficient rigour in WTO cases to obtain favourable rulings against China"; and (3) "even if the complainants managed to win such cases, China will just comply with the ruling on paper but not in substance." But they argue that "closer examination reveals that none of these really holds true," and they document the successes that have been achieved in challenging China's economic practices in past WTO disputes (p. 156). They also respond to concerns about difficulties with gathering evidence of Chinese practices, and they discuss strategies for bringing cases as part of a coalition of governments (pp. 166–170). Finally, they argue that "cases need to be selected strategically with an aim to addressing systemic issues and WTO-illegal trade practices generally and to causing changes to relevant WTO jurisprudence that would facilitate future actions against China's state-led market distortions via WTO litigation and trade remedies" (p. 183).

As to negotiations, in terms of where to address these issues, Gao and Zhou have a preference for multilateralism. They examine the alternatives, such as the Comprehensive and Progressive Agreement for Trans-Pacific Partnership (CPTPP) and the U.S.-China Phase One trade deal, and consider them to be inferior. In this regard, they note that "[w]hile the CPTPP SOE chapter was developed with China as a major target," it "has shown its lack of development and deficiencies when compared to China's WTO-plus obligations" (p. 153). And the Phase One deal "fails to address the more significant and systemic issues, such as China's SOEs and industrial policies and subsidies" (p. 171). For rules to have a real impact, they must be crafted multilaterally at the WTO.

6 Concluding Thoughts

Gao and Zhou have done an excellent job of countering the existing China trade narrative, and this effort will likely need to continue for many years because the proponents will not back down easily. One reason it is difficult to challenge the narrative effectively is that it has the force of powerful interest groups behind it. Gao and Zhou refer to Donald Trump's United States Trade Representative Robert

Lighthizer, who has called China an "existential" threat to the multilateral trading system and argued that China's system of state capitalism is inherently incompatible with the liberal world trading order (p. 185). Lighthizer was for many years a lawyer and lobbyist for the U.S. steel industry, representing clients who were trying to limit Chinese competition.[3] Lighthizer has continued his efforts after leaving office, writing op-eds and journal articles, and becoming involved with think tanks that advocate for restricting competition from imports. He and others will continue to push a particular narrative about China and the world trading system.

Several key areas for future work on countering this narrative are the following. First, it is important to note that just before China acceded to the WTO, the 9/11 terrorist attacks shifted the U.S. foreign policy focus away from China and towards the Middle East. According to a George W. Bush State Department official, in the summer of 2001, it looked as though China would be the main focus of U.S. foreign policy. However, after 9/11, Islamic terrorism took precedence, and China was downgraded as a priority.[4] Not only that, but in carrying out the War on Terror in the ensuing decade, the United States had to moderate its demands on China in a number of areas, including trade and human rights. The counterfactual of a scenario in which the United States spent the 2000s pressing China on economic reforms is an intriguing one, but we will never know how that would have turned out.

Second, Gao and Zhou make the point that "as a big economy, China does not capitulate easily and may instead (as it actually did) retaliate in kind [to unilateral actions] by imposing its own tariffs, resulting in a no-win situation" (p. 186). This point illustrates the limits of economic leverage. In the United States, there is a tendency to think that as the world's largest economy, the U.S. government can bend other governments to its will. The ability to do so has probably been overestimated in general, but in the case of China, it is clear that the impact of such actions is very limited. Can unilateral measures have a small impact on certain countries in the short term? Perhaps. But this approach will not solve systemic problems such as China's economic practices. And they will certainly not achieve this goal if people misunderstand the nature of the problem, as when many U.S. politicians and policymakers focus on issues such as the bilateral U.S.-China trade deficit.

And third, there is a lot of focus on WTO accession as the trigger for China's rise, with blame being assigned to the WTO or to the government negotiators who agreed to let China into the WTO. But looking at the economic trends in China in the 1980s and 1990s, it is clear that China's economic ascent was underway without membership in the GATT/WTO. WTO accession certainly had an impact, but China's economic power would probably not be significantly diminished in the absence of WTO membership. Indeed, if China had not joined the WTO, it would likely have focused on bilateral and regional trade deals instead, with significant liberalization still being achieved. Thus, arguments about China and the WTO miss the point to some extent, because even without a WTO deal, China would have become powerful

---

[3] See, e.g., Peterson (2018).

[4] Lester (2021).

economically and U.S. policymakers and politicians would still be panicking about China today. Indeed, in that scenario, it is possible that government negotiators who failed to agree to a deal to let China into the WTO would be the subject of criticism today, with the narrative being that the failure to let China into the WTO was the source of all the problems.

Gao and Zhou have done great work in providing an evidence-based and objective look at the concerns with China's economic practices and the role that the world trading system can play. Their latest book compiles all their work on the issue and sets out clearly the argument for a greater reliance on multilateralism to address the problems. One can only hope that the book will be read by key decision-makers and provide some pushback against the current narrative.

References

Lester S (2021) The place of China in U.S. Foreign Policy after 9/11 and China's WTO accession. International Economic Law and Policy Blog, 29 August 2021. https://ielp.worldtradelaw.net/2021/08/the-place-of-china-in-us-foreign-policy-after-911-wto-accession.html

Peterson M (2018) The making of a trade warrior. The Atlantic, 29 December 2018. https://www.theatlantic.com/politics/archive/2018/12/robert-lighthizers-bid-cut-chinas-trade-influence/578611/

Report of the Working Party on the Accession of China, WT/ACC/CHN/49, 1 October 2001

Thiessen M (2022) Who are the GOP's future leaders? Let's start with Mike Gallagher. Washington Post, 16 December 2022. https://www.washingtonpost.com/opinions/2022/12/16/mike-gallagher-gop-republican-leaders-marc-thiessen/

Simon Lester is the co-founder of the trade law and policy websites WorldTradeLaw.net and China Trade Monitor. Previously, he was the associate director of the Cato Institute's Herbert A. Stiefel Center for Trade Policy Studies, and served as a legal affairs officer at the Appellate Body Secretariat of the WTO. He has taught courses on international trade law at the American University's Washington College of Law, the University of Michigan Law School, and Melbourne University Law School.

Sergio Puig, At the Margins of Globalization: Indigenous Peoples and International Economic Law

Cambridge University Press, 2021, ISBN: 978-1-108-49764-0

Manjiao Chi and Xinhui Hong

International economic law and indigenous rights seem two separate areas of law that develop along parallel tracks. This is not true. In the era of globalization, indigenous peoples across the world are profoundly impacted by the expansion of transnational economic activities. Alarmingly, indigenous peoples have suffered from the loss of ancestral lands, pollution of the environment, erosion of their culture, and even the decimation of their populations.[1] The international community is confronted with the question more than ever before: can international economic law play the dual roles of promoting global economy and protecting indigenous peoples?

Prof. Sergio Puig's book, entitled "At the Margins of Globalization: Indigenous Peoples and International Economic Law", tries to conceptualize the above question and to explore a solution to it from a systematic perspective. It reveals that the economic, social, and legal status of indigenous peoples restricts their ability to defend their rights and interests, rendering them more marginalized and vulnerable.[2] To recalibrate the existing imbalanced structure of international economic law, the author contends that indigenous peoples should be brought from the margins to the center of discussion.

This contention is an alarming call. Over the past few years, there has been growing recognition of the importance of protecting indigenous rights in

[1]Extractive Industries Operating within or Near Indigenous Territories, 11 July 2011, A/HRC/18/35, https://www.ohchr.org/sites/default/files/Documents/Issues/IPeoples/SR/A-HRC-18-35_en.pdf, pp. 8–11.

[2]Puig (2021), p. 5.

M. Chi (✉) and X. Hong
Center for International Economic Law and Policy, School of Law, University of International Business and Economics, Beijing, China
e-mail: chimanjiao@uibe.edu.cn

M. Bungenberg et al. (eds.), *Asian Yearbook of International Economic Law 2023*,
Asian Yearbook of International Economic Law (2023) 2023: 227–230,
https://doi.org/10.1007/16517_2023_22, Published online: 22 April 2023

transnational economic activities. Literatures on this topic has flourished,[3] with a focus on certain specific fields,[4] industries,[5] or indigenous rights.[6] A comprehensive and systematic study of the relationship between international economic law and indigenous peoples is, however, a prerequisite to discussing how to integrate protection of indigenous peoples in international economic law. To fill this scholarly gap, this book uses a systematic approach to explore the effectiveness of international trade, investment, finance, and intellectual property laws in the accommodation of indigenous rights. It provides a unique perspective on the intersection between international economic law and indigenous peoples' rights and interests, which can help to mitigate globalization's passive impacts.[7]

At the Margins of Globalization explores a novel area but is richly annotated with references that summarize the achievement in international law and specific economic regimes regarding the protection of indigenous peoples. This book contains a thorough overview of the international economic legal system, informative case studies, and insightful analysis. What makes this book more remarkable is that readers may also benefit from the rich experiences of the author in the research area at the personal level.[8]

This book has three parts, each composed of several chapters. In the first part, the author discusses six main "narratives" on the negative impact of globalization. He contends that it would be partial and misleading to tackle the problem of the marginalized without considering the different perspectives on the discontent of globalization.[9] Then, the author innovatively provides a theory of "the cycle of susceptibility and exclusion," which illustrates the particular susceptibility of indigenous peoples to the negative consequences of global economic interdependence. Through a diagram, he explains how international economic agreements exacerbate vast disparities in both political and economic capabilities. Specifically, indigenous peoples have suffered from political harms, including illegitimacy and a shift in governance priorities, as well as economic harms, such as discrimination and inequality.[10]

The second part first analyzes the general protections of indigenous peoples under international law and specific economic regimes. After constructing a solid normative framework, the author examines the effectiveness of accommodating indigenous peoples' rights and interests in the four key fields of international economic law. He

[3] See, e.g., Borrows and Schwartz (2020), Binder (2015) and Foster (2012).

[4] See, e.g., Levine (2013) and Vadi (2018).

[5] See, e.g., Kleinfeld (2016).

[6] See, e.g., Hofbauer (2013); Nathaniah Jacobs and Tehtena Mebratu-Tsegaye (2021) Secure Land Rights Are Now More Important than Ever, Columbia Center on Sustainable Investment, 29 January 2021, https://ccsi.columbia.edu/news/secure-land-rights-are-now-more-important-ever.

[7] Puig (2021), p. xiii.

[8] Ibid., p. xiii.

[9] Ibid., p. 12.

[10] Ibid., p. 25.

points out that the international economic legal system can promote Indigenous peoples' rights and interests. To support this contention, the author presents case studies that show indigenous peoples' relative success in confronting the systematic challenges posed by globalization. According to the author, international economic law can act as a *shield* for indigenous rights protection, as well as a *sword* for their advancement, despite its imperfections.

Having discussed the impacts of globalization on indigenous peoples, the author attempts to search for solutions. While the author shows great sympathy for marginalized indigenous peoples, he does not take a radical view of isolating indigenous peoples from economic globalization. In the third part, the author adopts a more inclusive and practical perspective, proposing that there should be an expansion of using indigenous peoples' human rights within international economic agreements as a counterbalance to the imbalanced power created by the existing international business frameworks. [11] He proposes that indigenous perspectives should be incorporated into international economic law, including "respect for distinct beliefs about and forms of economic organizations; active commitment with communal self-determination; and recognition of individual and corporate duties toward our planet and future generations."[12] Only in this way can a more inclusive society and a fairer playing field continue to support global governance.

Overall, this book provides a broad substantive analyses of the intersection between indigenous peoples and international economic law. The author insightfully points out that protecting indigenous rights is a key litmus test for international economic law's legitimacy.[13] He proposed that the governing structure should include representatives of marginalized groups in treaty negotiations and international dispute settlement proceedings.[14]

The book is well-structured and perfectly combines theories and case studies. Among the theories covered are neoliberalism, global governance, and legitimacy. They provide the background for the arguments and the case studies. Many topics covered in this book are cutting-edge academically and practically, such as the right of states to raise counter-claims against investors and the *amicus curiae*. Moreover, the author analyses the provisions of newly signed international economic agreements, including CPTPP and USMCA. The case studies are presented in a storytelling manner, making them very lively and easy to read. Although the author has selected only two cases in each main field, they are comprehensive in their coverage of the main points and highly representative, demonstrating the depth of his research.

Further, what makes this book a unique contribution to the academic community is that the book presents a comprehensive and detailed analytical framework for further studying the relationship between indigenous rights and the various fields of international economic law. Notably, the inspirations derived from this book could

---

[11] Ibid., p. 4.

[12] Ibid., p. 148.

[13] Ibid., p. 121.

[14] Ibid., p. 132.

also be helpful to international organizations and grassroots movement organizers. For human rights scholars and indigenous rights advocates, for instance, this book could help better understand international economic law and how to use international economic law in defending and advancing the interests of indigenous peoples. In this sense, the influence of this book surely goes beyond the legal community.

References

Binder C (2015) Investment, development and indigenous peoples. In: Schill S, Tams C (eds) International investment law and development. Edward Elgar, Cheltenham, pp 423–452

Borrows J, Schwartz R (eds) (2020) Indigenous peoples and international trade: building equitable and inclusive international trade and investment agreements. Cambridge University Press, Cambridge

Foster GK (2012) Foreign investment and indigenous peoples: options for promoting equilibrium between economic development and indigenous rights. Mich J Int Law 33(4):627–691

Hofbauer J (2013) Foreign investments meet free, prior and informed consent (FPIC)-whose sovereignty? Aust Rev Int Eur Law 18. https://ssrn.com/abstract=2815859

Kleinfeld J (2016) The double life of international law: indigenous peoples and extractive industries. Harv Law Rev 129(6):1755–1778

Levine J (2013) The interaction of international investment arbitration and the rights of indigenous peoples. In: Baetens F (ed) Investment law within international law: integrationist perspectives. Cambridge University Press, Cambridge, pp 106–128

Puig S (2021) At the margins of globalization: indigenous peoples and international economic law. Cambridge University Press, Cambridge

Vadi V (2018) Heritage, power, and destiny: the protection of indigenous heritage in international investment law and arbitration. George Wash Int Law Rev 50:725–780

Manjiao Chi is a Professor and Founding Director of the Center for International Economic Law and Policy, School of Law, University of International Business and Economics, China. He holds BA, LLM and Ph.D. in law degrees. He is an editor of the Asian Yearbook of International Economic Law.

Xinhui Hong is a Ph.D. Candidate and Research Fellow at the Center for International Economic Law and Policy, School of Law, University of International Business and Economics, China. She holds LLB and LLM degrees from Xiamen University.

The manufacturer's authorised representative in the EU is Springer Nature Customer Service Centre GmbH, Europaplatz 3, 69115 Heidelberg, Germany. If you have any concerns regarding our products, please contact ProductSafety@springernature.com

Printed and bound by CPI Group (UK) Ltd, Croydon, CR0 4YY

30/09/2026

02225319-0004